I0817492

THE ROAD TO AUSCHWITZ

The Deportation of the Slovak Jews by the Hlinka Guard

WALTER S. ZAPOTOCZNY JR.

FONTHILL

For the Survivors

Fonthill Media Language Policy

Fonthill Media publishes in the international English language market. One language edition is published worldwide. As there are minor differences in spelling and presentation, especially with regard to American English and British English, a policy is necessary to define which form of English to use. The Fonthill Policy is to use the form of English native to the author. Walter S. Zapotoczny Jr. was born and educated in the United States; therefore American English has been adopted in this publication.

Fonthill Media Limited
Fonthill Media LLC
www.fonthillmedia.com
office@fonthillmedia.com

First published in the United Kingdom and the United States of America 2022

British Library Cataloguing in Publication Data:
A catalogue record for this book is available from the British Library

ISBN 978-1-78155-880-5

Typeset in 10.5pt on 13pt Minion Pro
Printed and bound in England

Preface

The Hlinka Guard has received little attention from historians. However, its story is worth examining, not only because of the part it played in the annals of Czechoslovakia, but also as an additional example of the Fascist movement in Eastern Europe and its treatment of the Jews.

The Hlinka Guard was formally established on October 8, 1938, though the first units had come into existence in July of that year. It disappeared with the Soviet conquest of Slovakia. In its time, it was a semi-independent part of Hlinka's Slovak People's Party. Father Andrej Hlinka, an ardent nationalist and bigoted Catholic, founded the party in 1918, shortly after the proclamation of the Czechoslovak Republic. Its aims, announced by its founder and leader, were to safeguard and promote the national life of the Slovak people and to fight the enemies of Slovak national, social, political, and religious life.

Although Hlinka's party never boasted a detailed program, its ideology, extreme nationalism, and a Catholic world view ranked high in the mind of its leaders. The brainchild of a bad-tempered and none-too-sophisticated priest, it was neither democratic in its debates nor elaborate in structure. Appealing to a poverty-stricken nation, it was, from the beginning, conscious of social and economic problems. Later, the so-called "Christian Social Thought," claiming to be based on encyclicals of Popes Leo XIII and Pius X, became the basis of its social policy. They discussed the relationships and mutual duties between labor and capital, as well as government and its citizens. All of its programs had religious, national, social, and constitutional values, and its ideology was based on papal encyclicals and was oriented mostly towards its Catholic electorate. The party rejected economic liberalism and the theory of class struggle popular among Socialists and Communists, who were, together with liberal atheists, considered to be the party's main enemies. Of primary concern was the need for some improvement of "the misery and wretchedness pressing so unjustly on the majority of the working class." The party supported the rights of labor to form unions, rejected socialism and unrestricted capitalism, while affirming the right to private property.

Besides promoting its leader's personal goals, the guard was to serve the Hlinka Party and the autonomous government as substitute for a military force. The government at Bratislava (the capital of Slovakia) not only had no troops of its own, but the units of the Czechoslovak Army stationed on Slovak territory were under Czech or loyal Slovak officers. Sports and gymnastic organizations, such as the Sokol or the Communist Gymnastic Union, were perceived as a threat to the new government leadership. But perhaps the most important use to which the guard was put was its deployment as a means of coercion and terror. It excelled in manhandling Jews, as a border-guard in charge of confiscating the property of emigrants, in terrorizing individuals and entire organizations, and in other tasks of a similar nature. The men also served as personal and parade guards for the party leaders and for celebrations. They were useful for mobilizing public demonstrations and suppressing the unwanted kind.

The Hlinka Guard was popular with the Slovak population, and enrolment soared. Dressed in black uniforms, high black boots, and gold-trimmed hats with a dangling tassel, they looked like a combination of Italian Fascist militiamen and comic-opera actors. In the streets, the guard co-operated with bands of ethnic Germans and carried on pro-Nazi propaganda. When the Czechoslovak Republic was nearing its end in March 1939, the guard actively opposed the Prague government, organized disturbances, strikes, and demonstrations, occupied public buildings, and helped to force the new state on the unsuspecting people of Slovakia. The Nazis owed much to the Hlinka Guard, who gave them the pretext for interfering in the internal affairs of the government.

The guard had often taken the lead in anti-Jewish measures and supervised Jewish labor and detention camps in the country. In the fall of 1941, Alexander Mach, chief commander of the Hlinka Guard, made plans for the construction of concentration camps in Slovakia and applied for instructors from Dachau. When, however, the Germans came with an offer to "absorb" the entire Jewish population of Slovakia, Mach seized upon the proposal, expecting that their eagerness to purge Slovakia of Jews would pay off.

This is the story of the Hlinka Guard and its complacency in the deportation of the Slovak Jews to Auschwitz and other death camps.

CONTENTS

Introduction

You will not need those anymore.

. . . a member of the paramilitary Hlinka Guards said to the young Jewish women when he took their earrings and gold chains.

The era of the First Slovak Republic, from 1939 to 1945, is one of the most controversial periods in Slovak history. Nazi Germany's rise to power and the outbreak of World War II, and all the consequences that came with it, have strongly influenced the study and assessment of the era. Slovakia's hope of achieving statehood is another current that intermingled in the disorderly World War II period. Roughly the same could be said about the personalities and organizations of the Slovak regime, particularly the Hlinka Guard. It was a militia of the Slovak People's Party named after Andrej Hlinka, a Slovak Catholic priest and politician, and the leader of the Slovak People's Party.

When the Hlinka Guard was established, many Slovaks perceived it as a symbol of the struggle for national emancipation, but it gradually experienced stagnation and a loss of membership because active members of the Hlinka Guard fervently participated in the persecution of Jews and the expropriation of their assets. When the Slovak National Uprising broke out in August 1944, the Hlinka Guard had its "moment of glory," especially when the Flying Squads (Hlinka Guard Emergency Divisions) of the Hlinka Guard entered the stage. The Emergency Divisions were established because the Germans did not trust the already disintegrating Slovak Army, which they blamed for their participation in the uprising. The Hlinka Guard seemed to be the best organization for fulfilling auxiliary and security tasks.

When the Slovak National Uprising broke out in August 1944, it brought new lifeblood into the Hlinka Guard. The members were able to resurface the old slogans about their own significance and their national role in Slovakia's proclamation of independence in March 1939. When the army failed, the Hlinka Guard were the only ones who were able to restore order, with the help of their German friends. They were essentially established to help resurrect the crumbling regime. Entering the squads was voluntary in the beginning. Although there were thousands of Hlinka Guard members, the willingness of Slovaks to enter its armed units was not as great as the commanders expected. Therefore, the high command of the Hlinka Guards began to issue draft cards, also sending them to non-members of the Hlinka Guard, who were simply afraid of risking their lives in military action and for whom the idea of being a guardsman was distant. However, during states of military emergency, their refusal to accept a draft card could lead to capital punishment.

When the Hlinka Guard movement was established, some people joined just because their favorite club or association, for which they could seek conditional renewals only after joining, had been abolished. Others genuinely believed in the national ideas the movement seemed to initially represent or wanted to help the failing regime survive. These types of guardsmen were less willing to risk their lives for distant ideas. However, others were lured by benefits that were offered to those who joined, and many Slovaks were able to improve their everyday livelihood. Some actively participated in persecutions, but most of them served as watchmen, and many of them immediately ran away from home at the first possible opportunity. It is estimated that 5 percent of the guardsmen participated in executions, and it is known that they were physically present during at least one mass execution where 282 people died.

The Hlinka Guard is a phenomenon that significantly affected life in Slovakia from 1938 to 1945. Despite its relatively short duration, for many historians as well as laymen, it remains one of the most controversial places in Slovak history. Works aiming at an examination of the Hlinka Guard can be counted on the fingers of one hand.

The issues of the Hlinka Guard should be seen in the broader context of the foreign and domestic political situation in the hectic period of pre-World War II, which had its roots in the period shortly after World War I. The guard did not exist only for itself and was tied to the socio-political life in its years of operation.

Therefore, for the overall understanding of the Hlinka Guard's role in the Holocaust, it is appropriate to examine the socio-political situation in the Slovak Republic, the overall nature of the organization of the guard, its goals, direction, outside influences, and its place in society.

1

Ideas of Slovak National Emancipation

The development of the Hlinka Guard must be followed against the background of the society and political events of the first twenty and thirty years of the twentieth century. It was during this period that conditions were created that aimed, among other things, to realize the ideas of Slovak national emancipation. The Hlinka Guard did not grow from the decision of one person or a narrow group of people, but its arrival in the second half of 1938 was the result of the Slovak solution of a state governed as a single power in which the central government was ultimately supreme. Separatist-oriented Slovaks in this period were mainly interested in the defense of Slovaks as a peculiar nation, which should be guaranteed by the creation of Slovakia within Czechoslovakia. The struggle for the autonomy of Slovakia played the most important role for Andrej Hlinka's Slovak People's Party during the whole period of the Czechoslovak Republic. The political objectives of the Slovak People's Party were sympathetic to many young Slovaks dissatisfied with the so-called "politics of Czechoslovak parties." Therefore, the entire process of the development of the Hlinka Guard continuously fed on the autonomous efforts of this party. The tragedy, however, is that this national emancipation process of the Slovaks culminated in the period of Nazi expansion in Europe. It is in this area the People's Party found an argument for its political goals.

In addition to the question of the constitutional organization of the republic according to the Slovak People's Party, several other factors were active in the '20s and '30s, driving many of its supporters dissatisfied with the current situation in the Czechoslovak Republic. One was the autonomy of Slovakia, as the idea of a united Czechoslovak nation was declared in the Constitution of 1920. This was important to many not only in the political but also in the ethnic sense. However, it was mainly frustration of Slovaks with economic conditions, which contributed to the turmoil. It is in these areas the People's Party found an argument source for its political goals. The predominantly young generation, especially in the early 1930s, looked at Czech clerks, teachers, or other workers as interfering with their own interests, and did not hesitate to show their resistance, if not outwardly, at least by membership or sympathy for the People's Party. These factors partly contributed to the consolidation of the Slovak People's Party's positions; mostly, of its profiling radical wing, on which the ideas for its creation had already matured in the mid-1930s. The search for the roots of Hlinka Guard until its inception must therefore be examined against the background of the development of the Slovak People's Party policy as a distinctive representative of the Slovak nationally oriented goals.

The Slovak People's Party could not have wanted a better atmosphere for its activities. It aroused a state of threat in the wider layers of the Slovak population and expanded the dissatisfaction thereby multiplying its constituency. Already during the 1920s, the People's Party gained prestige among the Slovak population despite the strong influence of national parties, especially the Agrarian Party, the Czechoslovak Social Democratic Party, or the Trade Party, which often based their practical policy on opposing the principles presented by the people's representatives. Using the press, these parties argued with the People's Party on the fundamental questions of the limitations of centralist Czechoslovakism and establishment of an autonomous government in the territory of Slovakia.

In the 1920s and 1930s, one of the largest political enemies of the Hlinka Guard in cities was the radicalized Communist Party. This was mainly related to the influx of rural inhabitants into towns and to the expansion of members of the socially weakest sections of society, mainly among the poor and unemployed agricultural or industrial workers.

The Social Democrats announcing programs like the Communists became one of the most important obstacles to the people's efforts to assert themselves in Slovak cities. The People's Party sympathizers conflicted with them especially at election rallies and during the speeches of party leaders. Politically angry radical Communists, as well as Agrarians and Socialists, who were seconded by zealous and equally radical people, did not hesitate to resort to physical assaults or murder. In the 1920s, bloody conflicts at rallies was nothing unusual. They escalated as early as 1920–1921 when the aim of the Socialists was even to assassinate Andrej Hlinka. As a result, in 1923, young Slovak People's Party policymakers began to organize the seeds of the predecessor of the Hlinka Guard, the Rodobrana (Home Defense/Nation's Defense).

The task of the young members was to protect the people's assembly parties, while respecting order. They were to set a good example of maintaining order, and by these examples and deeds help government authorities to maintain public order. Their role was far from insignificant. Since the early years, the violence at political rallies got out of control of the police forces and escalated. Police had to intervene in the countless rallies, but it was often the case that, despite the efforts and security efforts of the security forces, they failed to tame the angry mob who used everything available to them. It was not just stones or bricks, but also an arsenal of weapons ranging from sticks to metal rods or even firearms that were the exception rather than the rule.

It was in this climate, when a voter could not be sure of his health or even his life by attending a political assembly, that the predecessor of the Hlinka Guard was formed. The question of Slovakia's position in Czechoslovakia was strongly present in the constitution of Rodobrana, and later in the creation of the first Hlinka Guard organizations. Nationalist tendencies stirred the emergence of both organizations and became a catalyst for their practical activities. Their common feature was also the connection to Hlinka's Slovak People's Party, which was virtually the only party defending the interests of Slovak independence in parliament. Vojtech Tuka, the ideological creator of the Rodobrana, who did not conceal his sympathy for Mussolini's Fascist regime, was moving to the forefront in the party.

On January 31, 1923, Andrej Hlinka signed the arrangements, giving Rodobrane a structure like a party organization. Their task was to keep order, as police were helpless against irresponsible elements whose purpose was to terrorize the leaders and supporters of the People's Party. In addition to the basis of power in the implementation of the program of autonomy and to be available to the Party if it found, there was a suitable opportunity to fight for its goals in other ways.

The arrangement also included "ten commandments," which each member was obliged to observe:

1. Be faithful to your Slovak nation.
2. Follow your Slovak principles.
3. Confess publicly to your Slovak and Christian beliefs.
4. Honor and maintain law and order.
5. Defend everyone from violence.
6. Be devoted to your confreres.
7. Hold discipline.
8. Keep confidential.
9. Get new pedigrees.
10. Honor the freedom of other beliefs.

The program in the form of the "ten commandments" was not only an establishing document for its members, but it also demonstrated the Christian character of the organization. Its members were often seen in worship, which, in addition to them being religious, also showed their belonging to the nation in opposition to what the leadership called "pagan Czech morals." The anti-Czech accent associated with unbelief and Socialism was very strong in forming the organization. The *gendarmerie* (armed people) was the military component with jurisdiction in civil law enforcement and responsible for small towns and rural areas headquarters in the program, made sure that there were Slovak inscriptions everywhere. Despite the declared Christian foundations of the organization, the people's rallies echoed slogans against the presence of Czechs in Slovakia. "Shame on them, out with them, hang them or poison them" was heard everywhere. Several Czech parties had a common program based on similar principles. The Czech National Fascist Community essentially professed relatively similar ideas stemming from Fascist ideology as the Slovak Rodobrana, with especially strong emphasis on the idea of the self-governing position of Slovakia by the militia.

The question of the presence of Fascist ideas in Rodobrana played an important role in designing its program, and even imitated similar Fascist organizations abroad in some ways. It is therefore understandable that it was formed according to the model of the Italian Organization *Squadre d'Azione* (Action Squad) but considering the Slovak situation. In their press, the militia professed Fascist principles and, like the Italian Fascists, did not conceal the hatred of the Communists who, according to them, wanted to throw the Slovak nation into a "sea of fire and blood" in which it is already condemned to complete extinction. They have implicitly argued that the essence of Fascism was to preserve nation and state on sound national principles and on religious grounds. Only healthy nationalism, solid religious morality can keep a nation from being broken up and a state from anarchy. Rodobrana wanted to implement this Fascist idea in Slovakia.

An important role in the Slovak environment of the time was also played by traditional strong religious feeling and thus distrust of foreigners, especially Czech organizations and intuitions. Thus, the Christian orientation of Rodobrana was most significant, in addition to emphasizing the autonomy of Slovakia. The propaganda office of the Rodobrana added traditional anti-Jewish propaganda statements. They were favorable to anti-Jewish thinking, and they blamed the Jews for the difficult economic situation in Slovakia. Unlike other organizations with Fascist elements that were organized in Slovakia later in the 1930s, the Rodobrana membership base expanded at a rapid pace.

The fate of Rodobrana and Hlinka Guard are very similar in certain features. Both arose in a period that did not favor the politics of independence. Both organizations abused their position and exceeded their powers. Gradually they became more known for violence against political or other opponents than for the benefit of a party or nation. This phenomenon cannot be earmarked solely based on the link between the two organizations to the Slovak People's Party—it has deeper roots. These are linked to the political situation and in the case of Hlinka Guard, its power gradually increased following the rise of Nazi Germany and the introduction of anti-Jewish regulations.

The Rodobrana sought to cultivate, in common with many others paramilitary Fascist movements, a sense of mysticism among its members. All its members had to be practicing Christians, meetings were generally held in monasteries and other sites of pilgrimage and invariably began with a solemn Mass celebrated by a local priest. The Rodobrana was the first serious effort in Slovakia to popularize Fascism and attracted significant support. The authorities do not appear to take the movement particularly serious and had to ban it twice, first in 1923 and again in 1928. It was finally dissolved in 1929.

Anti-Jewish sentiment was not new in Slovakia. Jews have lived in the Slovakian region since the eleventh century. In the fourteenth century, nearly 800 Jews resided in Bratislava. Most Jews engaged in commerce and money lending. Two notorious blood libels occurred in Slovakia; in 1494, Jews were burned at the stake in Trnava, and in 1529, in Pezinok, thirty Jews were accused of wrongdoings and burnt at the stake. After the battle of Mohács in 1526, Jews were expelled from all major towns in Slovakia. In 1683, hundreds of Moravian Jewish fled to Slovakia seeking refuge from the Kurucz riots and the living restrictions of Moravia. Most of these immigrants settled in western Slovakia, bordering Moravia.

In 1867, the dual monarch of Austro-Hungary was established, and Slovakia became a part of Hungary, often considered Northern Hungary. For more than a millennium, Slovakian Jewry was closely linked with that of Hungarian Jews. The Hungarian parliament passed the Emancipation Law to promote assimilation among minorities, especially Jews. Government officials supported Jewish cooperation in industry and finance. The Jewish population grew exponentially, especially in small, secluded towns in Eastern Slovakia. Nevertheless, much anti-Semitism existed in Slovakia and nationalists refused to allow Jews to assimilate into their culture.

In 1882 and 1883, anti-Jewish riots occurred in several towns in Slovakia. With the introduction of the Reception Law of 1896, which placed Judaism and Christianity on the same equal level, the Slovak Clerical People's Party was formed. The party's main interests were anti-Liberalism and limiting Jewish influence in the country. The nineteenth century also gave rise to the Zionist movement. In Slovakia, eight local Zionist organizations were formed. In 1903, Bratislava held the first Hungarian Zionist Convention; the first World Mizrachi Congress was convened in 1904.

After World War I and the creation of Czechoslovakia in 1918, Jews were given the right to be considered a separate nationality in the country. Jews prospered not only in industry but cultural life. Jews held more than one-third of all industrial investments in country. In 1919, the National Federation of Slovak Jews was established in Piešťany, and the Jewish Party was created. On August 2, 1919, the *Jewish People's Paper* was first published in Bratislava. This paper played a crucial role in advancing the rights of the Jews in Czechoslovakia.

Under the influence of the Slovak Peoples' party, many Slovakians were incited against the Jews. In the 1930s, numerous anti-Jewish demonstrations were held in Slovakia led by the Nationalist Youth Movement and the German-speaking students.

2

The Hlinka Guard Forms

In the early 1930s, different attitudes occurred in the Slovak People's Party to the tactics of political struggle. Two groups emerged inside the party: the so-called moderates, grouped mainly around Jozef Tiso, and radicals, whose leaders were younger officials such as Alexander Mach and Karol Sidor.

The radicalization of young separatists in this period was not only a response to the government's centralism, but also one of the first efforts to create a new organization to replace the dissolved Rodobrana. Alexander Mach, as one of the main protagonists of the movement, later recalled that by the end of 1937, a view had been growing in the ranks of the radicals to recreating the Rodobrana, an organization that could act as the "guard of the defenders." Only the following year, however, given the foreign policy situation and the internal tensions caused by it in Czechoslovakia, did the young separatists have the opportunity to fulfill their plans. On January 5, 1938, Andrej Hlinka called for separation from the Czechs by saying, "If Prague does not hear us, if the Pittsburgh Agreement, and autonomy does not happen, then we will say goodbye to Prague." The well-known slogan "In the New Year to Attack!" ascribed to Mach would soon be fulfilled.

Note: In May 1918, a European politician and professor named Tomáš Garrigue Masaryk came to Pittsburgh, Pennsylvania, in the United States. He was advocating independence for the Czech and Slovak peoples in war-ravaged eastern Europe. The pact stated that all the signers approved of the Union of the Czechs and Slovaks in an independent state and that Slovakia would have its own administration, legislative assembly, and courts; the Slovak language would be the official language in schools and public life in the Slovak regions. The Pittsburgh Agreement helped boost the establishment of the new state, along with the support of President Woodrow Wilson.

The revolutionary, exciting style and rhetoric of Slovak People's Party at the beginning of 1938 also attracted many young people dissatisfied with the Prague government's approach to solving the Slovak question. This part of the youth became increasingly in favor of the radical wing of the People's Party.

Although Karol Sidor was the first man to be appointed as commander in chief of this new formation, it was Alexander Mach who persuaded the party leadership that the time was right to re-establish a paramilitary force in Slovakia akin to the former Rodobrana.

At the birth of the Hlinka Guard, Alexander Mach proved to be a good strategist. He was aware that the time was right to capture and target revolutionary sentiments. Already on June 11, 1938, he published an article in *Slovak Truth* entitled "Hlinka Guards," which proposed moving the separatist struggle to a higher, more active level. Among other things, he called for the creation of Hlinka Guards, namely, an organization responsible for gatherings, cultural events and press publications. His article found a response in many circles. Government censorship confiscated the whole load of *Slovak Truth* publications and imposed a three-month ban on newspapers. Despite censors' intervention, many of the issue got to the readers because the editors circumvented the censorship regulation and sent out many to all regions of Slovakia before confiscation. In the issue of July 1, 1938, in the article "Should we build our own guards?" Slovaks again suggested the creation of a new party organization based on Mach's call, but censorship hit again, and the newspaper had to come out with whited-out passages.

In his statements, Alexander Mach made a clear declaration of the need to create a new organization of a purely political nature, subordinated to the Slovak People's Party. His words fell on fertile ground among the young separatists all over Slovakia. The first Hlinka Guard organization was established in Bratislava, the second one in the Veľké Rovné and Trnava organizations. Similarly, Alexander Mach placed one of the first Hlinka Guard cells in Vienna. July 8, 1938 was the date of constitution of the Hlinka Guard in Trnava. The exact establishment of the first organization is difficult to determine as the name was not officially used everywhere by all separatists. However, the press and later propaganda mostly attributed the start of the Hlinka Guard in Trnava.

Parliamentary elections played an important role in the formation of the first Hlinka Guard organizations. Youth committed to Hlinka's ideas laid the foundations for future cooperation during the May pre-election agitations in favor of Slovak People's Party. In parallel, there were a number of groups who met only the night before the election, which often resulted in comic situations when they hung autonomous posters and met a group of supposedly hostile, which surprisingly hung the same posters, local Germans, with whom they found a common enemy in the Communists. In several cities, where the German group was more numerous, they even acted together in the pre-election struggles with the Communists.

According to later propaganda statements, just before the election, the Germans realized that the guardsmen were their best friends to fight for the common cause. It was timely for both groups to create a more significant form of political cooperation, as part of the guards had some sympathy for Hitler's policy and in particular his efforts to break up Czechoslovakia, which could mean strengthening Slovakia's efforts for greater independence. This topic became relevant only after October 6, 1938, when the Hlinka Guard logically started to focus on Germany as a power to co-operate with in the future of territorial changes in Central Europe, following the policy of the Slovak People's Party and the foreign policy situation.

While the organization was forming, the electoral struggle encountered several problems. Open activity in favor of the separatist idea was met by resistance from the repressive forces and could be classified as anti-state activity with the aim of breaking the republic. No less important was the attitude of the population. Open support for the electoral struggle in favor of the People's Party encountered bloody clashes with members of the opposing parties. Since such clashes were not unusual during this period, as part of the political culture of the pre-election struggle, guards used different types of weapons for defense. In the summer of 1938, it was mainly short sticks and belts. Later, short batons became a favorite weapon, perfect for intimidation and frequent physical attacks against their ideological and political opponents.

Some Hlinka Guards, depending on the region, established a contact with local party organizations. However, it remained only at the level of leaflet and print production and, in most cases, did not go beyond the technical security framework of the Slovak People's Party. Even the Trnava Guards could not create a wider background for a more sophisticated system of coordination of independence activities, but thanks to them the elections for the People's Party were victorious. More and more people showed interest in membership, which later caused the party and the guard serious problems. The young members wanted to create an organization with a wider nationwide scope, temporarily operating in a regional context, which would underpin the autonomist struggle. The specific structure of the membership was not yet crystallized in this period. The fact that it was established by youth determined the average age of its members in this period. However, they were in close association with the older structures of the party.

In particular, the involvement of older workers had become a hot issue, thereby bringing mutual cooperation to a qualitatively higher level. Cooperation with the People's Party had been beneficial for Hlinka Guard for several reasons. Although the guard could present their intentions to the public even without the party's knowledge, it lacked the funds, which the Slovak People's Party was able to allocate for its needs. Equally important to them was the support of officials and the consent of the nobility. The issue of membership of the Slovak People's Party was considered a necessity, even membership in the party was one of the conditions for admission to the guard. Each applicant had to submit an application to the Slovak People's Party. Therefore, during the second half of July, the Hlinka Guard made contact with senior officials of the Ministry of Defense of the Hlinka Guard. This step was a period of closer cooperation and networking between the two organizations.

The connection of the Hlinka Guard to the structures of the Ministry of Defense and its impact on the guard was increasingly noticeable, but the cooperation had so far only been carried out at the level of local organizations. This was mainly due to the fact that in the summer months, the Hlinka Guard was practically just a local association without a nationwide reach. This is understandable given the fact that only a small circle of people knew about its existence. It became known to the wider public only after the first articles were published in the press of the Slovak People's Party, which met with strong resistance from Czech and left-wing newspapers in a longer article called "Hlinka Guards." It warned against reviving the Rodobrana, under a threat that anyone who disagreed would be disciplined. Despite the objections to the new organization and, in particular, its connection to the ideas of the Rodobrana, it argued that if the Hlinka Guards was founded for the purpose of improving people's culturally, religiously and nationally, just as it is in other youth organizations of individual political parties, no one can object to their establishment.

Through the arguments on the newspaper pages, the Hlinka Guard was also known to the autonomous population, which was positively reflected in its organizational structure and the growth of its membership. Cooperation, largely initiated by the guard, developed primarily in a local environment. They did not want any local patriotism, but they wanted to capture the national movement all over Slovakia.

On October 6, 1938, one stage of the development of a young organization was completed, which over time had been transformed into an unmistakable power in autonomous Slovakia. The manifesto of the Slovak nation has pushed the efforts of the Slovaks towards their own self-governing establishment to a higher level. Even German observers could not fail to notice that the Slovak leaders were strongly opposed to "Jewish Marxism." The Hlinka Guard could thus look to the future in this spirit, as well as the exercise of the right of self-determination, with a prospect of rapid growth that was soon realized.

3

The Power of the Hlinka Guard Increases

After October 6, 1938, the power of the Hlinka Guard grew from day to day. More so because the movement began to spread rapidly all over the territory of Slovakia. This was also since the initial chaotic formation of regional and local organizations independent of each other had been replaced as early as October 6 by a coordinated organization through party members. The main impetus was the official foundation of Hlinka Guard in Bratislava on October 7, 1938 by Ján Dafčík, but mostly by Karol Murgaš, who became the soul of organizing the Hlinka Guard in the first months of autonomy. The chief and commander for life became Karol Sidor. The fact that he was the chief commander of the emerging organization was not a coincidence. His popularity among the population predetermined him to accept the position of commander of the organization, which according to the ideas of its creators, at least in the initial period, were to connect the Slovaks to equal status in a common state with the Czechs. Some point out that the fact that he became a lifelong commander of the Hlinka Guard was the main attraction for many still hesitant Slovaks to join the ranks of the guard. This was one of the reasons why the idea of setting up Hlinka Guard organizations was mainly associated with a change in the political scene. This gave a greater opportunity for Slovaks to organize themselves in national organizations, after October 6. Karol Sidor was a good personality to take over as commander of the Hlinka Guard because he had a positive attitude towards the forming of Guards during the tense days of September and the mobilization of the army. In his radio speech of September 23, 1938, in which he expressed support for mobilization, he took the opportunity to urge the youth organized in the guard to observe public order at critical moments. According to the guards, however, Sidor's effort to establish himself on the Slovak political scene also played a role.

The meeting of the Slovak People's Party in Piešťany concluded that the party should be the only representative of the Slovak nation to form the regime of autonomous Slovakia. The slogan "one nation, one party, one leader" became the main idea of forming the regime. The Hlinka Guard was tied to party structures in this process and its growth of power was directly dependent on the anti-democratic tendencies of the regime in transforming the Slovak People's Party into a *de facto* self-governing party. This was one of the reasons why the two institutions were in good agreement with each other in the early period of autonomous Slovakia. The guard saw in the party's efforts to wipe out political opponents the possibility of its growth of power. On the other hand, despite the various initial aversions of its moderate representatives, the Slovak People's Party could rely on the Hlinka Guard in formulating the regime. The guard thus made the transition to a one-party model more dynamic. The rapid increase in power of the Hlinka Guard, if not even the number of memberships, which in a short time reached the whole number of 100,000, was due to the politics of the People's Party. In a relatively short period, the party coped with political opponents and enforced more measures against various institutions and social organizations. Already on October 9, the People's Party suspended the activities of the Communist Party. A week later, on October 16, the Social Democratic Party was stopped. The other parties, except for the Slovak National Party, which, despite a similar program with the People's Party, stopped on November 4. According to some historians, the Hlinka Guard, on the one hand, acted as a back-up for the Slovak People's Party, an instigator, but also a repressor. Tiso already described it at a meeting of party officials on October 13, 1938 as "Sidor's sting organization," which, in his words, was not desirable, suggesting that the guard, as "Sidor's side government" be dissolved. This view was also expressed by the secretary general of the Slovak People's Party Martin Sokol. At the same time, he called for the guards to flow into the party's organizational structure and demand that they be banned.

He even commented on Murgas in radio broadcasts, from which the voice of the main organizer of the Hlinka Guard is often heard in those days, not only a lot of anger, but also the smell of "political alcohol." This was perhaps the most important of the reasons that helped the Hlinka Guard overcome the initial aversion of some conservative people. Although Karol Sidor defended it, he greatly underestimated its radicalization, especially on the issue of anti-Jewish focus. Sidor adjusted his approach so that he was assisted by ever-increasing winds of Fascism.

However, to understand the phenomenon of a remarkable increase in power, it is necessary to point out several phenomena that have influenced the organization and enabled it to establish itself very quickly on the Slovak political scene. After October 6, the party could only be small parts of the original state apparatus and therefore the Hlinka Guard appeared to be the most appropriate organization, which, despite the initial impulsiveness could become a power tool of the Slovak People's Party. Thanks to the party, the guard could push through changes in the state and society more quickly, which, among other things, led to the strengthening of the position of one party. The power increase of the guard was not only the People's Party and the factual help of the regime, but also the newly formed national committees.

The committees were formed in the first days after the declaration of autonomy, during a temporary confusion in society, and therefore their initial functioning is set in the context of these events. It was a revolutionary period. Declaration of Autonomy of Slovakia on October 6, 1938 in its consequences meant for Slovak People's Party and Hlinka Guard the fulfillment of the long-term dreams of Slovaks about their own administration of their territory. However, it had more far-reaching consequences for the Hlinka Guard than just the joy of the new government in Slovakia. The guard could step out of illegality and develop its activity without fear of police intervention and could develop a struggle for the creation of an independent Slovak state.

Radicalism in their ranks was largely understandable. According to the guards, there were still a lot of unreliable people and organizations in Slovakia, including Slovak authorities, schools, and other state and non-state institutions. Non-Slovak elements, especially Czechs, had to be dealt with as soon as possible, according to members of Slovak People's Party and Hlinka Guard. Czech dominance consisted mainly in the effort to eliminate Czech civil servants in crucial public offices.

After a new reallocation of power after October 6, 1938, a need emerged to change the current situation in favor of Slovak civil servants. For the most part, the political ambitions of the new regime understood that insisting on the state apparatus would have to be one of the priorities on the road to the creation of a new Slovakia. However, this process could not be carried out immediately. Mass unreasonable action could lead to a rupture with Prague, and the Slovak side did not immediately have adequate compensation for Czech employees. During this period, the foundations of the leadership of a new state power organization concentrated in Slovak hands were formed, but the People's Party did not have enough quality cadres from Czechoslovakia to immediately take power in Slovakia. It was not possible to meet the demands of radicals and Hlinka Guard for eviction of all Czech employees from Slovakia. The forming state apparatus was forced in individual cases to proceed in the sense of political amnesty by the exponents of the Czechoslovak regime.

In the first days of autonomous Slovakia, it was important for the state apparatus in the new political situation not to succumb to radical sentiments, not only in dealing with the relationship of Slovaks to the Czech clerical element, but also in relation to newly emerging state power. It was necessary to create a legally acceptable type of organization, an authority that would be able to keep Slovakia within the limits of the new state apparatus in revolutionary times. The Hlinka Guard seemed to be a suitable organization for the performance of this function, but it was not adapted to it by its very nature. It had not yet been accepted that the guard, as an organization whose membership was growing rapidly, was able to guarantee the required functions of a newly established state authority, albeit only as a subsidiary body to the authorities. Therefore, the need for the creation of committees that would temporarily bridge the gap between the government and the still legally functioning authorities of the former state power came to the forefront. Another equally important function of the committees was to effectively exercise control over state authority. Hlinka Guard could not suit the Prague government, which saw in it the mainstream of radical sentiment in Slovak society. A new power was created so that the Slovak government had something to rely on after coming to Slovakia.

The National Committee was formed in Bratislava on October 7, 1938. On that day, Jozef Tiso was appointed minister of Plenipotentiary for the Administration of Slovakia. The new government was established on the same day in Prague. However, it was considered only part of the Czechoslovak government until the formation, as outlined in the Act on the Autonomy of Slovakia.

Officially, the Slovak national committees formed all over Slovakia, established since Sunday, October 9, 1938, to help the government maintain order. Their creation was preceded by a call spread by the press and radio saying:

> We call on all our proven to take the initiative of forming the Temporary Slovak National Committees. Let them consist of proven Slovak nations and especially make sure that they maintain good contact with the other language populations. Temporary Slovak National Committees should assist the municipal councils and municipal councils so to maintain order and preserve the Slovak national property, which simultaneously means a de facto assumption of power in all Slovak municipalities and towns, will arise. Please send us brief reports on the creation of Temporary National Committees.

This challenge was addressed by Karol Sidor, who refused to participate in the formation of a new government. The Hlinka Guard was supposed to implement their regulations, which they were to apply to society. For this reason, the connection of the guard with the national committees was necessary and important for Sidor. Not that he was directly agitating for the creation of Hlinka Guards. In connection with the calls for the establishment of new temporary bodies, however, almost all over Slovakia both organizations were founded in fact together. The task of the national committees in the first days after October 6, 1938 was, among other things, to maintain peace and order in the autonomous territory, but in fact they did the opposite. Not a day passed that anti-Jewish and anti-Czech activities took place in Slovakia. This started the day after the declaration of autonomy. On Friday October 7, demonstration meetings were held in the evening to celebrate the establishment of the first Slovak government. These events were the first to point out the possibility of misuse of the Hlinka Guard, even though it had not yet been absorbed by the organization. The party's presidency also raised the issue of further direction or even the abolition of the Hlinka Guard.

The joyful mood of autonomy was expressed by thousands of people, mostly students and youth, by the burning of many lanterns. On the other hand, many predominantly young, radicalized Slovaks chanted hateful slogans, such as "Slovakia to Slovaks, Palestine to Jews, Jews Out, Czechs Out." Through them, the radicals expressed their long-stoked views on solving the relationship to non-Slavic and dangerous state elements. In many places they expressed their radicalism by stripping national flags from schools and offices and from the stores of Czech traders.

Interconnection was evident in several local committees with local Hlinka Guard organizations. Important guard members were elected to the committee, so there was a tendency to blot out the boundaries between Hlinka Guard and committee. This was mainly due to the ambiguity and unconsolidated situation. It is certain, however, that Hlinka Guard was closely linked to the national committees, in particular by the notion of guardians of national property, peace, and personal security and by carrying out the tasks of its extended arm, a kind of executive power and organized force. On one hand, the guard, in cooperation with the committee, received a partially legal basis for its activities. Guardians often, practically throughout the existence of the Hlinka Guard, claimed rights under the authority of executive bodies, not only on civil matters, but often interfered with things that did not fall within their responsibility. It was partly from ignorance, especially during the period shortly after October 6. At that time, there was considerable inconsistency in the interpretation of rights as regards the competences of the specific components of the state apparatus, and of the Hlinka Guard as a newly created organization, despite the efforts of the Hlinka Guards Headquarters to create a framework for guard activities.

By March 14, frequent disputes arose between the Hlinka Guard and security authorities or authorities over competences, mainly in security matters. The servicing members of the National Committee, mostly the guardsmen, did not hesitate to control even military personnel, which in the military circles caused a sharp wave of criticism toward the National Committee. The army mainly referred to the order of Hlinka Guard Number 5 on the prohibition of the mixing of civilian persons into military matters, noting that only the *gendarmerie* and military supervisory authorities are entitled to control military personnel. Hlinka Guard members even stopped military non-commissioned officers and searched their cars, apparently exceeding their powers defined for both Hlinka Guard members and National Committee.

The cooperation of the Hlinka Guard and the National Committee was also purpose-built, resulting from the specific development of the Hlinka Guard in a specific municipality or town and consisted in linking its functionaries to the national committees and the local People's Party organization. The guard did not perform only the tasks assigned directly by the committee. In many places where the guard was organized in parallel with the National Committee, or was already in place before its constitution, the guard commanders, who had a function in the national committees, could often apply the committee's resolutions directly by official Hlinka Guard interconnectedness of both institutions.

Local Hlinka Guard organizations, committees, as well as the commissioners, took a negative view of the violent events, but they did not condemn anti-Semitism as such. In the posters, they just announced that "if the Jewish issue will not be resolved, it will destroy national property and damage the prestige of the new

Slovakia." The National Committee and the Hlinka Guard, however, condemned in the spirit of the People's Party policy on anti-Jewish riots, not because of the fight against antisemitism, but because of the destruction of national property and damaging the prestige of the autonomous Slovakia.

The Hlinka Guard was already so established in Slovak society at the end of 1938 that cooperation with the national committees did not have to entail the approval of its activities from official offices. Nevertheless, the existence of national committees was coming to an end. In their own words, "the National Committee fought for the rights of Slovaks and Slovaks and had the merit in that jobs vacated by employees who harmed Slovakia and the Slovak people." The dissolution of the National Committee was decided by the Presidium of the Regional Office on November 8, 1938 and the government of the Slovak Republic on December 19, 1938. The increase of the powers of the Slovak People's Party as a supervisory body over the activities of the state administration undoubtedly contributed to their disappearance. In a new situation at the turn of 1938 and 1939, the committees no longer found any justification and were lost in the past.

Many of the committees have exceeded their powers, contrary to government orders, hand in hand with local People's Party organizations and the Hlinka Guard. Despite their proclaimed function, they often became powerful authorities. The execution of their orders was carried out by the Hlinka Guard, which was closely linked to them. It became a kind of prolonged hand of committees, which disappeared at the turn of 1938 and 1939, when their activities the establishment of government power was not necessary.

4

The Structure of the Hlinka Guard

After the declaration of an autonomous Slovakia at the beginning of October 1938, the guard was still a voluntary organization, a kind of association, which gained more influence. One of the most active guard organizers in the first days and months was Karol Murgaš. The Nazis also understood his role and influence in organizing the Hlinka Guard. According to them, "he was the decisive man of the Hlinka Guards." More importantly, however, he was extremely capable, clear and energetic in German circles, whose relationship with the Germans was more than positive. He was often given the attribute as almost the only Slovak politician who was a "friend of Germans."

Although deputy chief commander of the Hlinka Guard was Alexander Mach, he was reportedly fully engaged in his other tasks and was unable to cope with directives and organizational orders. Even the German authorities did not consider him the most capable man for organizing the Hlinka Guard and put more emphasis on good relations with Murgaš, who even commented on Mach in one of his later reports that his pro-German belief was only temporary and adapted to the current political situation. On October 9, the Organizational Schedule of the Hlinka Guards was signed which was only a temporary proposal. According to this proposal, the guard was a voluntary guardian of Slovak national property and Slovak national ideals, of which only a man of the "Hlinka spirit" could be a member. The guard could continue to build a new Slovakia.

On the German side, the guard was given great importance during the period of autonomy. It is also noticeable that German advisor Laurenz Karbus was sent to Bratislava during this period to act as an advisor for the Hlinka Guard, especially in the field of armaments. Karol Murgaš did not object; on the contrary, he accepted the German advice and instructions. The beginnings of the Hlinka Guard's formation were also supervised by German officials, who were to ensure that the direction of the guard and the formation of its organizational structure matched most German ideas.

The basis of the organizational structure was to become 100-men groups, consisting of two halves. There were four teams in each hundredth and three teams in each section. The guard gradually gained a wide range of powers, but their performance depended on the commitment of the individual commanders and the capabilities of the headquarters, due to the lack of good-quality officers. Many of the tasks were overseen by the local commanders, who determined the direction of the guard. For example, they decided on the admission of new members. Given the absence of practical coordination from the highest places in the formation of Hlinka Guard organizations, it was essential that the state apparatus, in view of the growing influence of the guard, unify the whole process.

The situation at the end of October 1938 was also addressed by the presidency of the autonomous government, which issued an official opinion on the organizational structure of the Hlinka Guard. The order reflected the tasks of the Hlinka Guard in the Slovak society and tried to turn it into an organization based on solid foundations. The Hlinka Guards were organized throughout Slovakia, mostly together with the establishment of the National Committee. According to the government, the highest commander of the Hlinka Guard was also the chairman of the Central Slovak National Committee.

The main headquarters of the Hlinka Guard in Bratislava, which was the highest-ranked component of the organization, consisted of three chiefs and seven departments. Karol Murgaš was appointed chief of the organization headquarters. His task was to issue organizational orders and to maintain contacts with the Slovak army officer corps, which, according to the guards, should be instrumental in building a strong, national, and free Slovakia. Later, longtime Chief Commander Alexander Mach was appointed chief of the political section and was in charge of the political education based on Andrej Hlinka's ideas, in the spirit of the late political party. Later, the tasks of the spiritual administration were specified by a special statute in 1939, when Ladislav Jurkoviè became a representative of the main spiritual affairs for Hlinka Guard. The appointment of an evangelical spiritual leader was a step towards improving relations between Catholics and Protestants in the organization, but their relationships remained tense until the end.

In addition to the spiritual department, six other departments were set up to stand by their leaders. Many of them later largely influenced the formation of Slovak history in the years 1938–1945. The deputy of the Slovak Parliament, Pavol Čarnogursk, became the head of the propaganda department. The social department was headed by Imrich Vashina and Jan Horacek. The establishment of a separate department for the Academic Hlinka Guard, headed by Vilom Kovárom, was also appreciated by the university students. The young academics were ordered to fulfill the tasks of the helpers of the promotional headquarters, but at the same time they should also be available for the administrative functions of the individual chiefs. The Railway Guard, although formally subject to the orders of the Hlinka Guard, had a relatively autonomous position within the guard, unlike the other constituents. The only vacant department in the Hlinka Guard remained the health department in October 1938.

The highest command within the organizational structure of the Hlinka Guard was the Main Command. Regional headquarters fell under the direct authority of the Hlinka Guard according to the Land Order Number 2. The regional headquarters consisted of a regional commander, aide, a propaganda and intelligence officer, a scribe and an arms master. The Land Order stated that each regional headquarters should at the same time maintain an economic section made up of a commander, two scribes, and a storekeeper.

District, city, and local headquarters were hierarchically located under the regional headquarters. The smallest unit in the hierarchy of the organizational structure of Hlinka Guard Headquarters was the local headquarters. The commanders of the guard were to become certified people and autonomists, but it was not possible to meet due to the lack of high-quality commanders. The guard fought with this problem practically until the end of the existence of the Slovak State; as such, complications accompanied the selection of suitable candidates for command positions in the emergency sections of the Hlinka Guard.

On October 28, 1938, the role of Hlinka Guard in society was greatly enhanced by Decree Law Number 15 on the dissolution of all paramilitary organizations and the recognition of the Hlinka Guard as the only military organization in the territory of the Slovak Republic. Despite not being sympathetic to several members of the Hlinka Guard, the government of the Autonomous Land of Slovakia again helped the Hlinka Guard strengthen its position and influence and social life, which grew at a staggering pace in this period. The government believed that the Hlinka Guard was the most suitable alternative through which it could try to solve several problems of Slovak society.

One of the government's priorities was the monopoly of the party's power, which the Slovak Government Decree of October 28, 1938 immediately dissolved all paramilitary and military organizations operating in the territory of the Slovak country, including the National Guard, Union of Freedom Guard, National Rifle Unity, Peasant Horse, Shooting Unity, Danube Guard, and similar organizations. Armed formations of Sokol gymnasiums, workers' gymnasium units, and Czechoslovak Eagle units were disbanded as well, but the associations were not dissolved. In addition to these associations, the cessation of activities affected mainly Jewish associations, and were forcibly dissolved. Many of the associations, however, disbanded spontaneously (e.g. the Czechoslovak Cyclists Club) and decided to voluntarily enter the Hlinka Guard. The Hlinka Guard became the only authorized organization on the territory of the Slovak land and acquired the right according to build its organizational network on the territory of the Slovak Republic.

During this period, the guard intervened in several spheres of social and political life. According to the Decree of the Slovak Government Number 287/1938 of November 3, 1938, the guard was to help all authorities and security authorities in their performance, to care for the religious-moral and patriotic education of male youth from eighteen years, and with the help of trained officers educate their membership in military discipline and spirit of defense.

Although the constitutional changes in Czechoslovakia in November did not substantially affect the influence of the central government in Prague on the organization of the armed forces, they contributed to strengthening the position of the Hlinka Guard in Slovakia and created room for improvement of its organizational structure.

Against the background of military training in the Hlinka Guard, an interesting battle began to unfold with the Hlinka Guard for a position at the expense of the competing German organization, the *Freiwillige Schutzstaffel* (Voluntary Protection Corps' or FS), which tried to achieve the position of military defense of the population to reach a position similar to Hlinka Guard. Hlinka Guard, especially in nationally mixed areas, lost membership at the expense of the German organization.

To be a full-fledged Hlinka Guard organization, Hlinka Guard officials also had to solve the problem of providing uniforms for its members. The Hlinka Guard uniform had undergone several changes during the development of the organization. Even though in the general public, the Hlinka Guard was mainly associated with black, in the early period some guards had blue shirts. Hlinka Guard only went to black later. Yet, many of the guard members, because of the financial demands of the guard's uniform, did not own a uniform. Its components were so expensive that many members of the Hlinka Guard could not afford them at all and were often confined to caps and boots. In many villages, it was common to see men dressed in local costumes with guards' caps instead of uniformed guardsmen. Several headquarters tried to help their subordinates with the procurement of uniforms and organized boxing matches where they collected entry fees. From the proceeds, it then bought guards uniforms or accessories.

The Hlinka Guard was reworked into an influential power in autonomous Slovakia during December. Already in October, it was recognized as the only military organization in the territory of the Slovak land. It began to gain even greater influence in this area when its statutes were approved based on Government Regulation Number 70 of December 5, 1938. At the same time, the government disbanded sports clubs in the country and assigned their property to the Hlinka Guard. The property of the associations meant a significant benefit for Hlinka Guard, since the financing of the guard to this point was based mainly on donations and subsidies of sympathizers.

In addition to the profits from the assets of the dissolved associations, which were not always certain, Hlinka Guard was financed from several sources. The state contributed to the guard for certain expenses. Under Government Decree No. 2200 of September 25, 1939, the state was to cover expenses such as headquarters and salaries of employees from the state budget. Therefore the guard had to find other sources of income that would cover its functioning or help solve the acute problems of dressing guards in uniforms. One way of obtaining funding was to apply for subsidies sent by Hlinka Guard headquarters to districts, towns, or counties. In addition to this source, the popular form of raising funds was the organization of sporting and cultural events, but also the proceeds from the so-called cinema licenses, as individual Hlinka Guard headquarters operated dozens of cinemas throughout Slovakia. Perhaps the most profitable was the Jewish property acquired by the guards in the form of coercion, forcing the Jews to contribute to the Hlinka Guard account often by considerable sums.

In addition to the organizational changes were the provisions laid down by Organizational Order Number 5 covering conditions of admission to the Hlinka Guard. Until then, virtually everything was free to the respective commander to determine, which should be modified by organizational orders in the sense that every member of the Slovak state and any Christian could be accepted as a member of the guard, if he fulfilled precisely specified conditions. This wording followed the approved statutes of the Hlinka Guard by decree of the government of December 5, 1938. It was determined that every guard must be crime-free for the admission to the organization (except for the punishment for autonomous activity), morally pure, should also live a family life, and not be an alcoholic. Other conditions of entry into the guard also included 100 percent healthy without apparent physical problems and no anti-autonomist activity before October 6, 1938.

One of the basic principles in admitting a new membership to the Hlinka Guard was that each new member would only be admitted as a guard without considering military rank and social status. Nevertheless, many Slovaks reported to the guard with the prospect of functions or command rank, which, in their opinion, could later serve to gain additional benefits.

5

The Guard Increases Attacks on Jews

Being a member of the Hlinka Guard brought advantages. It is precisely the many benefits made available from the guard's legitimation that attracted more to its rank. In addition to the radical supporters of humanist politics, they were the most radical supporters of persecution against the predominantly Jewish population. Although the guard's activities could not be perceived solely as anti-Jewish actions, even though they formed the largest part of their agenda until March 14, 1939, it was these events that were visible from the outside that most reflected Slovak society. Many of the guards were active in the most brutal crackdowns on Jews, and gradually the role of the guards in the process of resolving the Jewish question within the state apparatus became official.

It is very difficult to separate the issue of the guards' riots and attacks against Jews, which were often ordered from above and prompted by superiors' orders, and whether they resulted from the application of the regime's anti-Jewish legislation. On the one hand, the guards on their own initiative persecuted mainly Jews, on the other hand they were gradually involved in the anti-Jewish measures of the government as an executive body. Not all the activities of the guard were directed against Jewish citizens. Czechs and ordinary Slovaks often became the target of guard arbitrariness. They often did not suit them politically, or by attacks against them, guardsmen tried to solve their personal problems.

In the period before March 14, 1939, the guardsmen exceeded their powers as an auxiliary body of the security forces and authorities and, from their arbitrary position of guardians of Slovak property and lives and intervened in several spheres of socio-political life. Security forces and the state apparatus therefore criticized many of the guards' persecutions. During the period of autonomy, there had been several cases of investigations of guards for offenses committed on Jewish citizens. It is obvious from many sources that the guards were aware of their position, but the possible prosecution was often not a threat to them. Already in this period, there were many cases of abuse of Jews and forcibly confiscating their property under the threat of torture and physical punishment. One of these cases happened in Sered, near Trnava, on the right bank of the Váh River, where the guards registered all Jews and added to the list the amount each Jew was to pay from 100 to 4,000 crowns (4,000 crowns is equivalent of 73,949 in today's U.S. dollars). As the district authority pointed out: "every Jew who pays this sum should have received a picture of Andrej Hlinka, namely Jews who donated smaller sums received a smaller image, and Jews who donated more money received a larger image." Many Jews in the city were put in prison at Hlinka Guard stations and were released only after they had paid the required sums, often in excess thousands of crowns.

During the autumn of 1938, there were numerous anti-Jewish actions of smaller groups, in which young Slovaks acted aggressively. Hlinka Guard members may have appeared among the troublemakers, but, as in other similar cases, their participation may not have been the rule. Anti-Jewish events of this nature arose many times spontaneously when a larger group of friends met. They would break the windows of the homes of Jewish owners or attack lonely Jews at night on the streets of the city. Many Jews lived in fear of attack and did not go out at night. Disturbances and attacks were regular, especially in the first two months of 1939. Jews complained, for example, that day after day they were attacked without any reason, and their windows are being broken. In a letter dated January 5, 1939, Jewish leaders asked Prime Minister Jozef Tiso to intervene because the district office did not want to intervene, and the municipal police would do nothing.

In many cases, although it was not the guards, but many of the offenses took place under the guard. The organizational unpreparedness and the influx of membership made it possible for all elements to enter it, which soon began to act out their own grievances and prejudices. The air of hatred and fear became a breeding ground for people who aimed for the simple discharge of aggressive appetites or self-enrichment. The pursuit of a career and the prospect of easy profit were often the driving force behind their actions. Under the auspices of the protection of their property, they demanded from the Jews and wealthy citizens more and more money. One example is the case of Rudolf Held, who demanded money from affluent citizens, while answering the questions why he wanted the money, he said, "I don't need to legitimize it, but you know who I am," showing the Hlinka Guard double-cross patch. He even threatened the maid that he would blow up the house of a financial advisor if she did not send him money. He went to the houses of Jews and some non-Jews, and on the pretext of being a guard and guarding them, he demanded cash from them for protection. He was detained but released along with several anti-Jewish rioters shortly after March 14.

There were so many similar members hiding behind the Hlinka Guard name that the leadership of the guard tried to distance themselves from their causes by claiming that they were not members of the Hlinka Guard. Already at the beginning of October, there were cases of enrichment of individuals across the whole of

Slovakia, who were allegedly entrusted with collections for the expenses related to its functioning under the supposed Hlinka Guard auspices. As a result, on October 17, the Hlinka Guard issued an order in which it stood up sharply against the "parasites" both inside and outside the guard.

These and similar actions, however, were mostly hooliganism and many Hlinka Guard members failed to participate, although among the troublemakers were certainly members of the Hlinka Guard. However, they took part in them on their own, without the official patronage of the organization. Much more dangerous were, so to speak, officially, or tacitly, actions taken of guard officers against Jewish people and their property. These radicals practiced these actions from the first days after the declaration of autonomy. In the narrowly understood powers of the Hlinka Guard, they often interfered arbitrarily, especially against the economically active Jewish population and former members of the Communist Party or various "enemies of Slovak life."

In November 1938, Jozef Klein, a Jewish fashion and knitwear shop owner, reported that Hlinka Guard members have been standing in front of his house were not letting any customers in since November 16, 1938. He suffered considerable material damage and had to close his shop. During this period, the guards stood in front of almost every Jewish shop and warned shoppers that there were plenty of Christian shops in the city where they could shop without the support of the Jews. Some Hlinka Guard commanders offered themselves to Jewish fellow citizens to protect them from attacks and secure their property against damage. For example, the Hlinka Guard commander in Slovenské Raslavice, for a fee of 10,000 crowns from the Jewish religious community, promised to maintain order in the community so that the Jews could live happily and carefree with non-Jewish fellow citizens.

Several of the Hlinka Guard commanders were selected from the ranks of teachers, lawyers, and doctors, especially in the initial period. They often became commanders shortly after the establishment of the organization; many of them entered the guard with idealistic ideas and assumed the functions of local commanders in the villages simply because no one was better suited to this position in the village and enjoyed proper authority as public persons. Many, however, condemned the manifestations of violence against Jews, tried to prevent looting of Jewish taverns and shops, for which they became unpopular in the guard and were later practically sidelined.

In addition to anti-Jewish attacks, the guard was engaged in several activities to defend Slovak interests. According to the guard's own words, they were careful, for example, to observe the closing hours and evening peace in the businesses and streets. They even became a sort of guardian of morality. According to their statements, they confiscated naughty French magazines in the businesses and tried to purify social life, which they, however, often understood very narrowly and from the position of the radicals. In fact, this activity was not the primary part of their work. It is possible that they were given orders from the commanders to observe public life, and at the same time to observe the peace of the night but intervened especially when it was disturbed by Jews or Czechs.

In many cases, they often acted impulsively and without legal basis. In most of the disputes, they objected to the fact that they were defending the narrowly understood Slovak interests that the guard had in their view as a guardian of Slovak lives and property. By defending Slovak interests, the guardsmen did not argue only in actions against the Jews. Czechs, who were already on the list of many members of the Hlinka Guard before March 14, also became the target of their attention. In mid-December 1938, guards forced open the door to the home of a local Czech teacher who was beaten and ordered to leave the city within forty-eight hours. Similarly, they attacked pupils of a wine school of Czech nationality, whom they bullied and kicked and, like their teachers, ordered them to leave the Slovak territory. Such anti-Czech riots were not new and occurred almost immediately after the declaration of autonomy.

In one case, guards carried out repression mainly against Jews directly on behalf of authorities, respectively, Jozef Tiso. By November 1938, Slovakia lost 21 percent of the territory in favor of Hungary, it was one of the impulses for the prime minister to punish the Jews for alleged co-responsibility on this act.

As a result of the Vienna Arbitration, Czechoslovakia was obliged to surrender the territories in southern Slovakia and southern Carpathian Ruthenia south of the line and inclusive of the towns in the area. Slovakia lost 10,390 km square with 854,277 inhabitants—503,980 Hungarians (58.99 percent), 272,145 Slovaks or Czechs (32.43 percent), 26,151 Jews (3.06 percent), 8,947 Germans (1.05 percent), 1,825 Ruthenians, 14,617 other and 26,005 foreign citizens, according to the Czechoslovak census from 1930.

The guard was thus provided a convenient opportunity to prove its readiness and organization even in the fall of 1938. The judgment of the Vienna Arbitration provided the Slovak People's Party and the Hlinka Guard strong propaganda to nourish nationalist sentiments of the indignant population. It showed growing aversion to the activities of the Hungarian authorities in the allocated territory. After the Arbitration, the help of the Hlinka Guard to the government in carrying out guard duty became invaluable.

According to the order of Minister Pavel Teplanský, the Hlinka Guard was to conduct searches of various kinds throughout Slovakia to prevent capital exports from Slovakia. Especially in areas closely adjacent to the occupied territories, members of the Hlinka Guard were heavily deployed, often illegally. The task of the guard in conjunction with the *gendarmerie* to carry out guard service and related searches of persons, especially at train stations and roads, was to prevent the transfer of more money and valuables outside Slovakia. In the event of seizure, they were supposed to issue confirmed, signed records at *gendarmerie* stations, which would give these actions a hallmark of legality. However, in many cases the practice was different because of the complexity of the process. Hlinka Guard members issued receipts for confiscated sums on the spot, often leading to inconvenience and complaints from passengers at *gendarmerie* stations or directly at district offices. The money seized by the guards mostly went to the account of local or district Hlinka Guard headquarters or flowed in different directions, often to the Hlinka Guard in Bratislava. In some cases, guards showed over-zeal, which could often have unpleasant consequences for people who did not carry any valuables and their luggage or motor vehicles, which had to be thoroughly inspected. At the same time, there were instances where members of the Hlinka Guard performed guard duty not on behalf of and without the assistance of the security authorities. For this reason, the district authorities issued orders to all notaries and *gendarmerie* to ensure that the actions taken were lawful, in particular that Hlinka Guard members should under no circumstances go beyond their authority to conduct searches of vehicles and persons in the absence of security authorities.

The Vienna Arbitration was undoubtedly a great injustice on the Slovak nation, which was skillfully used by some political leaders, often acting emotionally, to attack the Jewish population as a whole. They blamed them for the loss of the southern territories of the country. In several cities, anti-Jewish demonstrations were held, even in Jewish property was destroyed or other violent acts against Jews committed, as if with the tacit consent of the police.

The anti-Jewish riots that swept through Bratislava and the subsequent response of the Slovak government were triggered by one event in addition to the unfair judgment of the Vienna Arbitration. On the eve of the Vienna decision, on November 1, 1938, the Hungarian youth organized a rally in front of the Carlton Hotel, attended by foreign journalists, requested the annexation of Bratislava to Hungary. The police not only arrested several young Jews who took part in the demonstration, but also found a leaflet on which said: “Fascist hatred of engulfed and racist poison soaked by Slovak chauvinists, know that we will not be your victims. If you chase us, we will all return. Long live a great liberal Hungary!”

The Jewish demonstrations for affiliation with Hungary were not just a matter of November 1. The Bratislava Jews had already asked the city to be affiliated with Hungary and outraged not only Slovaks, but also politicians from the southern territories of the country.

On the day of the Bratislava riots, Jozef Tiso was visited by Jozef Faláth, Hlinka Slovak People’s Party, and Jozef Kirschbaum, leader of the Academic Hlinka Guard. In the presence of Adolf Eichmann, an employee of German Security Police in Vienna and the editor of the weekly *Völkischer Beobachter Kun Goldbach*, they presented a plan to solve the problem by deporting impoverished and foreign Jews to the ceded territory. In addition to Eichmann, Kirschbaum, and Faláth, the meeting was also attended by Juloslav Janek, the commander of the third district of Bratislava Hlinka Guard.

The mood towards the Jews was clearly sharpened throughout Slovakia to the extent that the command of otherwise relatively pragmatic Jozef Tiso ordered district authorities to notify all district and *gendarmerie* (an armed police officer) stations, as well as the head of units of the Hlinka Guards of southern Slovakia to detain Jews in their districts and with their family members transport them on trucks across the new border.

On the first days, especially on the night of November 4 to 5, the *gendarmerie* and Hlinka Guard units were exporting entire Jewish families in trucks and buses to towns and villages beyond the line set by the Vienna Arbitration. With regard to foreigners of Jews employed and self-employed, additional instructions were issued to systematically and gradually resolve the Jewish issue so as not to harm the economic interests of the Slovak country. From Slovakia, only Jews, foreign nationals, and those who did not have a right of residence in the village where they stayed were required to leave. At the same time, their apartments and business rooms were to be sealed and their money and passbooks seized. The Hlinka Guard worked closely with this action, but most of the deported Jews came back, either on their own initiative, or by the Hungarians put back to the border with deportation documents. However, the measure was halted on November 7, as the southern areas had finally come under the administration of Hungary. The Jewish issue was still in its infancy at that time, but the Hlinka Guard showed a high level of enthusiasm and participated directly in anti-Jewish intervention.

The measures during the evictions of Jews affected not only the Jews themselves, but also Czech citizens who were also exposed to Hlinka Guard terror. The reputation of Hlinka Guard who had nothing to do with it except the patch on the sleeve was spoiled by the troublemakers. In the ranks could be found a number of parasites. The Hlinka Guard leadership tried to cleanse them. However, this was not entirely possible. Indeed, many of them, as in the wider Hlinka Guard, held important positions in the functional apparatus. The commander-in-chief of the Hlinka Guard, Karol Sidor, due to growing problems with the influx of such parasites, on February 3, 1939 stopped the admission of new members. It was necessary for the special district offices to examine their political and moral credibility. This step brought the organizational structure of the Hlinka Guard to a higher level of quality, but a number of non-compliant members of the Hlinka Guard remained active, some even in leadership positions. This was the situation in the guard at the end of winter 1939, when the level of efforts of some of its members for statehood increased.

6

Hlinka Guard and the Declaration of Independence

March 1939 was a time of great social and political change for the Slovaks. Since gaining autonomy on October 6, 1938, the territory of Slovakia had undergone a profound socio-political and territorial legal development. However, the declaration of autonomy of the Slovak land was only a step on the road to full self-determination for the Slovak People's Party and Hlinka Guard radicals. It was only an essential and as short as possible episode on the road to independence. The Hlinka Guard from the narrowly understood idea of the guardian of Slovak property and lives gradually evolved into an influential power force in Slovakia and interfered in virtually every sphere of socio-political life. At the same time, the guards expressed their dissatisfaction with the constitutional organization of the Czechoslovak Republic since the end of 1938. The situation in Czechoslovakia was also closely monitored in Nazi circles, which gradually increasingly supported radicals grouped mostly in the Hlinka Guard in an effort to accentuate the ideas of the creation of the Slovak state.

Slovak representatives did not hesitate even emphasizing the Slovak demands for greater independence from the Czechs. The greatest support was sought by the radicals in Germany, who followed up with the belief that they would provide help in solving the relationship of the Slovaks with the Czechs. On the other hand, from the perspective of 1938, they correctly understood that Germany would soon become a major player in changing borders in Central Europe, giving them a strong impetus to engage with German officials. Already at the beginning of November 1938, Vojtech Tuka, a private person at that time, officially met with German Deputy State Secretary Ernst Woermann, who, among other things, raised the question of Slovakia's future direction and its relationship to the common state with the Czechs. He refused to give definite guarantees because they were waiting for a suitable opportunity for and even more vigorous intervention than in the fall of 1938.

On February 2, 1939, Vojtech Tuka met Adolf Hitler in Berlin and basically put the fate of his nation in Hitler's hands. At a meeting attended by Slovak leader Franz

Karmasin, Hitler appealed to Tuka that only a declaration of state independence could help the Slovaks to find a way out of the difficult situation that crystallized in connection with the German claims to the Czech territory and the efforts of the Hungarians to expand their northern borders. On February 5, 1939, Alexander Mach spoke words that became a symbol of later events in March. In his statement, he declared that the condition of the nation's survival is only statehood.

On the very day of Tuka and Hitler talks, some Czechoslovak ministers met in Unhošť, in the Nouzov Forest, for whom the organizer of the meeting, General Alois Eliáš, proposed that they try to reverse the development in Slovakia by military intervention. He also counted on the fact that the Hlinka Guard could try to prove to the outside world that the call of Hlinka Guard for independence was the will of broad masses. According to him, it was therefore necessary to ensure that guards and Slovak Germans did not attempt a coup. This could discredit the intervention from abroad as a suppression of the will of the nation.

In his plan, Eliáš rightly assumed that German intervention was more than possible because of the peaking tensions. However, the German intervention, together with some colleagues, considered it a better solution. "The second case, the disintegration of the state by external intervention, is better for us if we have to choose between two evils. The world will be convinced that Hitler forced the Slovaks to declare themselves independent and break away from the Czechs," he concluded.

Tensions were exacerbated by Tiso's speech as prime minister of February 1, 1939, in which he responded to Tuka's previous statements on the road to Slovak statehood. Among other things, he claimed that "we are building our own state, our Slovak state, on the soil of the Assembly. We cultivate the ideology of the sovereignty of the Slovak nation." On the basis of his speech, an article on Slovak statehood was published in the *Slovak* newspaper, which pointed out that the fate of Central Europe and thus of Slovakia could no longer be determined without the great German nation. Seeing the historical possibility of imposing the requirement of secession from Slovakia, Austrian governor Arthur Seyss-Inquart came to Bratislava for negotiation. He tried to convince Tiso that Hitler's proposal to immediately break away from the Czechs and thus break the common state would not only suit Germany but also Slovaks, for whom this was the only right solution.

The statements of the Slovak representatives on the Slovak statehood did not radically affect the process of the disintegration of Czechoslovakia, as Germany and its efforts to conquer the Czech territory played a major role. However, they accelerated the concerns of Czech politicians about the integrity of the common state, and thus de facto the German intervention. In this tense situation, Karol Sidor, Pavel Teplanský, and Jozef Tiso went to Prague to defend Slovak autonomy. Negotiations began on Thursday March 9, 1939, which failed to complete due to sudden events.

Before the events of March, Czech politicians considered Hlinka Guard to be relatively strong, so they tried to push it into legal limits and create it into an organization whose task would be mainly military education. However, due to its lack of armaments, it underestimated it from the military point of view. In early March, the Hlinka Guard was virtually unarmed. Several weapons, especially revolvers and older rifles from World War I, could have been in private possession, but the real power of the Hlinka Guard could not be sufficient against better armed Czech troops and *gendarmes*. In many places, the guardsmen tried to stand up to the soldiers they wanted to prevent from coming from the Czech Republic, for example, on railways. The main job, however, was to organize a sort of militia by creating Hlinka Guard patrols armed with private weapons, which point to the determination of the guards not to surrender. In several cities, it was the guardsmen who organized demonstration marches, often with the active support of representatives of the German minority.

Against the organized army, however, just emotion was not enough. The guards needed high-quality and especially numerous equipment. Some of the weapons were owned by the guard in 1938, when it was passed the property of the National Guard. In addition to weapons in private possession, if necessary, the guardsmen could use different knives, clubs, or boxers, as in Rodobrana, especially in street fighting in many places. However, the occupation of Slovakia changed the situation. Weapons began to flow to Slovakia, mainly from the territory of the former Austria. In total, several thousand firearms were transported or smuggled in various ways in the territory in a relatively short time. In addition to the assistance of German friends and foreign Hlinka Guard, guardians in the regions obtained weapons mainly from warehouses of district offices and occasional assaults. It was often the case that guardsmen, often with the support of the Germans, attacked *gendarmerie* stations in which weapons were stored.

Several *gendarmes* of Slovak nationality also decided to switch to the Slovak side with his weapon. The intervention was unanswered by many *gendarmes* or soldiers of Slovak nationality. Mostly, however, Slovaks in the *gendarmerie* corps or in the army were already isolated from the impact on the course of events. For example, in Bratislava, soldiers of Slovak nationality were included in special squads, which could not be used in the event of an alarm. On March 10, engineer squads were created in the capital to occupy roads between cities and create roadblocks with machine guns. Although their commanders were Slovaks, they did not know who to fight or how to act in case of emergency.

The situation in those turbulent days was different in the cities and different in the countryside. While in larger cities more *gendarmes* were deployed to occupy important buildings and offices, these were mostly smaller groups in the countryside, which were supposed to ensure order and ensure that the citizens were aware of the proclaimed law. They put this message on the columns and corners of the houses, but guards in many removed them. Also, as far as possible, members of the Hlinka Guard in the villages organized demonstration marches for singing the guard's songs that mostly ended in front of police stations. The relationship of the guardsmen against the Czech power representatives was greatly escalated, the arrest warrants were issued to the commanders and the local guard's headquarters and the *gendarmes* seized their documents, cash, and passbooks. The practice to secure the Hlinka Guard commanders was common almost everywhere, but in some places the detention was not often realized for interesting reasons. Commander of the Hlinka Guard in Zemianske Kostol'any resisted arrest and was shot, and by far it was not the only case. According to predetermined instructions, they were also to confiscate radio receivers so that the guards and the population could not be radicalized, in particular, through the Slovak broadcasting on Vienna Radio. But they did not succeed everywhere. According to orders, the local Hlinka Guard headquarters were on standby duty and, as in cities, Hlinka Guard patrols were formed. However, everything depended, as always, on the commanders and the specific village.

Although the anger of the guards was directed mainly against the Czechs, in the southern districts the relationship of Hlinka Guard escalated with local Hungarian citizens. In many places, the situation had become so severe, the residents asked the Hungarian government for protection against the guards. The vigorous attitude of the guards, especially in cities, and the support of some German minority activists who actively assisted the guards in many places Germany's policy, were a surprise for the army and *gendarmerie*. They counted that they would not oppose the army for the prevalence of their weapons.

A crowd of thousands gathered in Bratislava and on the streets of Trnava, similarly in Spišská Nová Ves, Prešov, practically all over Slovakia in feeling that fundamental changes were taking place. The Hlinka Academic Guard was also activated. According to the participants, almost 8,000 people gathered in front of the government building alone, largely Academic Guards, who heard the speech of their commander, Joseph Kirschbaum; however, they shot into the crowd, injuring several people.

Most military measures were abolished on March 1 and 13. Even Slovak soldiers, in order to distinguish themselves from their Czech colleagues, began to wear the guard patch on their sleeves. The guard also became a symbol of the struggle for Slovak independence. This is also evidenced by the fact that the relations between military detachments and the guard were at a good level as the Slovak commanders took over the army barracks from the Czech predecessors in the presence of the armed units of the Hlinka Guard. Despite the fact that the common state with the Czechs was coming to an end, they did not organize the guards in Bratislava until the declaration of statehood.

The guard continued to maintain its activity mainly in the area of solving the Jewish question. In March 1939, the guardian efforts were supported by the establishment of an independent Slovak state on March 14, 1939. This date became one of the most important milestones for the Hlinka Guard in the coming years, which its members gloriously celebrated annually. Later, after the declaration of Slovak independence, the guard's participation in the March events was used for propaganda. State propaganda realized the need to take advantage of these events. The guard did indeed play an important role in them, especially in the larger cities where it organized marches, demonstrations, and established a form of militia. In a short time, it managed to mobilize a relatively large number of her members who decided to stand up for the common cause.

For Slovaks, however, predictive words of General Eliáš, who already in February counted on the fact that German intervention would mean that the Czechoslovak state-law continuity will remain after the war and eventual defeat of Germany, were accepted. The Slovak State was not formed by a direct German regulation, but undoubtedly under its strong pressure. This had negative consequences on certain features. However, it did not hinder the guards at all. They organized marches in cities to express their joy at the completion of their efforts, according to them, for a fairer constitutional arrangement. The guardians recognized the role of Germany in this process and tried to present Hlinka Guard as a pro-Nazi organization. Immediately after the declaration of the Slovak state, Adolf Hitler received thank you telegrams from the Hlinka Guard commanders for providing a helping hand.

7

Hlinka Guard in the First Months of Independence

Following the *Anschluss* (annexation) of Austria to Nazi Germany in March 1938, the conquest and breakup of Czechoslovakia became Hitler's next ambition. The incorporation of the Sudetenland into Germany that began on October 1, 1938 left the rest of Czechoslovakia weak, and it became powerless to resist subsequent occupation. Moreover, a small northeastern part of the borderland region known as Zaolzie was occupied and annexed to Poland ostensibly to protect the local ethnic Polish community and as a result of previous territorial claim.

On March 15, 1939, one day after the proclamation of the Slovak State, the German *Wehrmacht* moved into the remainder of Czechoslovakia, and from the Prague Castle, Hitler proclaimed the Protectorate of Bohemia and Moravia after the negotiations with Emil Hácha, who remained as technical head of state with the title of state president. However, he was rendered all but powerless. The real power was vested in the *Reichsprotektor*, who served as Hitler's personal representative. The office and title were held by a variety of persons during the Protectorate's existence. In succession these were:

March 16, 1939–August 20, 1943:	Konstantin von Neurath, former foreign minister of Nazi Germany, minister without portfolio until 1943. He was removed from office after Hitler's dissatisfaction with his "soft policies" in 1941, although he still held the title until his official resignation in 1943.
September 27, 1941–May 30, 1942:	Reinhard Heydrich, chief of the SS-*Reichssicherheitshauptamt* (Reich Main Security Office) or RSHA. He was officially only a deputy to Neurath, but in reality, he was granted supreme authority over the entire state apparatus of the Protectorate.

May 31, 1942–August 20, 1943: Kurt Daluege, chief of the *Ordnungspolizei* (Order Police) or *Orpo*, in the Interior Ministry, who was also officially a deputy Reich Protector.

By and large, not all Hlinka Guard practices and activities performed during the days before and after March 14, 1939 were accepted by most Slovaks. The dissatisfaction of its activities caused some of the population to be concerned about their violent actions and enrichment. One form of enrichment of guards was a guard service at the state border in connection with the expulsion of Czech employees from the Slovak territory.

On March 14, orders from the main headquarters directed the Hlinka Guard to pay increased attention to all persons who, for whatever reason, would leave Slovakia and take away valuables and cash. In doing so, it was particularly important that they take no more than 500 crowns with them. Everything else was to be withdrawn after a receipt was given in order to prevent the outflow of capital from the Slovak territory. The Hlinka Guard issued similar orders to subordinate headquarters during the night of March 13–14, 1939. Orders were given to subordinate headquarters that fleeing Jews and Czechs were to be searched, and money and treasures from each person were to be taken away.

Similarly, as during the evictions of Jews to Hungarian territory after the Vienna Arbitration, in which several guardsmen worked eagerly, some of them may have been convinced of the necessity of their removal, others of selfish desires hoping for relatively decent earnings. The money and valuables were to be handed over to the county authorities for confirmation, but in many cases, they were kept to themselves. All other property, including passbooks and jewels of Czech citizens, had to remain in Slovakia. As the writer of one of the insurgent chronicles stated: "we can be sure that many valuables would stick to Guard's fingers." Czech officials tried to mitigate the harsh measures for at least a part of the employees, especially from the army. Although all Czech soldiers were supposed to be disarmed, the Czech side tried to ensure that the departure from Slovakia took place in an orderly manner.

In addition to the seizure of property, however, guardsmen were also involved in the deporting of persons, especially those of Czech nationality from the Slovak territory. The guardsmen did not hesitate to use methods which had little to do with the democratic society and humanity in the expulsion of Czechs. They violated letter secrets, disturbed domestic peace and order, or interfered with the operation of companies with non-Slovak owners.

The fact that the anti-Czech mood ruled among the radicals after the proclamation of the Slovak state can be clearly documented in the statements of several official people, even Catholic priests. They certainly disagreed in many ways with the radicalism presented by the guardsmen during their displacement, yet their comments were also found in the Hlinka Guard. Catholic priest and Slovak parliamentarian Vojtech Plechlo said in a marginal relation to the Czechs that "after twenty years of marriage we have now divorced Czechs and this marriage will never be renewed anymore." The well-known priest Alexei Isakovich drew attention to the diversity of Slovak and Czech history, pointing out to the fact that while the Slovaks adhered to Christian principles, "Czech history proved the result of a dispute between God and the nation, that began with the collapse of statues, founding an independent church and ending with the collapse of an independent state." He saw the fall of the Czech Republic and the establishment of the Protectorate of Bohemia and Moravia as a course of history that cruelly deals with injustice committed by the Czechs on the Slovak nation and the German nation.

After March 14, the guardsmen were not satisfied with the pace of the removal of Czech employees from Slovakia. Their attacks on the Czechs after March 14 continued, and even intensified, in many areas. After March 14, however, the newly formed Slovakia had to face a much more serious enemy: Hungary, which occupied Transcarpathian Ukraine and began to claim other territories. The first days of Slovak independence cannot therefore be described as peaceful. A great and unexpected blow was struck by German, which through its army occupied the territory north of the Váh River and seized the military material there. The Germans even considered using the territory of Slovakia as a suitable article for trade for territorial concessions in favor of Germany.

The guard in the first days of independence performed various security tasks, no longer as a purely independent organization, but as a part of the Slovak Army. Their orders stated that its members who had military training were subject to the mobilization order of the military chief of the Hlinka Guard. According to the same order of March 16, the Hlinka Guard stood at the disposal of all authorities ensuring the security of the Slovak state—that is, the Slovak police, *gendarmerie*, and guard as the executors of the government of independent Slovakia and as such stand under absolute military discipline. Hlinka Guard, by its official assignment under military command, tried to point out the need to improve military discipline in the guard, which was important due to the ever-increasing attacks of Hungarian separatists in the southern regions of the country.

The reorganization in the Hlinka Guard was necessary also because the army was still undergoing the process of transition to Slovak hands, and thus in a possible military conflict, the state could not adequately defend itself. It was all the more important that the conflict with the southern neighbor was concluded. Although Hungary recognized the Slovak state almost immediately after its inception, but considered the issue of borders, especially in its eastern part, open, which ultimately meant later Hungarian intervention in the east of the country.

The degree of reliability of the Hlinka Guard depended mainly on its discipline, which was closely tied to the command. Since the Hlinka Guard did not have enough high-quality military trained officers, its actual combat usability could be different according to areas and command. Although the Hlinka Guard units in the militarily threatened areas should be subordinate to military command, but when they were to enter the territory of eastern Slovakia, which was most threatened by fighting, there was a rather small commitment in the ranks of the guardsmen. The guard from western Slovakia mostly did not move to eastern Slovakia, so it could be argued about the willingness or unwillingness of its members to enter the endangered areas. It is certain that it, too, was later marked by relations with the military, claiming that the Hlinka Guard had allegedly attempted to occupy important and lucrative positions in the interior, while the soldiers themselves had to face the Hungarian attack as soldiers, and often the troops themselves praised individuals for their merit in defending borders. However, there was not always positive comments about guards and their participation. SS-*Sturmbannführer* Friedrich Polte in his report of March 13 on the guard, said that with her deployment was not optimal. In particular, he criticized the lack of discipline of the guards and their non-military behavior.

The guard commanders had to deal with many cases when their subordinates refused to take military conscription and thought to exclude such guards from Hlinka Guard. Hlinka Guard command sought to influence public opinion in favor of guards, highlighting their participation in the fight against the enemy as the brave sons of the nation.

8

The Seizure and Aryanization of Jewish Property

On March 8, 1939, the Ministry of the Interior of the Slovak Republic Number 3747/1939 issued a regulation to supplement the status of *gendarmerie* stations so that there were temporarily recruited members of the Hlinka Guard, but who were to be trained militarily and reliable. The members of the Hlinka Guard were to be protected as authorities of the state, but importantly, they were subject to the orders of the *gendarmes* and their superiors. They were subject to *gendarmerie* regulations and even judicially subject to *gendarmerie* law. This regulation was not repealed until June 15, 1939, when the status of the corps was supplemented by *gendarmes* for duty. According to the decree, the members of the Hlinka Guard, who had been at police stations so far, were to be released.

The Hlinka Guard during less than three months helped to solve the burning situation in the *gendarmerie*, but without the authorization of the superior *gendarmerie* bodies took several measures, which not only embarrassed the *gendarmerie*, but also police and authorities. They claimed the powers of the security authorities, carried out screenings of persons on the platforms, legitimized various persons, carried out house searches, seized possessions, detained persons who were assumed to be hostile to the Slovak state, or accused them only for selfish reasons. The situation itself had to intervene by the Ministry of the Interior, which on April 5, 1939 pointed out that some of the members of the Hlinka Guard had recently been claiming the powers of state authorities and arbitrarily interfering with their competence. Therefore, it had to find that Hlinka Guard does not belong to the performance of the security service:

> A member of the Hlinka Guard, unless authorized by the competent authority, was not entitled to legitimize, arrest or seize property. Members of the Hlinka Guard may operate in the performance of the State Security Service solely under the authority of the competent State Security Authority. In such a case, they are not subject to the decisions of the Hlinka Guard headquarters, but solely to the orders of the authority which gave them permission to perform the state security service.

The guardsmen were very brutal especially when it was a question of seizure of Jewish property, unlawful detention of Jewish people at Hlinka Guard headquarters, or their frequent arrests and beatings. A well-known guardian official, county commander of the Lower Guardian County, Jozef Bányai, replied to the question about the growing number of complaints. On the press pages in 1938, he had already attacked those who accused the guards of irresponsibility and attributed various acts to them, declaring willingness to investigate individual cases of lapses if there were guardsmen involved: "I would be very pleased, if they told me who was blackmailing the Jews for guarding, who was shopping in stores and not paying. Hlinka Guard cannot be held responsible for any wrongdoing of people who were not Guardsmen."

On the one hand, he correctly pointed out that not all Hlinka Guard members were committed to attacking the Jewish population and that it was only natural that he, as a senior official, had to defend an organization of which he was one of the highest representatives. On the other hand, it is certain that the guards took part in many cases of robbing or beating Jews, of which Bányai certainly knew, but tactically remained silent.

The state authorities were aware of the danger of the spread of arbitrary, often brutal, intervention by the guards against the Jews. Multiple seizures with the appropriation of Jewish property were proven. The best-known are cases of seizure of cars or radio receivers as well as larger financial sums. As is evident from several cases, the seizure of motor vehicles, which they did not hesitate to use for private purposes, became very popular among the guards. In its complaint addressed directly to the Hlinka Guard, the Slovak Trade Union of Private Officials drew attention to the economic impact of confiscation of business and private vehicles by guards.

Radio receivers were to be taken mainly from persons. According to Hlinka Guard reports, however, they were all returned, except those pieces that allegedly their owners did not take back. Even though they called on them by a decree that the return ended on November 25, 1939. However, all had been sealed and set only to listen to selected stations. In addition, the guard owned several radio receivers that were donated to Hlinka Guard as an institution.

A very widespread way of enriching the guards was to force the property of Jewish citizens by force, torture or threats. Hlinka Guards were perhaps most interested in the process of Aryanization. The First Aryanization Law was passed in April 1940. Through a process known as voluntary Aryanization, Jewish business owners could suggest a qualified Christian candidate who would assume at least a 51-percent stake in the company. Under the law, fifty businesses out of 12,300 were Aryanized and 179 were liquidated. Party radicals and the Slovak State's German backers believed that voluntary Aryanization was too soft on the Jews.

At the July 1940 Salzburg Conference, German negotiators convinced the Slovaks to replace several members of the cabinet with reliably pro-German radicals. Ferdinand Ďurčanský was replaced as interior minister by Alexander Mach, who aligned the anti-Jewish policy of the Slovak State with that in Germany. Another result of the Salzburg talks was the appointment of SS officer Dieter Wisliceny as a Jewish adviser for Slovakia; he arrived in Slovakia in August. He aimed to impoverish the Jewish community so it became a burden on non-Jewish Slovaks, who would then agree to deport them. Wisliceny convinced the Slovak parliament to pass a law creating the Central Economic Office, led by Slovak official Augustín Morávek and under Tuka's control, in September 1940. The Central Economic Office was tasked with assuming ownership of Jewish-owned property. Jews were required to register their property; their bank accounts were frozen, and Jews were allowed to withdraw only 1,000 crowns, later 150 crowns, per week. Jews were forbidden from owning motor vehicles, sports equipment, or radios. The 22,000 Jews who worked in salaried employment were targeted. Non-Jews had to obtain Central Economic Office permission to employ Jews and had to pay a fee of 50–5,000 crowns. The licenses had to be renewed periodically. By mid-1940, the position of Jews in the Slovak economy had been largely wiped out.

A second Aryanization law was passed in November, mandating the expropriation of Jewish property and the dismissal of Jewish employees. In a corrupt process overseen by Morávek's office, 10,000 Jewish businesses (mostly shops) were liquidated and the remainder, about 2,300, were Aryanized. Liquidation benefited small Slovak businesses competing with Jewish enterprises, and Aryanization was applied to larger Jewish-owned companies, which were acquired by Aryan-owned competitors. In many cases, Aryanizers with no experience in business struck deals with former Jewish owners and employees so the Jews would keep working for the company. The Aryanization of businesses did not bring the anticipated revenue into the Slovak treasury, and only 288 of the liquidated businesses produced income for the state by July 1942. The Aryanization and liquidation of businesses was nearly complete by January 1942, resulting in unemployment for 64,000 of 89,000 Jews. Manufactured Jewish impoverishment was a pressing social problem for the Slovak government, which it solved in early 1942 by deporting the unemployed Jews.

The redistribution of Jewish property into the hands of non-Jews had become a great attraction for many Slovaks. Seeing that the path to achieve it would be easier with the support of the Hlinka Guard, many future Aryanizers began to report to the ranks of the Hlinka Guard. Again, it strengthened the ranks of those who were more interested in their own benefit than in the interests of the nation so vigorously declared by propaganda.

9

The Role of Hlinka Guard in Consolidating the Regime

After overcoming the initial problems in the consolidation period, the guard ceased to be just an organization whose main feature was arbitrary interference in security issues. It began to co-operate with the representatives of the state, at least in part. In addition to the security tasks traditionally assumed by the guard, referring to the function of a guardian of Slovak property, order, and lives—which became the source of many disagreements within—it became interested in solving various ailments of Slovak society. These were mainly issues of a social nature, which began to dominate the pages of the periodicals. In *Gardista*, articles more often appeared on the struggle of the "Hlinka Guard against the bidders" against which they wanted to crack down on the Hlinka Guard.

Even though the Hlinka Guard continued to organize anti-Jewish speeches that went beyond its authority, the Hlinka Guard's primary direction of action was to become social and economic. But the guards did not proceed to suppress anti-Jewish activity simply because it was required of them. On the other hand, involvement in controls within the economic sphere could bring many advantages to many Hlinka Guard members. It is interesting that the guards were also mixed in matters that fell under the authority of the *gendarmes* or the business board. They were helpful in solving various economic problems, although they often exceeded abilities.

In connection with price increase, the guard focused mainly on the increase in the price of food articles, because a large part of the traders in this sphere were Jews. The guards either intervened directly or through commanders linked to the local Slovak People's Party officials to intervene in order to solve the problems of price increases in mostly Jewish shops. Based on one of these guard denominations, the Bratislava Regional Office ordered the *gendarmerie* and the district office to deal with cases where Slovak traders were helpless against the "inhuman terror" of the Jews.

Guardian figures were often not based on truth, but document Hlinka Guard's efforts to interfere in economy. However, in addition to the activity of eliminating

Jews from economic life, the Hlinka Guard had also been activated in other economic issues and in the fight against the so-called "Jewish Czechoslovaks." In this context, the guard was to interfere in the issue of supply control, in the period especially after September 1, 1939, when Germany attacked Poland with the help of the Slovak Army. For example, the Hlinka Guard headquarters had been made aware that cases of premature closure of imported goods stores were multiplying and, as traders reported, this was because there appeared to be a large increase in buyers and people seem to be starting to accumulate stocks for fear of scarcity.

The Hlinka Guard also made claims for the protection of national interests, drawing attention to another area of the economy of the young state—the revival loan. However, its activities were not only primarily aimed at helping the government, but against the background of officially formulated action to consolidate the regime. It did not hesitate to attack former Czechoslovaks by pointing out their lack of national sentiment to benefit of the Slovak state. However, the guard's participation in the economic recovery loan support action was not an arbitrary Hlinka Guard action but a planned action of the regime. The guard had a significant hand, especially in pointing out the lack of underwriting of Czechs or Jews. In this process, the guard was supposed to become an auxiliary instrument of the regime, which planned to attack non-Slovak citizens of Slovakia so that it could subsequently blame them for their low participation in underwriting. The Hlinka Guard actively cooperated with the party and its representatives and were members of commissions to put pressure on selected groups of citizens. The efforts were aimed at ranks of the so-called rich Czechoslovaks, Jews, or Czechs.

Jews and supporters of the former regime were also targeted by the Government Decree of April 4, 1939 on political riches, which decided to take action against the "Czechoslovak bourgeoisie" and "capitalists." Mach, as the chairman of the Commission for Political Riches, became the main hope of the radicals in the Hlinka Guard, as his speeches often showed an obvious edge against these groups of the population.

The Hlinka Guard also became an important aid in the elimination of manifestations of resistance hostile to the regime, using in particular its knowledge of the situation of individual towns or villages and intended to become a decisive force in the fight against opponents of the state system. In other words, its role in this process was mainly to intimidate real or supposed adversaries. Measures in the economic area were mainly directed against the Czechoslovaks and Jews. However, a large part of the Slovak capital was in the hands of the Germans against whom the government could not intervene for understandable reasons, and therefore the cleansing of management posts and the introduction of Slovaks was an area of involvement. Therefore, the government directed all its attention in the economic field against the restriction of Jews in corporate management, in which it had unreserved support from the Hlinka Guard. Despite all the disagreements that occurred between organizations, guards, and parties, this trend practically unequivocally accepted both institutions, which differed mainly in the form they had be used to eliminate Jews not only from the economy, but from life in Slovakia in general.

On April 18, 1939, in an effort to clarify the status of the Jew, a government decree on the definition of the concept of a Jew and guidance on the number of Jews in some liberal professions was issued. The decree read as follows:

Government Decree on the Definition of the Concept of a Jew

PART ONE

Definition of Jew.

§ 1.

(1) A Jew shall be considered, irrespective of sex and nationality:

1. who is, or was of Israeli faith, even though he converted to a Christian faith after October 30, 1918,

(2) who is, or has been, un-confessional and comes from at least one parent of the Israeli religion;

3. who comes from the person referred to in points 1 or 2 (except for a descendant who himself has transferred to a Christian faith before 30 October 1918),

4. who has entered into marriage after the date of entry into force of this Regulation with the person referred to in points 1 to 3 for the duration of that marriage,

5. who, after the date of entry into force of this Regulation, has lived with the person referred to in points 1 to 3 in the non-marital community, as well as the descendants, born in such a community.

(3) The exception shall be provided by the Government in cases of special consideration.

§ 2.

(1) In disputed cases, whether a person is considered to be a Jew under this Regulation shall be decided by the district office in the district of which the person has his / her residence (stay).

(2) An application for such a decision may be made by both the person who is disputed whether to be considered a Jew, or by another person (natural or legal) if he / she proves his / her legal interest that it matters to the other a person considers a Jew or not. The decision may also be initiated by the Office or a court.

(3) Appeals against the decision of the district office are admissible within 15 days from the date of issue of the assessment (Section 2, Section 72 of the Decree of January 13, 1928, No. 8/28 Coll., On administrative continuation) to the Ministry of the Interior. The appeal must be lodged with the district office which decided the case. Ponos to the Supreme Administrative Court is not admissible.

PART TWO

On the Guiding of the Number of Jews in Certain Liberal Professions

In Advocacy.

§ 3.

The number of lawyers is determined by four percent the total number of enrolled members of the relevant chamber.

§ 4.

(1) The surplus of attorneys (attorneys-at-law) shall be deleted from the list of competent chambers, namely from the Office.

(2) The following shall be deleted:

(a) do not have their annual taxes, levies, charges or other public charges settled;

(b) they are not dependent on this profession according to their state of wealth or their earnings in another job,

(c) they do not actually practice;

(d) do not adequately control the state language,

(e) they are not desirable in this profession of other important public interest.

§ 5.

(1) For reasons of necessity or for other special considerations worthy of reason, as long as they persist, the Ministry of Truth may leave Jewish lawyers in their profession beyond the number permitted under § 3.

(2) The number of admissible members may not exceed ten percent of the total number of members of the relevant chamber.

§ 6.

(1) The deletion pursuant to § 4 shall be ordered by the committee of the relevant chamber,

(2) An appeal against the cancellation order shall be admissible within 15 days to the Ministry of Truth. The appeal shall not have suspensory effect. The appeal shall be definitively decided by the Minister of Jurisdiction.

§ 7.

(1) A Jewish attorney may only represent a page - a Jew, unless there is no other lawyer in the district of the district court where he has his seat,

(2) These provisions also apply to substitution representation, both between lawyers and lawyers.

(3) Associations, any commercial and economic companies and other legal persons, other than legal persons pursuing the interests of Jewish religion and Jewish culture, do not fall within the notion of a site which could be represented by a Jewish lawyer.

(4)Infringement of these provisions has legal consequences as if the site were not represented at all. These consequences are the responsibility of both the property and the disciplinary commission of the advocate-Jew, in terms of property liability, against the creditor or his heirs.

§ 8.

The Minister of Truth may allow a public notary to represent a litigation page in a district court in his district where there is only one lawyer or where there is more solicitors, but none of these solicitors can or does not want to represent the site. Permission may be resisted at any time by the Minister of Truth, on a proposal from the relevant Chamber.

In Public Notary.

§ 9.

A Jew cannot be a public notary.

In the Profession of Editor.

§ 10.

A Jew can only be an editor of a Jewish journal, that is to say a journal which is expressly designated as such and pursues the interests of Jewish religion and Jewish culture.

Common Provisions.

§ 11.

In the event of termination of service with respect to this Decree of Government, it shall apply to it and to the provisional provision of the Decree of 18 April 1939, no. 65 Sl. On shortening the notice period for service relationships, regulated under private law, and on surrender on termination.

§ 12.

The offense is committed and punished by the competent district court with imprisonment associated with work obligation within three months and a fine of 1000 to 5000 pieces:

(a) who, while excluded from the pursuit of his profession, continues in that profession,

(b) who employs or allows the employment of a person excluded from that profession,

(c) who in any way, directly or indirectly, allows a person excluded under this Regulation to continue the profession of detached person;

(d) who is guilty of an offense referred to in Section 7.

(2) A member of the Bar and Public Bar Association who has been guilty of the provisions of points a) -d) shall also lose his profession and shall be deleted from the list of the relevant chamber.

(3) Conditional suspension of the sentence imposed pursuant to this Section is excluded.

PART THREE.

Final Provisions.

§ 13.

This Government Decree shall enter into force on the date of its announcement; it will be met by the Minister in the agreement with the ministers involved: Dr. Tiso, Dr. Tuka, Dr. Fritz, Dr. Ďurčanský, Medrický, Dr. Pružinský, Chatll Sivák, Stan Fritz.

During the consolidation of the regime, the Hlinka Guard was not only active in economic matters, it also sought to eliminate any dissatisfaction with the ideology of the new state. By knowing the local circumstances, it could contribute to consolidating its power while strengthening its positions in the state. It often proceeded in line with the regulations and efforts of the state to eliminate its own opponents. The state apparatus used it as a means of power against various groups of the population. The guards could thus cope with, for example, the Communists, whom they could almost persecute with impunity by helping the government.

In addition to participating in the fight against whispering campaigns by Communists, the guard was very willing to take part in an action against the spread of anti-state leaflets, whose dissemination was mainly done by supporters of the former Communist Party. The guardsmen had a significant advantage over their enemies in knowing, together with the police, former political parties, and actual anti-regime activists.

The Hlinka Guard police were mostly patrolling and controlling activities in public areas, buildings, or social facilities, often giving them the opportunity to cope with the various "ailments" of the society, but also with political opponents. During inspections, the guard members often checked the observance of morality, closing hours or things that pointed to forms of passive resistance to the Slovak state. The inspection of hotel trades was entrusted to the Hlinka Guard on the basis of the Circular of September 8, 1939. It was canceled only in March 1940, after the authorities could already perform the tasks entrusted to them by law. In the guest rooms they checked whether there are traces of the former regime, in particular flags, badges, or paintings of exposed representatives of the former Republic, which often gave their guests a negative opinion on the socio-political situation in the country.

In connection with this and similar cases, the Ministry of Interior responded by means of the Presidium, saying that paintings, busts of Masaryk, Beneš, and Czechoslovakia that have not been removed from the offices and public rooms so far must be removed by the owners. Calling the *gendarmerie* into this and similar actions would be a senseless waste of power and time that could be used more effectively, so the Hlinka Guard it seemed to be the best means of carrying out this and similar orders.

The status of the guard in the state became the subject of a special government meeting at the end of May 1939, which significantly influenced its later relationship with the army, the party, and the government. Several of the proposed preconditions for determining the direction of the guard and its subordination to the party were not fulfilled. Special attention was paid to Tiso's unfortunate proposal for mandatory membership of the guard, from which he wanted to create a mass organization affiliated to the party and carrying out military missions. With his vision of compulsory membership, Jozef Tiso not only pursued the objectives of subordinating the guard to the People's Party. His well-intentioned idea, however, was inapplicable to the socio-political situation at that time and was doomed.

The resolutions of the meeting were finally approved at the meeting of the Party Bureau on June 5, 1939, which also agreed to create Rodobrana as a kind of elite corps within the Hlinka Guard.

10

The Role of the Guard Increases Sharply

Before the government was able to comment on the issue of compulsory membership in the Hlinka Guard, the role of the guard increased sharply in connection with the participation of the Slovak army in the anti-Polish campaign. In the August *Gardista*, anti-Polish articles began to appear more and more frequently. Alexander Mach, in his intentions of rescuing and regaining Slovak territory, mentioned in his speech at the end of August that "every Slovak is willing to grab weapons for the purpose of returning the torn territories to Slovakia." As a result of similar statements on August 23, 1939, zealous guards attacked and damaged the Piotr Kurnicky apartment in Bratislava. Articles and speeches advocated the recovery of illegally taken territories in favor of Poland after World War I and in 1938. Many of them were written by Karol Murgaš, who, according to German observers, belonged in the past together with the Sidor and Ďurčanský wing.

According to a regulation of the Ministry of National Defense, reservists were called to arms to serve in the Hlinka Guard. The Hlinka Guard was entrusted with the calling of persons over thirty-five years of age which could not be carried out by the military administration. There was also an effort to conceal general mobilization, as Slovakia officially did not declare war on Poland. According to the chief military command, the official assignment of the Hlinka Guard was to work with the military authorities to ensure the defense of the state.

The guard had been in permanent use since August 6, 1939, when it was ordered to perform various important services in the districts. According to this order, all Hlinka Guard headquarters were to be set up around the clock and local headquarters were to draw up lists of all non-military guards, soldiers over thirty-five, and Jews from nineteen to forty-five years old. The border district was ordered to be ready immediately. They were to especially observe important bridges and roads communications and track suspects. For this purpose, the guardsmen were divided into groups to be in charge of performing important tasks and reporting both day and night to the night service, which operated at all Hlinka Guard headquarters.

The Hlinka Guard, in the months of August–September 1939, received a number of advantages that represented a great concession of ruling power against the radicals. Guards in border and object protection could even use the right of requisition, bringing them virtually to the level of the army. Headquarters were given the explicit right to confiscate for the needs of the guard private cars and trucks, which was justified especially in the guard tasks and ensuring the transport of material to the north of Slovakia. On September 9, it issued an order informing the guards that the Ministry of the Interior had sent all district authorities a guideline to comply, in cooperation with the *gendarmerie* and the police, with requests from the guard headquarters, in particular relating to seizures of cars and radios. The guard also reopened older requests for the confiscation of Jewish radios or cars. Again, with the help of the state apparatus, it obtained a legal basis for repression against the Jewish population and political opponents.

The guard became an organization with previously unimaginable powers. Its prestige and value had increased to such an extent that it was necessary to reflect on its reorganization in order to perform the tasks entrusted to it as efficiently and with the least possible abuse. In particular, the issue of compulsory membership resonated from government meetings on the future functioning of the Hlinka Guard.

Hlinka Guard members were certainly aware of their position in society and tried to use it for their own benefit. Guardians did not hesitate to use their rights immediately. By order of September 14, 1939, for example, the Hlinka Guard local and district headquarters were given the task of drawing up lists of licensees:

> To deal with Jews and Slovaks who do not behave as required by state interest (outrage, spread false news, behave passively, etc.), licensed Guardsmen should have applied for these licenses in a short time. Each Guardsman should also observe Jewish, Czech, Czechoslovak, or semi-philosophical and other persons who are working against the Slovak State, and against the Slovak Government. It is necessary to collect material that bears witness to the activities of these persons, witnesses, as well as a written record of their anti–state acts or speeches directed against the Slovak–German alliance.

The persecution of the internal enemy increased disproportionately in the period shortly after the outbreak of the war with Poland and the Hlinka Guard's involvement. With the government Decree Number 310 of December 1, 1939, the Hlinka Guard, among other duties, were assigned mainly tasks in the implementation of military training. Assistance to the army in the implementation of military training was not new for the guard. Similarly, it tried to use the Czech–Slovak government, which in 1938 invited the guard to carry out military training of Slovaks. By the end of 1939, the idea of engaging the Hlinka Guard in the post-war training process had become current again.

The use of Jews in work crews had become a source of easy earnings for some guards. Opportunities for their enrichment were the so-called Jews' labor camps, which provided them with a relatively decent income. At the end of 1939, especially at the beginning of 1940, there was a severe winter all over Slovakia, which was remembered as one of the strongest. The towns and villages were virtually impossible to walk in because of the amount of snow, which is why the Hlinka Guard set up a snow-shoveling labor camp for Jews following many of the regulations on the defense education of Jews. According to later investigations, the Jews worked in groups for forty days under the supervision of the Hlinka Guards. The highlight of cynicism was that any Jew who did not bring a snow shovel with him could borrow one at Hlinka Guard Headquarters for a small fee.

The military education meant for Hlinka Guard the necessity to participate in the education of the population in the form of lectures. It was a good opportunity for the guards to spread their thoughts among the wider population. In the Annex to the Order of January 1, 1940, the main headquarters highlighted to the commanders, the main task in addition to training on ideological lectures. Cultural officers had to instruct the guards before the start of military training that training means winning a fight that may not even take place on the front: "A well–trained, well-prepared nation will, by its discipline and readiness, deter the enemy or force it to meet the legitimate demands of the Slovak nation."

The Hlinka Guard was assigned to the auxiliary work in the implementation of military training got them into the area which was reserved for the army. The army's cooperation with the Hlinka Guard was not the best. Guards often complained about the army's unpreparedness to take courses and their unwillingness in carrying out military training. According to the Zilina County Command, the army even refused to provide the guards with the manuals and literature needed to carry out military training.

11

The Salzburg Conference and Reorganization According to the German Model

In mid-July 1940, Adolf Hitler invited Jozef Tiso, Vojtech Tuka, and Alexander Mach to a summit held in Salzburg, Austria. Tiso first met privately with German Foreign Minister Joachim von Ribbentrop, who informed the Slovaks that Germany considered Slovakia within its *Lebensraum* (living space), and therefore justified interference in Slovakia's internal affairs. He demanded that Tiso renounce his goal of a Catholic clerical state and dismiss Ďurčanský, due to his attempt to maintain communication with the Western powers and keep friendly relations with the Soviet Union. In another meeting, Adolf Hitler hinted that failure to comply would leave the Slovak State at the mercy of Hungary, by revoking the protection guarantees that Slovakia had obtained in the 1939 German–Slovak treaty.

The Slovaks requested a revision of the Vienna Arbitration. Specifically, they wanted six districts to be returned to Slovakia: Vráble-Šurany, Lučenec, Jelšava, Košice, north Sátoraljaújhely, and the Sobrance District. According to the Slovak foreign ministry, these areas contained 209,000 Slovaks and 100,000 Hungarians.

Ďurčanský was replaced as interior minister by Mach, who aligned the anti-Jewish policy of the Slovak State with that in Germany, while Tuka became foreign minister. Jozef Kirschbaum was dismissed as secretary-general of the Slovak People's Party, while Konštantín Čulen, the head of the propaganda ministry, was replaced by the radical Karol Murgaš. Nevertheless, the Germans recognized that the radical candidates were not as competent as the men that they replaced and were therefore careful not to go too far in demanding influential offices for them. None of the Slovak leaders, except Mach, was happy with the result of the negotiations.

After the Salzburg Conference, the Hlinka Guard began a new phase in the development of the organization. It was not so much related to Mach as to the trend outlined during Salzburg negotiations at the end of July 1940. Hlinka Guard, in the words of its chief commander, openly declared the ideas of the Slovak version of National Socialism. Already after their arrival in Slovakia, the most skilled people who played an important role in Salzburg spoke to the crowd from the balcony of the National Theater in Bratislava. Vojtech Tuka spoke words that for a long time influenced the direction of Slovakia. German observers closely followed the Slovak post-Salzburg internal political development and in regular reports informed their superiors about the political situation in Slovakia.

These reports often mention the Hlinka Guard, which was intended to become a tool to enforce and implement the new efforts. The Nazis pursued their political interests by putting them in crucial positions in the state. The idea of the Salzburg talks was, in fact, that the power given to Jozef Tiso was to be redistributed to the hands of Tuka and Mach from the summer of 1940, in the expectation that they would stand by the ideas of the new Europe with National Socialism applied into practice.

After Salzburg, the guard had become one of the tools of the dispute over the nature of the direction of the state and sought to meet the expectations imposed on it by radical groupings. The re-elected Commander Hlinka Guard Mach later confessed to giving a speech, but the words of his ideological leader grounded him so much that he did not know how to respond. "I had a speech ready that meant something. I wanted to emphasize what I said before March 14 in Vienna in the presence of Karol Sidor against the excessive celebration, we will not imitate anyone—who imitates will cut!" Mach gradually became one of the most aggressive supporters of the idea of Slovak National Socialism. His collaborators often criticized his beliefs about National Socialist ideas. According to several sources, he behaved differently in public and in private. He became an example of a man who was so tied to the regime that he could not imagine his existence without him.

Karol Danihel, a longtime collaborator of Mach and for some time the chief of Hlinka Guard, recalled that Mach was not precisely political at first, but after Salzburg he began to express National Socialist thinking. His speeches often contradicted each other, day by day. One day he spoke for National Socialism, the next day he cursed it privately. The Nazis did not make any illusions about the ideology of National Socialism in Slovakia taking deeper roots. They were aware that many Slovak leaders saw National Socialism as a need and a necessity.

After the July events, the Hlinka Guard gained enormous influence in the state. Shortly after the Salzburg Conference, Otomar Kubala became chief of the guard and the German advisor for the Hlinka Guard SS-*Obersturmbannführer* Viktor Nageler arrived. Berlin was very interested in making Slovakia a model satellite state with its own administration, but it wanted to steer it according to its ideas. This is one of the reasons why after the Salzburg negotiations that Nageler came to Slovakia. Advisors sent by Germany were supposed to participate in shaping the state in the sector they were assigned. The Hlinka Guard became one of the Nazi priorities. At the end of July 1940, Joachim von Ribbentrop called the appointment of a Hlinka Guard, along with Jewish police, propaganda, and economic advisors, necessary.

Immediately after Nageler's appointment, he was behind several ideological changes and efforts to transform the guard according to German models. The

German envoy assumed that advisory work could generally be the more successful if it would be non-political. The adviser was to be considered as an expert and act in that sense. His activity was to serve state as a whole by counseling, but not to individual power or interest groups.

Nageler became, however, an example of a buffer who was drawn into a battle between two rival groups who tried to influence the events on the Slovak political scene. Less than a month after his appointment, he decided not to leave anything to chance and began his journey through the Hlinka Guard district headquarters. He tried to get into the problems of the organization and especially tried to get to know its organizational and personnel apparatus. He made a good impression in the guard's commanders and gained a lot of good contacts, which helped him to better penetrate the secrets of Hlinka Guard and orientate himself in his new position. Shortly after his arrival, however, he had to struggle with the distrust of the guards. In the first weeks of his tenure, not even Kubal or Mach looked at him as an advisor, but as more as a cop trying to limit their decisions. But after about six weeks, he said: "tensions have relaxed and, over time, a quite cordial friendship has evolved." Nageler did indeed interfere with the history of the Hlinka Guard, but his mistake was that he did not solve the problems from a political perspective.

In November 1940, Nageler initiated the establishment of the Bojnice Castle School for training Hlinka Guard commanders. During autumn, the final preparations of the course were finished. The deputy commander of the Hlinka Guard had to visit all district Hlinka Guard headquarters and find out the actual status of headquarters and memberships. After the inspection, the course participants were identified. After visiting the headquarters Kubala expressed satisfaction with the functioning of district and local staffs, however, he noted that "even with good experience everywhere, there is a certain lack of exemplary organization."

Among other things, the reorganization of the Hlinka Guard, which was being discussed more and more in connection with the German Guard's plans during this period, was to be followed and discussed at the course. The first important step of the reorganization was the later abolition of the Hlinka Guard county headquarters. The property of the headquarters was to be taken over by district commanders. In county settlements, the abolished headquarters were replaced by less demanding county inspectors who were employed by Hlinka Guard. The trainee who achieved the best results at the course could also become a county inspector. For the district commanders, the gain of the post of county inspector was very motivating, because unlike the unpaid honorary function of the district commander, the inspectors would be paid functionaries of the headquarters.

The function of county inspectors was control, disciplinary, and administrative. Each had at least once a quarter to conduct an unannounced inspection of all district headquarters. In particular, the county inspectors oversaw examining the commanders' skills of the district commanders, the work of Hlinka Guard officers, the functioning of the office and, in special cases, the local commanders could also be inspected with the participation of the district commander.

In the context of the reorganization of the Hlinka Guard and the effectiveness of the activities of the district headquarters, each district headquarters set up a paid aide, who only worked for the Hlinka Guard and would be its employment. Kubala, together with Nageler, realized that the organization was not possible without the permanent functioning and handling of the agenda, which has grown considerably by using the guard for various auxiliary actions of military education and later took an initiative in the process of anti-Jewish measures. The Nazis realized that the guard had to be internally reorganized. Even the guards themselves gradually adopted the rhetoric and began to admit mistakes from the past, which were to be solved with the help of "German friends." The Hlinka Guard had not established and developed accurate records. German organization also affected this area. The Hlinka Guard made the system of registration of membership more transparent and issued each members ID cards.

The legitimacy was the wearing of badges or uniforms, which many guardsmen who were not members of the Rodobrana, abused and wore a badge to which they were not entitled. The use of the Hlinka Guard coat of arms was unified and its violation made criminal. By order of Hlinka Guard Number 5, it was forbidden to use the uniforms of any badges except the guard's blouse, on which the guardsman could have affixed a badge accompanied by a record of legitimacy.

The use of uniforms was tightened. The uniforms of the guardsmen were divided into service and walking. A member of the Hlinka Guard could only use a uniform for service, and consisted of a field cap, blouse, black shirt, black tie, black ratchets, and boots. Those guardsmen who wore blue shirts had as soon as possible to replace them with new black ones. Walking uniforms were to be used on solemn occasions. The guard without rank could use a service uniform and non-commissioned officers and uniform officers—which differed from the service brigadier—long pants and walking belt. In the event of social events, they were to wear a white shirt.

Gradually, the organization introduced rules, which were designed to prevent guards from dishonoring the uniform, for example, by inappropriate behavior. In the guard's uniform, the members of the Hlinka Guard had, in addition to the usual ban on visiting Jewish businesses and shops, a ban on going to the taverns or conducting business activities such as doorstep selling, etc. Therefore, in the autumn of 1941, the Hlinka Guard issued orders to subordinate guards to stop wearing uniforms in the course of personal gain. Similarly, guards were forbidden from wearing Hlinka Guard uniforms at dances and entertainment organized in public rooms.

One of the efforts to reorganize the Hlinka Guard according to German models was the emphasis on the previously neglected health issues. Even this seemingly insignificant part of the guardian life has been criticized and reorganized by the Germans. Hlinka Guard therefore to uplift the military component in the guard introduced the so-called week of guard's greeting. According to them, Hlinka Guard was supposed to be the elite of the Slovak nation, a selected team to protect against enemies at the time of need and be guardians of Slovak interests at the time of peace. The Hlinka Guard role was briefly expressed in a uniform greeting, "Watch!" This greeting was developed to express Slovak self-confidence, pride, courage, and readiness. The salute was their legitimacy, it was to be a badge of their unity and belonging.

"Whoever is ashamed to raise his hand to greet his friend or acquaintance, is ashamed of his Slovak conviction and is able to betray his nation and state." Main headquarters Order Number 5 of August 15, 1940 ordered the use of a single "Great salute" to all guardsmen and was to remind them in the way of greeting "German friends." "Let our salute continue to remind us of the great German nation's friendship with which we fought for freedom and independence. It is a greeting not only to the history of the culture of all mankind and to the history of Slovakia, but it is a greeting to a new world, a new Europe."

The Hlinka Guard also introduced the use of Hlinka Guard badges on a civilian suit. Until then, guards often violated the principles and wore badges to which they were not entitled. In the summer of 1941, a new salute changed to "Slovak to the Guard! *Der Deutsche grüßt: Heil* Hitler!" Many guards linked the greeting "To the Guard!" With the greeting "Be praised by Jesus Christ!" to which the Hlinka Guard had to respond by issuing an arrangement that stressed that both greetings do not contradict each other but should not merge.

One of the manifestations of the Hlinka Guard reorganization in the spirit of National Socialist ideas was the almost ubiquitous accentuation of Slovak–German friendship. In his memoirs, Milo Urban, the editor-in-chief of *Gardista*, recalled how grotesquely Mach's order was for him to include at least one photograph of Hitler in almost every *Gardista* issue. From the positions of the guard, the relationship between Hlinka Guard and *Freiwillige Schutzsstaffel* was glorified.

As in other issues, propaganda statements have not always coincided with reality. The cooperation between Hlinka Guard and *Freiwillige Schutzsstaffel* depended on a particular region. In many places, the Germans created their own "living communities" and their relationship to Hlinka Guard practically did not develop. In mixed Slovak–German areas, guards and public officials even considered the *Freiwillige Schutzsstaffel* to be a competing organization on education and guidance issues. Nevertheless, their cooperation was predetermined by their presence at various public holiday celebrations, adventures and demonstrative marches through the city streets. The towns, state authorities and the guard almost always invited local Germans to their activity, who, like the guardsmen, sent their members to them. The unity of the Slovak–German friendship through the friendly union of Hlinka Guard and *Freiwillige Schutzsstaffel*, however, gradually began to deteriorate. Official propaganda continued to reinforce the impression of the unholy alliance of the two nations, which "gradually became a fighting community for the better future of the common homeland and for a new Europe."

All Hlinka Guard orders were mainly external modifications, which were to help restore the guard's lost reputation in society and military elements. An important part of the reorganization was Hlinka Guard courses, which were to help the guard to the desired goal of becoming an elite nation. The military training instructors were non-commissioned officers and officers of the *Waffen*-SS, who, however, were mainly concerned with verifying physical fitness. Ideological lectures were given to various influential guardsmen and propagandists who instilled in the participants the National Socialist idea in the spirit of Slovak–German friendship. As Otomar Kubala put it: "the purpose of the school was to train Hlinka Guard officers. They were then supposed to set up Hlinka Guard schools in each district so that the whole Hlinka Guard would achieve greater military value."

For the first course, the Hlinka Guard called upon the district commanders, by special letters sent to each commander separately. For cost-effective reasons, it was recommended contacting the nearby commanders who had the car to come together. Each commander was to wear a black guard uniform and carry blue sweatpants, sweater sweatpants, black leather trainers, as well as washing, shaving, and cleaning supplies, stationery, notepad, and paper. The guard dagger was also mandatory.

Selected Hlinka Guard units and ordinary guards were divided into three categories (twenty to thirty years; thirty to forty years; and over forty years), with individual categories having adjusted scores for test results. Guards were to undergo various disciplines, such as a demanding 3,000-meter run, a 5-km march with a short-term load after waking up at 2 a.m. in a uniform, helmet, and military backpack, in which two bricks were placed for the load, or various sports disciplines taking place on the sports field. The intelligence service was also challenging, during which the guardsmen were supposed to wade through the Nitra River, to reach the designated bridge undetected and to submit a written report at the designated location.

Training schools were also set up for selected guards at the SS center in Sennheim, which was initiated again by Nageler. The Sennheim course was a sort of culmination of the guard's advancement. Its successful completion meant for the guard obtaining the defense badge, which was obtained by mastering the basic disciplines. It was a successful completion of some disciplines of light athletics, swimming, cycling, military walking training, which included shooting rimfire rifle and throwing a grenade in all positions. The badge consisted of crossed swords, from which grew the Slovak double cross. It was lined with a laurel wreath and was worn on the left pocket of a blouse. In addition to physical screenings, the guards also attended a series of ideological lectures mostly in German, where their instructors, mainly from the SS, initiated the concepts of National Socialism. Only successful graduates of the Hlinka Guard district schools, who had proved their work in favor of Hlinka Guard, were to be selected for the SS schools.

The Germans, through Nageler, understood the importance of the guard as a strengthening of its position in Slovakia and tried to contribute to its better functioning according to German models by military elements and organizing Hlinka Guard schools. According to his ideas, the guard was to become a choir of selected individuals who, after reorganization, would gradually begin to occupy positions in the state apparatus. Although he failed to accomplish this task, his proposals to improve the functioning of the organization meant a significant step forward for the guard.

Similarly, courses in Germany were attended by the commanders of Hlinka Guard selected units, which were also established after the arrival of Nageler. Therefore, the selection criteria for the Hlinka Guard members were high. In addition to physical fitness, selected candidates also had to undergo racial screening in several phases. Prospectively, even in Berlin, the most capable individuals would later recruit into the *Waffen*-SS. Nazi plans to deploy the Slovaks in the *Waffen*-SS persisted until 1945. The fact that it was not only the plans of a few Slovak Germans, but also supported by high-ranking representatives of Germany, is evidenced by several indications. In one of his letters, Himmler even mentioned that he had suggested to Mach that young disposable Slovaks report to the *Waffen*-SS, which Mach reportedly nodded enthusiastically. Racial screening was one of the first steps to the idea. According to a report by Herbert Buchtal, a physician trained by the *Waffen*-SS Supplementary Office, only 8 percent of the guards passed the stringent criteria applicable to the Germans during the first review of the Bratislava Guards. However, despite relatively bad results, Nageler continued his efforts.

According to the Hlinka Guard memorandum of March 5, 1942, Hlinka Guard students achieved excellent results, for which the chief of staff gave them praise. In special order to the district commanders, the role of the Hlinka Guard at that time was to participate in the military education of the population. One of the most important tasks of the Sennheim course was to create appropriate new cadres to better carry out military training. The classic guardsmen wore distinguished and gray-green uniforms with a modified cut. However, many people were mistaken for Hlinka Guard uniforms with German uniforms, often resulting in comical situations. The first time the guardsmen of these units appeared in Bratislava, the inhabitants wondered why the Germans had Slovak orders. In *Gardista*, this question was aptly answered by the chief of the Hlinka Guard:

> Although the black uniform is nice to represent, it is unsuitable for service and exercise. This has been pointed out in the Hlinka Guard for half a year. So, we were looking for a practical color and even a uniform. We saw the most practical color in the one worn by HM members. But there is also a mistake. Our soldiers are terrified that this color and such uniform is very wrong, as our anti–aircraft units have a similar uniform. Ash color would not be bad, but FS has it. So, we had to look for something between the color of ash and green. That there will be people who object to this color and uniform? Well, the main thing here is under the uniform. The rest is all secondary. And there is a brave Slovak heart.

After the end of the course in Germany, courses for selected units were to be continued in Bojnice under the supervision of several prominent figures of Slovak political life from autumn 1940, until 1942.

12

Changes in Hlinka Guard after the Salzburg Conference

As a result of the new tasks assigned to the Hlinka Guard, in particular with regard to the control and implementation of anti-Jewish regulations, there were several reorganization changes in the Hlinka Guard. Already in 1941, the guard took steps leading to the initial revision of membership. Organizational Order Number 5, which was prescribed conditions for admission to the Hlinka Guard, later guided the guards during the revision, especially during the following year. According to the organizational status sent to Hlinka Guard headquarters in the Hlinka Guard order of April 9, 1941, only a Slovak citizen of Slovak nationality was admitted on the basis of a voluntary application could become a member of the guard. The applicant could only be admitted after a one-year waiting period. The prerequisites for its admission included moral preservation, political integrity, Aryan origin, and physical ability. Even physically unfit candidates could be admitted to the guard, but they could only perform intellectual work and could not wear a uniform. The Aryan origin of the guardsmen was to be proven by the background of both parents and grandparents. Every guardsman admitted, under the order of April 9, was to receive from the Hlinka Guard district commander a document that entitled him to wear a uniform and Hlinka Guard badge. The duty of each guard member was to take the prescribed oath when joining the organization:

> I swear to the living God that the law of eternal leader Andrej Hlinka.
> For God's life, for a nation of freedom will be the highest order.
> I swear I will faithfully obey the orders of my superiors and,
> I would rather fall than betray. So Lord God help me.

One important milestone in the development of the organizational structure of the Hlinka Guard was the publication of the disciplinary code of the Hlinka Guard. With the staff regulations of the Hlinka Guard and the disciplinary code, which had been in force for a long time, the basic model of the internal organization of the guard was created with precisely specified rules for its members. The maintenance of the discipline was, according to the staff regulations, the primary task of each guard. Each guardsman was to express, in accordance with the guidelines contained in this document, obedience to his commander.

The code stated that he who disobeys his commander, who violates the principle of discipline, sins against the state, threatens the freedom and happiness of his fellow citizens, is a pest and an enemy of the whole. If the guard violated the regulations of the Hlinka Guard staff regulations, he could be punished on the basis of the Hlinka Guard disciplinary code, which also introduced the so-called disciplinary committees. They had the power to investigate and assess such conduct of Hlinka Guard members who had been damaged or compromised by the guard's reputation. However, several guardsmen were hurting the good reputation of the Hlinka Guard regularly, and the statute of disciplinary committees gradually became only paper without practical use. Many Slovaks tried to get into the guard because of the undisputed advantages resulting not only from the legal right to preferential employment, but also from the advantages of anti-Jewish legislation.

The guardsman had to meet the requirement of political integrity, in particular a positive attitude towards national and Christian ideas in the Hlinka spirit. He had to swear:

> I declare on my honor,
> that I have never been to the Freemasons and Rotary club,
> that I am of Aryan descent,
> that I live an ordered family life,
> that I always and officially keep secret,
> that I will not do anything against Hlinka Guard, the Party, against the interests of the nation and against the independence of the state.
> When I learn circumstances that could harm the nation and the state, I will announce them at the appropriate place.
> I will execute all orders that will be my superiors the.
> I declare that I am aware of the penalties that will catch me when my certificate would not be based on the truth and when I would did not fulfill the promise.
> I declare that I am aware of the obligations arising from the oath.
> To the guard!

According to propaganda statements and orders, the role of the Hlinka Guard in the military education after the issuance of the new directives was mainly to lead all citizens to the need for uniform cohesion and national sentiment. The work in the military education was to be directed for general welfare and army. The main goal of all-useful work was to form and educate a new person according to Christian, national, and social principles when working on the Slovak goals. The guards were supposed to clean the roads, modify the sidewalks, and take care of the urban greenery, but these tasks remained almost on paper.

In this period, Hlinka Guard was fully engaged in the Jewish question. Efforts to resolve the relationship with the army thus remained largely at the level of the statements of resilient unity and occasional meetings of troops at the onset. But the reality was different. This relationship gained new importance in early September 1944 by creation of Hlinka Guard emergency units, which were supposed to be a replacement for the army, because it was in critical days of the nation, according to the guards had totally failed.

13

Implementation of Anti-Jewish Regulations

The anti-Jewish legislation of the Slovak Republic became a breakthrough in the Hlinka Guard members' persecution efforts. On this basis, Jews became second-class citizens and gradually their rights were increasingly restricted. The guardsmen also dealt with the issue of Czechs remaining in Slovakia even after the removal of a large part of Czech employees. However, the anti-Jewish agenda became the most important part of the organization's active work until the outbreak of the August 1944 uprising. Some guard members disagreed with the brutality that many of their fellow members had shown, and they were no longer interested in actively participating in the organization. This is one of the reasons why the guard lost a large amount of membership in the early 1940s and stagnated. It lost many of the functions it had previously performed and was degraded to an anti-Jewish organization in the eyes of the public.

According to one Nazi report, this period was even "rightly described as a ravage and gradual death of the Hlinka Guard." In German eyes, the Hlinka Guard was merely an organization that, at the outset, seemed strong enough to lead the Jewish question to a solution. However, under fire from the authorities on the one hand and lured by the Jewish with money on the other hand, the Hlinka Guard was unable to take decisive action. The state apparatus assigned to the guard the role of a subsidiary body in anti-Jewish legislation, which gave the organization an increasingly distinctive and virtually the anti-Jewish character. Since the Salzburg Conference, the guard's pressure to address the Jewish question had increased. Not until the summer of 1940 did the Hlinka Guard pay much attention to this area, but from the Salzburg Conference, according to the guards, in this respect, they had a new mission.

Following Salzburg, not only the process of adopting anti-Jewish regulations, but also the process of collection, was sped up. Aryanization Act Number 10 of September 1940 empowered the Slovak government to resolve the Aryanization of Jewish property without parliamentary participation. Shortly after that came the second Aryanization Act Number 303 of November 1940, which no longer counted on the voluntary Aryanization on the basis of co-ownership. The transfer of assets could be 100 percent or partial, thus the Jewish original owner could have retained no more than 49 percent of the assets and business profits. However, the original Jewish owner could no longer make any decisions and his participation in the business was purely technical. The issuing of the laws of Aryanization brought a lively response among the guards. They had allowed many radicals to reach profitable businesses based on personal contacts or activity. As the writer of a report to the Foreign Office in Berlin said, "unprecedented cases of corruption" were too common in Slovakia.

Hlinka Guard activities in the Aryanization process varied from case to case. While some guards were satisfied earning money from the Jewish property that the Jews had worked on, others were dissatisfied with it and robbed the property of the owners. Some guards did not even hesitate to furnish the flats of Jewish owners, who were deported to the Nazi concentration camps. In many cases, not only the affected Jews complained, but the actions of the guardsmen were also considered outrageous for a large number of high-ranking citizens.

In the period of the Slovak Republic, many of the guards became rich. In the end, however, they often fled, as other similar radicals whose rapid career was tied to the anti-Jewish legislation of the Slovak Republic. Together with the retreating exponents of the Slovak state, they mostly went to Austria before the advance of the Red Army and left their family and acquired property in Slovakia. There were many guards in Slovakia at that time. Many did not hesitate to sell their moral principles to the prospect of easy profit and benefited from the advantage of the Aryanization process. Of course, not all guards engaged in profitable enterprises, but the legislation of the Slovak Republic allowed them to gain a more favorable position in this area. That is why the guard and its membership were attractive to many profitable Slovaks.

On the other hand, a large membership base had begun to be thinned, in particular with regard to the brutality of Hlinka Guard in this area. For the guards, the advantage was that in the Aryanization process, the guard as an organization could participate legally on the basis of anti-Jewish legislation. The party, together with the Hlinka Guard, agreed that in each municipality where there was at least one Jewish enterprise, a commission consisting of a chairman, an economic officer, and a secretary of the party's local organization, a local commander, and a promotional or social officer of the Hlinka Guard could draw up lists of Aryanizers who had already applied for Jewish business.

When deciding on the allocation of a business, very important information was to be taken into account in addition to information on party membership, since the applicant was registered as a member of the Hlinka Guard. Hlinka Guard membership and contacts could help many Slovaks to hold Jewish businesses.

In addition to Jewish vehicles and homes, the guardians were also interested in the process of adopting anti-Jewish orders. They often criticized them and considered it necessary to be as strict as possible against the Jews. Through the press, the Hlinka Guard called for the acceleration of Aryanization and the strict observance of anti-Jewish measures. In addition to the traditional accusations of Jews being Communist, propaganda alleged manifestations of Jews expanding in Slovakia in the first half of 1941. These were, of course, inadequate claims, but they were part of anti-Jewish propaganda. They criticized, for example, the "stretching" of Jews in towns, in the Tatras mountain range that straddle the border of Slovakia and Poland, or in the capital, but criticism was prompted by the brutal behavior of the Jews in the means of transport. Almost every day brought news of the obsesses of the Hlinka Guard.

On March 18, the express train was overcrowded with Jews. They were in every car and in all classes. In one wagon, there were five traveling in uniform and two guards not in uniform. When the Jews were taking too many seats, they called on the Jews to make room for the Aryans. When the Jews received it with a mocking smile and did not move from their seats, the guards simply chased them into the wagon where there were more Jews, and then put the Aryans back into the cars to "cleanse them completely from the Jews."

Hlinka Guard members suggested setting up a special department for the Jews to determine when they must be allowed to travel and to prevent the Aryans from being forced to sit with the Jews on trains. Legislative measures were soon adopted in the form of a decree of the minister of Transport and Public Works of October 9, 1941, which excluded the travel of the Jews in the first-class cabins and sleeping wagons and ordered that they can only travel in third-class wagons labeled "For Jews." Similarly, guardsmen treated Jewish citizens the same way in buses. On the basis of the aforementioned decree, they were allowed to travel without class restrictions, but in the case of a large rush of boarding passengers, Aryans took precedence over the Jews. When Hlinka Guard members violated the law, they did not avoid investigation, but the vast percentage of cases of violence against Jews went unreported to the security authorities.

Guards were recruited for the auxiliary work of the security authorities on the basis of the Hlinka Guard Law of July 4, 1940. According to it, they should cooperate in maintaining public order and public security. In 1941, their role became even more pronounced when the implementation of anti-Jewish regulations was added. In anti-Jewish actions, the Hlinka Guard gained extensive powers. In 1941, the Ministry of the Interior issued guidelines for members of the Hlinka Guard authorizing them to carry out ancillary control in the maintenance of anti-Jewish measures, in which it defined the powers of guards. The guardsman was obliged to detain and show the Jew to the police office if he could not legitimize him or the Jew committed an offense. He could also enter any publicly accessible room and, in the case of the persecution of a Jew who might have escaped or suspected of seriously breaking the law, into a Jewish private apartment, but only if the police were involved.

These regulations were just paper arrangements that the guards did not hesitate to break many times, without remorse. If the guard had a legitimate suspicion of a Jew committing the offense or actually came across a Jew, he could search him without cause. However, as in the case of persecution and intrusion into private Jewish flats, this legislation did not mean anything to the guardsmen, who at all costs intended to enrich himself due to the misfortune of the Jewish fellow citizens. Although the Hlinka Guard issued orders in which its subordinates warned that interference with the powers of the security authorities was unlawful, it had to find that, despite the bans, there were still cases where subordinate headquarters intervened on various matters of intervention and others directly at central offices.

The property of the Jews who had been transported was to be sealed and seized. It was supposed to be guarded by the guards along with the mercenaries, yet many things from Jewish flats were stolen. Every guardsman was entitled to reimbursement of lost profits, and the amount for which he was doing this extra work was set at 5 crowns per hour, which was relatively decent earnings. According to the headquarters, the guardsmen, who had valid legitimacy to participate as an auxiliary body in security control measures against Jews, should intervene in cases where Aryans concealed Jewish valuables. Security authorities often did not respond, even though they were certain that the Jews kept their valuables, such as paintings, carpets, or furniture, before being transported by Aryans. *Gardista* articles or leaflets pointed to the problem of so-called "White Jews" who, according to them, helped the Jews in their plan to rule the world. Already in the middle of 1939, a demonizing, strongly anti-Jewish-oriented leaflet, *Sisters and Brothers*, appeared; according to this leaflet: "The Jewish international monster is beginning to crawl out tongues of fire and with them to burn peaceful and happy Slovak souls." In their endeavor, they were to be supported by White Jews, "who were so stunned by the glitter of the Jewish golden calf that they lost patriotic sentiment and common sense."

Government Decree Number 184/1939 set the policy on regulating the number of Jews in medical practice. According to the Hlinka Guard, it was found that the Jews had not respected and circumvented the regulation. Allegedly, secretly, and with the help of the population, which was introduced Jewish propaganda, the practice of medicine continued. Wearing a civilian suit, the guard's job was to watch marketers who refused to sell goods before 10 a.m. and then sell these goods after 10 a.m. to Jews. The order was circumvented so that Jews would buy at certain hours. The Aryans were shopping for them on the market before 10 a.m. and carrying the goods directly to the Jew's home. Hlinka Guard members were to follow them and intervene. However, the State Security Center went further in its proposals and suggested that, through the Hlinka Guard, the guards would also consider whether it would be expedient to prohibit Jews from buying poultry in order to tighten its price to Aryans.

On the basis of its observations, the price of poultry was disproportionately high, mainly because the Jews bought it in bulk. In connection with the economic activity of the Jews, the Hlinka Guard also ordered the guards to observe whether their trafficking was "within the limits of the merchandise and place of business" and whether public officials did not buy from the Jews, even if was not explicitly necessary. The members of the Hlinka Guard were also to observe that Jews did not purchase daily consumables in large quantities and that non-Jewish retailers were not supplied by Jewish wholesalers, since there were still cases where individual food articles are only available to Jews. In the context of the fight against the "White Jews," the guard's priority was to monitor public officials and their contacts with Jews, as well as whether Jews maintained contacts with officials. The Hlinka Guard was supposed to be a leading force in the struggle against these dubious individuals who, in their view, were using the moderate procedure and committing unprecedented heavy, political and criminal actions causing great despair. As in the past, it was to be the Hlinka Guard, which in every place and in any case intensively follow every progress of the Jews, who would uncover their Jewish helpers and not allow them to arbitrarily gamble with the spiritual and material possessions of the nation.

As a result of these and similar regulations, the Propaganda Bureau proposed simplifying the control of Jews. Since various anti-Jewish measures had recently been issued for security reasons, such as banning certain places (better cafes) or detaining Jews on the streets after a certain time in the evening, it was important, according to the office, to improve the system of Jewish selection. The Propaganda Bureau therefore suggested that the Jews should be marked in a prominent place with a certain sign so that the security authorities could more easily check compliance with the anti-Jewish regulations. In the Šariš-Zemplin county since April 1941, Jews were obliged to wear a 3-cm-thick yellow tape. On the basis of decrees of the Ministry of the Interior, the guardsmen were also invited to control measures which ordered the Jews to wear yellow stars and mark houses in a similar way. Guards also checked for compliance with the provisions of the so-called Jewish Code, a government decree adopted on September 9, 1941.

The Jewish Code, adopted by the totalitarian regime of Hlinka's Slovak People's Party after years of systematic persecution of Jews, was the most extensive legal norm of war-time Slovakia. By integrating all previously issued anti-Jewish laws into one regulation, and by introducing a racial definition of the term "Jew" into Slovak law, it effectively finished a major part of the process of stripping the Jewish population of Slovakia of their civil and human rights. The entire ordinance is included here as it provides us with an understanding of the position of the Slovak government towards Jews.

Ordinance of September 9, 1941, on the Legal Status of the Jews
(Source: EuroDocs, European Studies, (Provo: Harold B. Lee Library, Brigham Young University)

198/1941 Sl.z. Regulation of September 9, 1941 on the Legal Status of the Jews.

The Government of the Slovak Republic pursuant to Section 1 of Act No. 210/1940 Sl.z. orders:

GENERAL PROVISIONS.

Definition.

§ 1.

(1) The following shall be considered to be a Jew under this Regulation, whatever their gender:
(a) who comes from at least three, depending on the race of Jewish grandparents;

(b) a Jewish blend that originates from two according to the race of Jewish grandparents [Section 2, and if:

1. was, or became, a member of the Israeli (Jewish) religion on 20 April 1939,
2. after 20 April 1939, he married a Jew (lit. a)],
3. comes from a marriage with a Jew [c. (a)], concluded after 20 April 1939,
4. comes from illegitimate contact with a Jew [c. a)] and was born as an illegitimate child after 20 February 1940.

(2) A Jewish grandparent according to race within the meaning of the provisions of this Regulation shall be deemed to belong to an Israeli (Jewish) religion.

§ 2.

The following shall be deemed to be a Jewish mixer under this Regulation:

(a) who comes from two according to the race of Jewish grandparents (§ 1, paragraph 2), if according to § 1, point. b) does not consider himself a Jew,

(b) who comes from one according to the race of the Jewish grandparent (§ 1, paragraph 2).

§ 3.

(1) The continuing complaints to the competent authorities, courts and bodies of public corporations and institutions shall, in cases where this is strictly necessary for their decision (measure, etc.), require the party to confirm that he is not a Jew, heavily Jewish blend.

(2) Authorities, courts and authorities (par. 1) shall not request confirmation pursuant to par. 1, if they are aware from the documents submitted or otherwise that the party is not a Jew, then the Jewish mixer.

(3) 1 are issued by municipal (district) notary offices—in Bratislava the State Registry Office—competent according to residence.

(4) For persons not residing in the territory of the Slovak Republic, a certificate is issued (paragraph 1) by the State Registry Office in Bratislava.

(5) In doubtful cases, whether someone is a Jew, a Jewish mixer or not, the Ministry of the Interior decides. Both the party and the authority, court or body of a public-law corporation may apply for a decision.

(6) The matrix lifts necessary for the issue of the certificate pursuant to par. 1, expressly issued and designated as such, shall not be subject to stamp duty or levy. The amount of remuneration that church registrars are entitled to collect for these lifts shall be determined by the Minister of the Interior in a decree.

§ 4.

The following are to be considered as Jewish associations under this Regulation:

(a) a public company if at least half of the partners are Jews (Jewish associations) and at the same time if at least half of the participation in the profits of the company belongs to Jews (Jewish associations);

(b) a limited partnership if at least half of the limited partners and at least half of the public partners are Jews (Jewish associations), or if at least half of the participation in the profits of the society belongs to Jews (Jewish associations);

(c) a participating company or cooperative, if more than one quarter of the members of the Board of Directors are Jews, or if at least half of the principal amount belongs to Jews (Jewish associations); in so doing, account shall not be taken of members of the Management Board who are foreign nationals and who are permanently resident in a foreign country,

(d) a limited liability company if at least one quarter of the executives are Jews, or if at least half of the share capital belongs to Jews (Jewish associations),

(e) Mining, if a quarter of the members of the administration are Jews, or if at least half are Jewish (Jewish associations);

(f) a legal person (association, foundation, fund, etc.) or other body of persons or property whose purpose is to promote Jewish interests, or at least half of which are Jews (Jewish associations), except where they are constituted by special legal entities regulations.

§ 5.

The Jewish or non-Jewish nature of the association (§ 4) is determined by the Central Economic Office in doubtful cases.

PART ONE

Personal status

TITLE I – Registry

§ 6.

(1) The municipal (district) notary offices—in Bratislava the Police Directorate—keep a register of Jews residing within their jurisdiction.

(2) The Police Headquarters in Bratislava shall also keep records of those Jews who reside in the territory of the Slovak Republic but who do not reside there.

(3) On the basis of records pursuant to par. 1 and 2, the Ministry of the Interior keeps the central register.

(4) Jews are obliged to report the data and their changes necessary for the records according to par. 1 and 2.

(5) Details of keeping records and reporting duty (paragraph 4) shall be determined by the Ministry of the Interior.

§ 7.

Those who knowingly fail to comply with the reporting obligation pursuant to Section 6 shall be punished for a violation by the district (state police) office with a financial penalty from Ks 100.- to Ks 10.000.-, which in case of unenforceability shall be closed from 1 day to 15 days.

TITLE II – Label

§ 8.

(1) Jews are obliged to wear a Jewish sign. Details of the shape of the sign and the manner of its wearing, as well as general exceptions, in agreement with the minister responsible to the minister, shall be determined by a decree in the Official Journal.
(2) Other designations in connection with the name (surname) or firm of a Jew (Jewish association) may be determined by the minister responsible.
(3) He who does not wear shall not use the markings according to para. 1 or 2 of the punishment shall be punished by a fine of between Ks 100 and Ks 10,000 for the offense by the district (state police) office, which is to be closed from 1 day to 15 days in the event of unenforceability.

TITLE III – Restrictions on marriage and intermarriage.

§ 9.

(1) It is forbidden to marry between a Jew (a Jew) and a non-Jew and between a Jew and a Jewish mixer [§ 2].
(2) Who deliberately marries against the prohibition in para. 1, punish the offense for imprisonment of up to 3 years and loss of office and electoral rights.

§ 10.

Conscious extramarital sexual intercourse between a Jew and a gentile is punished as a crime by imprisonment up to 5 years.

§ 11.

Criminal continuation for offenses under Sections 9 and 10 falls within the jurisdiction of regional courts.

TITLE IV – Exclusion from the right to vote and from public office.

§ 12.

(1) Jews do not have the right to vote and are not eligible to be elected to the Assembly of the Slovak Republic or bodies of public corporations.
(2) A Jew cannot be appointed as a functionary of the state and public corporations and institutions at all.
(3) 1 and 2 also apply to Jewish mixed persons (§ 2) and to the non-Jewish spouses of the Jews, but only as it concerns passive voting rights.

§ 13.

(1) A Jew cannot be a member of the Hlinka Slovak People's Party, registered parties of national groups, or a member of the Hlinka Guard, the Hlinka Youth, the *Freiwillige Schutzstaffel* and the *Deutsche Jugend*.

(2) The officers or non-commissioned officers of the organizations referred to in para. 1, neither a Jewish mixer (§ 2) nor a non-Jewish husband of a Jew.

§ 13.

(1) A Jew may not be appointed as an expert, appraiser, interpreter, judge layman, bankruptcy trustee, forced trustee in judicial or other continuation, guardian, guardian, except as guardian and guardian for guardian or guardian-Jew.
(2) 1 also applies to Jewish mixers, referred to in § 2, point. a).

§ 14.

(1) A Jew may not be appointed as an expert, appraiser, interpreter, lay judge, bankrupt a trustee, a custodian in court or otherwise, as guardian, guardian, excluding the appointment of a guardian and guardian for a guardian or guardian-Jew.
(2) 1 also applies to Jewish mixers, referred to in § 2, letter. a).

TITLE V – Ineligibility to public services.

§ 15.

(1) A Jew shall not be employed in the service of the State, including in the service of public corporations and public institutions at all, including public policyholders, including their or subsidized institutions, enterprises, funds and facilities, except for Jewish cultural, cult and socio-health institutions as well as the Jewish Center.
(2) 1 shall also apply to Jewish mixers, referred to in § 2, point. a). The officer and non-commissioned officer of the armed forces or the mercenary may not be a Jewish mixer referred to in § 2, point. b).
(3) 1 also applies to the non-Jewish spouses of the Jews.

TITLE VI – Inability to practice some of the liberal professions.
Part One.
Ineligibility to public notary, advocacy and civil engineering.

§ 16.

(1) A Jew cannot be:
(a) by a public notary (a non-public outline);
(b) by a lawyer (lawyer);
(c) civil engineers.
(2) 1, para) and b) also applies to Jewish mixers referred to in § 2, letter a) and b). a).
(3) 1, point (a) a) applies to non-Jewish spouses of Jews.

§ 17.

(1) The offense is committed and punished by a competent district court imprisonment of up to 3 months and a fine of between 1,000 and 5,000 Ks:

(a) who, in accordance with § 16, is excluded from pursuing his profession, continues in it,
(b) who employs or allows the employment of a person excluded from that profession,
(c) who in any way directly or indirectly allows a person excluded pursuant to Section 16 to pursue the profession from which he / she is excluded.
(2) A member of a public or bar association, as well as a member of the relevant engineering organization of interest, who has been guilty of the provisions of par. 1, point (a) 1 letter b) and c), loses the right to practice and is deleted from the list of the relevant chamber (organization).
(3) Conditional suspension of the sentence is excluded.

Part Two.

Ineligibility to practice medical and veterinary practice.

§ 18.

(1) Jews may not practice medical and veterinary practice.
(2) 1, because it is a medical practice, also applies to Jewish mixers, referred to in § 2, point. a).

§ 19.

(1) The offense is committed and punished by a county (state police) office with a fine of 500 Ks to 50,000 Ks, which in case of un-recoverability is to be closed from 5 days to 30 days:
(a) who, in accordance with § 18, is excluded from the practice of medical and post-veterinary practice,
(b) who, in the exercise of a medical or post-veterinary practice, employs or enables the employment of a person excluded from the practice;
(c) who, in any way, directly or indirectly allows the person excluded from him to pursue the medical practice.
(2) Conditional suspension of the sentence is excluded.

Part Three.

Ineligibility for practicing medical practice and pharmacy rights.

§ 20.

(1) A Jew cannot practice medical practice.
(2) A Jew may not be the owner or concessionaire of a public pharmacy with real, radical or personal rights.
(3) 1 shall also apply to Jewish mixers, referred to in § 2, point. a).

§ 21.

(1) The offense is committed and punished by a county (state police) office with a fine of 1,000 to 100,000 Ks, which in case of un-recoverability is to be closed from 10 days to 60 days:
(a) who, in accordance with § 20, is excluded from the pursuit of his profession therein continues,

(b) who employs or allows to employ a person excluded from this profession,
(c) who in any way directly or indirectly allows a person excluded under § 20 to continue the profession from which he / she is excluded.
(2) Conditional suspension of the sentence is excluded.

TITLE VII.

Work obligation and restriction of personal, domestic freedom and letter secrets.

Part One.

Work obligation.

§ 22.

(1) Jews between 16 and 60 years of age, if they are not doing work according to § 38 of the Consumer Act, are obliged to do the work ordered by the Ministry of the Interior.
(2) For persons referred to in para. 1 the job is procured; the hard work is organized, and the working conditions are determined by the Ministry of the Interior.
(3) 1 does not apply to Jews who are authorized under § 43, para. 1, who, according to § 258, para. 2 may remain in their current occupation, as well as for Jews who are subject to the provisions of § 256, provided that the relevant permission or exemption is valid.

§ 23.

The work carried out pursuant to Section 22 shall not establish employment (service) relationship and the persons performing it shall not be subject to public insurance.

§ 24.

Anyone who disobeys the order (§ 22) to start work, also the one who does not do the ordered work, or carelessly executing it or leaving it without the consent of the Ministry of the Interior, punishment for the offense of the district (state police) office with a financial penalty from 100 to 10,000 Ks, which in case of non-enforceability is to be closed from 1 day to 15 days.

Part Two.

Personal and home search.

§ 25.

The State Security Authorities may at any time carry out a personal search of the Jews, even without a written order from the authority or court.

§ 26.

(1) The State Security Authorities may at any time carry out a search at the Jews and at the Jewish associations, even without a written order of the authority or court. Otherwise, the provisions of Part II apply. of Act no. 293/1920 Sb.z. and n.
(2) 1 also applies to enterprises (factories) and other rooms of Jews and Jewish associations.

Part Three.
Limitation of letter secrecy.

§ 27.

(1) A Jew (Jewish association) as the sender of any postal item (letters, parcels, etc.) inland traffic is obliged to indicate on it his exact address and easily identifiable mark (a Jewish star).
(2) Who violates the provision of para. 1, shall be punished by the District (State Police) Offense for Penalty Offenses from Ks 100 to Ks 10,000, which in case of unenforceability is to be closed from 1 day to 15 days.

Part Four.
Restriction on residence.

§ 28.

(1) The Central Economic Office may, in agreement with the Ministry of the Interior, impose on Jews the obligation to move out of a certain municipality (city), while at the same time imposing an obligation to move to a certain municipality (city).
(2) The Central Economic Office may, in agreement with the Ministry of the Interior, determine the districts of district offices or individual municipalities (towns) to which Jews may not immigrate.
(3) The Central Economic Office may impose on Jews the obligation to move out of a certain part of the municipality (city) and at the same time may impose the obligation to move to a certain part of the municipality, generally or in individual cases.

§ 29.

(1) The Ministry of the Interior and its subordinate public administration authorities may restrict or prohibit Jews from staying in certain municipalities (towns) or in certain parts thereof (squares, streets, parks, swimming pools, etc.), as well as restricting or forbid visiting certain businesses (spas, inns, cafes, exhibitions, etc.).
(2) Infringement of restrictions or prohibitions issued pursuant to para. 1, punish the district (state police) authorities with a fine of 100 to 10,000 Ks, which in the case of unenforceability to be closed from 1 day to 15 days.

TITLE VIII.
Limitation of federal and assembly rights as well as press rights freedom.

Part One.
Federal Law and the Jewish Center.

§ 30.

(1) It is forbidden to establish Jewish associations or Jewish organizations [§ 4, lit. f)] except for Jewish religious communities.

(2) Who violates the provision of par. 1, punish the district (state police) office with a fine of 500 Ks to 50,000 Ks, which in the case of unenforceability to be closed from 5 days to 30 days.

§ 31

(1) The only organization of Jews living in the territory of the Slovak Republic solely called to represent their collective interests is the Jewish Center, based in Bratislava.
(2) The Jewish Center is a public interest corporation; its members are all persons considered to be Jews under § 1.
(3) The Jewish Center shall be subject only to the supervision of the Central Economic Office; its commands and modifications are binding on it.

§ 32.

The details, in particular the internal organization, the bodies of the Jewish Center and the rights and obligations of its members, as well as the supervision (Section 31 (3)), are determined by the Central Economic Office.

Part Two.
Right of assembly.

§ 33.

Jews may not hold public gatherings or escorts and may not attend other public gatherings.

Part Three.
Restricting freedom of the press and publishing literary and other

§ 34.

(1) A Jew may not be a publisher, an editor (responsible editor), or a contributor to any magazine, except for a magazine published by the Jewish Center.
(2) Jews (Jewish associations) may not have any periodical or non-periodical magazine. No one else may publish a magazine serving their interests.
(3) 1 and 2 shall also apply to Jewish mixers referred to in § 2, letter a). a).
(4) Who violates the provision of par. 1 to 3, punish the district (state police) offense for fines from 100 Ks to 10,000 Ks, which in the case of unenforceability to be closed from 1 day to 15 days.

§ 35.

(1) In the territory of the Slovak Republic, it is not possible to print or otherwise reproduce, or to put into circulation (demonstrate) the spiritual (scientific, literary, musical, visual, etc.) product of a Jew, even under a foreign (code) name. This does not exclude the use of these products for scientific purposes.

(2) Prohibition under para. 1 also applies to spiritual products of Jewish mixers, referred to in § 2, point. a).

(3) Who deliberately violates the provision of par. 1 and 2, the District (State Police) Offense shall be punished by a fine of between 500 Ks and 50,000 Ks, which in the case of unenforceability is to be closed from 5 days to 30 days.

TITLE IX.

Restrictions on matters of cult and education.

Part One.

Cult buildings.

§ 36.

(1) Members of the Israeli (Jewish) religion and Jewish religious communities may carry out their cult acts only in buildings whose appearance does not appear to be buildings intended for religious acts.

(2) Jewish synagogues and prayer rooms must be adapted according to par. 1 to 1 July 1942; otherwise they will be owned by the state on the date stated by the District (Municipal Notary) Office. Details of the adjustment will be issued by the Minister of the Interior.

Part Two.

Prohibition of ritual slaughter.

§ 37.

(1) Jewish ritual slaughter of any livestock and animals, as well as cutting, selling and any consumption or use of meat and meat products derived from ritual slaughter shall be prohibited.

(2) Failure to maintain the provisions of para. 1 district (state police) authorities as a financial penalty from 100 Ks to 10.000 Ks, which in the case of unenforceability to be closed from 1 day to 15 days. In case of repetition of cod, the offense is closed from 2 to 30 days.

Part Three.

Education restrictions.

§ 38.

(1) Jews shall be excluded from any study at all schools and institutes other than public schools and courses specifically established for them.

(2) Jews, whether individuals, religious communities or corporations and institutes, may not establish any school or educational institution—except for popular schools—and may not acquire the education provided by such schools or institutes by private teaching.

(3) Testimonies of Jews from schools and educational institutions issued abroad cannot be notarized.

§ 39.

(1) Schoolchildren—except for those who are nationals of recognized Christian churches—may fulfill their school obligation only in special folk schools or classes designated for this purpose by the Ministry of Education and National Enlightenment.

(2) Personnel and material costs of folk schools (classes) referred to in para. 1 are obliged to pay the respective Jewish religious communities. Details will be determined by the Ministry of Education and National Enlightenment.

§ 40.

The aim of retraining Jews may be to set up special courses for them, the costs of which will be borne by the Jewish Center.

TITLE X.

Employment restrictions.

Part One.

Helpers in Jewish households.

§ 41.

(1) Household helpers—Non-Jews may not be employed in Jewish households.

(2) A household in which the majority of its members are Jews is considered to be Jewish.

(3) Servants, governess, etc. are also considered to be household assistants, even if they do not live in the home or in the employer's apartment.

§ 42.

Violation of the provisions of Section 41 is punishable by the police (state police) authorities as a violation of a financial penalty from 500 Ks to 50,000 Ks, which in case of un-recoverability is to be closed from 5 days to 30 days.

Part Two.

Employment.

§ 43.

(1) The employment of a Jew in any service, employment or apprenticeship is possible only after the permission has been granted (para. 3).

(2) 1 also applies to the employment—for free and for free—of Jewish family members employed by Jews; authorization under para. 1 is not necessary in cases where the employer is the State, its enterprises, institutes, funds, etc. or in cases where state

authorities order a Jew to work according to the Decree-Law No. 129/1940 Sl.z.

(3) Authorization under para. 1 shall be granted (extended) by the Central Economic Office. The granted (extended) authorization may be withdrawn at any time by that authority.

§ 44.

(1) An employer shall be obliged to submit an application for a work permit pursuant to Section 43; 2 employee.

(2) An application for an extension of a work permit must be submitted no later than the 30th day before its expiry; until the request is fulfilled, the Jew can remain in his current job.

§ 45.

A service, work or apprenticeship contract concluded with a Jew for whom a (extended) work permit has been granted is only valid as it does not contradict the terms of the granted (extended) permit.

§ 46.

(1) The authorization to employ a Jew shall be granted only to a specific person (employer), to a particular occupation or to a particular undertaking (establishment), to a particular Jew (employee), for a specified period of time.

(2) A Jewish employee who, depending on the nature of his work, often changes his or her job (laborers, laborers, housewives, etc.) may be granted a work permit for a certain type of employment for a certain period of time. This permit may also be subject to conditions for both the employer and the employee. Such an employee may be employed without further authorization for the duration of his employment.

§ 47.

(1) If an application for a work permit is refused, as well as in the case of its withdrawal or refusal to renew it, and in the event of a late application (Section 258 (1)), the employer is obliged to cancel the employment, employment or apprenticeship immediately. , two weeks' notice, depending on whether they are employees of higher service or employees of others. If an employee is entitled to surrender or other remuneration on the basis of a service contract, in addition to a fixed salary, he shall be entitled under that title to a maximum of three months' fixed salary.

(2) Jewish employees dismissed from service (employment or teaching) in respect of the provisions of Sections 43 to 46 shall not be entitled to provision (retirement) or other benefits if they are entitled to them in addition to the ordinary entitlements under Act No. 26/1929 Sb.z. and n., pursuant to Act no. 221/1924 Sb.z. and n. and legal regulations amending these laws. If the dismissed Jewish employee has contributed to a special pension or other similar base or fund with the employer, the contributions paid by him / her will be refunded at 5% interest. This payment may also be made in installments, but not later than 1 year from the date of release.

§ 48.

Violation of the provisions of Sections 43 to 47 is treated as a violation by the district (state police) authorities by a fine of 1,000 Ks to 100,000 Ks or by closing from 10 days to 60 days. In the event of unenforceability, the financial penalty should be converted into a closure from 10 days to 60 days.

TITLE XI.

Representation and prohibition of interventions.

§ 49.

(1) A lawyer may represent a Jew only in cases where representation by a lawyer is mandatory under law, or in cases where the continuing office or court deems it necessary and imposes this. Otherwise, continuing before the authorities, courts and bodies of public corporations and institutions can only be a Jew's agent to the Jew.
(2) 1 also applies to a public notary who is authorized to represent the site before the district court pursuant to § 8 of Government Decree no. 63/1939 Sl.z.
(3) A representative of the Jew according to para. 1 can only be a self-sufficient Jew who is relative to an ascending relative of an ascending or descending branch, married or sibling. In addition, the business owner-Jew (§ 37 and § 43 of the Commercial Code) may also be the agent of the business owner in matters relating to the operation of the business.

§ 50.

(1) Anyone who knowingly violates the provisions of Section 49 shall be punished for imprisonment by the regional court by imprisonment of up to two years and a fine of up to 10,000 Ks, which in the case of unenforceability shall be converted into a substitute sentence of imprisonment within three months.
(2) A gentile who, without authorization, turns to an authority, court or body of a public corporation, institution (intervention) to defend the right or interest of a Jew, shall be punished by a regional court for imprisonment of up to five years and a fine of up to 10,000 Ks in case of unenforceability it will be converted into a prison sentence within 3 months.
(3) Conditional suspension of the sentence referred to in para. 1 and 2 are excluded.

TITLE XII.

Other restrictions.

§ 51.

Jews cannot acquire the right to possess or carry weapons.

§ 52.

Jews cannot be authorized to fish.

§ 53.

A Jew cannot drive a Slovak motor vehicle (§§ 1 and § 12 of Act No. 81/1935 Coll., Et al.), Nor to obtain permission to manage it.

§ 54.

(1) The Minister of Transport and Public Works shall stipulate the manner of traveling of Jews on state railways as well as other public transport means by a decree in the Official Newspaper.

(2) The Minister of the Interior is empowered to impose other restrictions on Jews with regard to travel, by means of a decree in the Official Newspaper, which may impose financial penalties of up to 5,000 Ks for failure to maintain these restrictions.

§ 55.

(1) Jews and Jewish associations, as well as a member of a household in which there is at least one Jew, cannot be granted a concession for the possession of a radio receiver or for the possession of a radio transmitter.

(2) 1 also applies to the non-Jewish spouses of the Jews.

§ 56.

(1) Passports, passport cards and temporary passports may be issued to Jews only with the permission of the Ministry of the Interior (State Security Central) for a maximum period of one year.

(2) 1 also applies to the non-Jewish spouses of the Jews.

PART TWO.

Property rights.

TITLE I

Restrictions on the acquisition of rights in rem and trade licenses.

§ 57.

Jews and Jewish associations cannot acquire property and other rights in real estate except in case of inheritance.

§ 58.

Jews and Jewish associations may not take over or rebuild industrial, commercial or trade enterprises, acquire or acquire or acquire a trade license.

TITLE II.

Restriction on the freedom to dispose of property.

§ 59.

(1) The validity of legal acts concerning the transfer, extinction, change or restriction of the ownership or other rights of Jews, non-Jewish spouses of Jews, as well as Jewish associations to movable or immovable property and rights whose ordinary value exceeds 500 Ks, a written authorization from the Central Economic Office

is required. This amount may be increased or decreased by the Central Economic Office by means of a notice published in the Official Journal. In the case of live and dead inventory used for farming, it gives written permission and increases the amount of 500 pieces of this inventory, heavily reducing the State Land Office.

(2) 1 shall not apply to acts of non-resident foreign nationals, rental of rooms in dwellings, transfers of cash, transfers of goods in the ordinary course of business of production, trade or other trade, legal acts in agricultural and reinsurance activities agricultural operating loans, as they do not exceed the framework of sound management, and for cases of transfer of agricultural property pursuant to Section 150, par. 1 of this Regulation and pursuant to § 26 of Act no. 46/1940 Sl.z.

(3) Loading according to para. 1 (b) economic operators (establishments), their parts and accessories are prohibited; the provisions of Sections 167 to 190 shall apply to such treatment.

(4) The prohibition referred to in para. 3 does not apply to the disposition (disposal) of economic enterprises (factories), their assets, accessories of non-Jewish spouses of Jews. The prohibition referred to in para. 3, does not apply to the disposal of participations, shares and kitchens; irrespective of their value, these may be disposed of with the permission of a commission established by the Slovak National Bank pursuant to Government Decree No. 113/1939 of which the representative of the Central Economic Office is also a member for the permits pursuant to this paragraph. The authorization may be issued only with the agreement of the representative of the Central Economic Office.

§ 60.

(1) The Central Economic Office shall be obliged to collect for the permit according to § 59, para. 1 and 4 in favor of the Fund for the Support of Jewish Emigration (§ 215) a benefit of 20% of the regular (municipal) value of the subject of the legal act, to the burden of persons (associations) referred to in § 59, para. 1. This benefit is not subject to the authorization pursuant to § 59, par. 4 in the case of permits for Jews (Jewish associations) who are foreign nationals and who do not reside in the country. However, if the subject of the authorization is the deposit or cancellation of a mortgage, or if the treatment is based on an official (judicial) decision, the Central Economic Office may refrain from levying the benefit. The enforceable decision of the Central Economic Office on the levying of the benefit pursuant to this paragraph is an enforcement order pursuant to § 90, para. 2 of Decree-Law no. 8/1928 Sb.z. and n. In cases according to § 59, para. 1, last sentence - this benefit is collected by the State Land Office in favor of the Land Reform Fund.

(2) Details of the continuation and collection of the benefit shall be regulated by the Central Economic Office with the approval of the Prime Minister—by the State Land Office with approval of the Government—and shall be published in the Official Newspaper.

§ 61.

Violation of the provisions of § 59 is punishable by the district (state police) authorities as a violation of financial penalty from 10 Ks 500.000 Ks or by closing from one day to 6 months. The unenforceable pecuniary penalty should be converted into a closure from 1 day to 6 months. The objects of the legal act can be declared forfeited.

TITLE III.

Restricting the handling of cash and securities.

Part One.

Obligation to deposit cash on passbooks.

§ 62.

(1) Jews, non-Jewish spouses of Jews and Jewish associations are obliged to deposit cash in excess of the amount specified in § 63 on deposit books, in their own name, at a financial institution authorized to accept deposits on books.

(2) Cash shall be deposited no later than 3 days after its receipt.

§ 63.

(1) Persons referred to in § 62, para. 1, may not carry more than:

(a) corresponds to their standard of living and that of their family, but not more than 1,000 Ks per person,

(b) is necessary for the transfer of an undertaking or for the execution of an authorization, but not more than 5% of the turnover achieved in the last year.

(2) The Central Economic Office may reduce or increase the amount referred to in para. 1.

Part Two.

Tied accounts.

§ 64.

(1) All payments to the Jews, to the non-Jewish spouses of the Jews, and to Jewish enterprises and Jewish associations may only be made on the beneficiary's escrow account at a financial institution specified in the list specified by the Ministry of Finance in agreement with the Central Economic Office. This list is published by the Ministry of Finance in the Official Newspaper.

(2) Subject to this Regulation, the persons, undertakings and associations referred to in para. 1, to receive any payments other than those referred to in paragraph 1.

(3) 1 and 2 shall not apply to Jewish enterprises which are under temporary administration.

§ 65.

(1) Persons (associations of persons), referred to in § 64, para. 1, shall notify the financial institution that their account is bound under this Regulation.

(2) Financial institutions shall be obliged to designate the escrow accounts (§ 64, para. 1) as Jewish and to notify them to the Central Economic Office.

§ 66.

Restricted salaries, payments for goods and services in the course of the operation of an undertaking or in the exercise of an occupation need not be deposited in a tied account (Section 64 (1)), if cash payment is usual.

§ 67.

The payer is obliged to remit payments to a tied account with a financial institution (Section 64 (1)), which the payee designates. If the beneficiary does not designate such a financial institution, the payment shall be deposited into a tied account with Poštová bank.

Part Three.
About safekeeping.

§ 68.

(1) Jews, non-Jewish spouses of Jews and Jewish associations are obliged to deposit in a deposit, in their name, at a foreign exchange bank or other domestic financial institution according to a list specified by the Ministry of Finance in agreement with the Central Economic Office, fixed values (effects) and securities of a similar kind. The deposit must take place within 8 days after the acquisition of the individual securities, after the exchange of the securities and lots whose tied custody has been exchanged or is required by special legislation.
(2) The obligation to fold according to par. 1 does not apply to the lottery tickets of the Slovak Class Lottery, nor to securities and lottery tickets, which are bound by safekeeping by special legal regulations.
(3) The obligation referred to in para. 1, also affects the non-Jewish holder (detainer) of the values (effects) mentioned therein if they hold them for the persons (associations of persons) referred to in para. 1.
(4) The rights that are in the securities remain unaffected by the composition.
(5) List of financial institutions according to para. 1 shall be announced by the Ministry of Finance in the Official Newspaper.

§ 69.

The provisions of § 68 shall also apply to articles of gold or platinum, to their alloys to each other or to other metals, even if those articles are only partly of gold or platinum (alloys), and also to gems and pearls; however, they do not apply to:
(a) wedding ring own and wedding ring of deceased husband,
(b) tooth substitutes of precious metals, if used as such;
(c) goods which are the subject of the normal exercise of a trade or other trade activity (goldsmith's, jeweler's, watchmaker's, dental, etc.).

§ 70.

Transfer passbooks of persons (associations of persons) referred to in § 68, para. 1 to other persons (associations of persons), as well as to transfer securities from one financial institution to another, possibly only with the permission of the Central Economic Office.

§ 71.

Persons, associations of persons), referred to in § 68, par. 1, they may set up safe deposit boxes and closed safekeeping in addition to deposits pursuant to Sections 68 and 69 at the financial institutions only with the permission of the Central Economic Office.

§ 72.

Withdrawals from deposits (Sections 68 and 69) from safe deposit boxes and closed custody (Sections 71) are admissible only with the permission of the Central Economic Office.

Part Four.

Restrictions on withdrawals from deposits and accounts.

§ 73.

(1) Jews, non-Jewish spouses of Jews and Jewish associations may, from deposits in passbooks or check or other accounts—regardless of whether they sound in name, password, etc.—including tied accounts according to § 64 to § 67, kept at the same or at various financial institutions, including Postal Savings Bank, to collect a maximum of 500 Ks per week for the maintenance of themselves and their family members, unless special regulations stipulate otherwise.
(2) The Central Economic Office may reduce or increase the amount referred to in para. 1.

§ 74.

Withdrawal in cash or by voucher from deposits and accounts referred to in § 73 above the rate specified therein shall be admissible without the specific permission of the Central Economic Office only in respect of taxes, levies, charges or other liabilities to the State, local authorities and by a public insurance institution, or in respect of the payment of actual operating costs or salaries for services the need of which will be demonstrated to the paying financial institution by the production of documents. The accuracy of these documents and the need to reimburse the running costs in respect of Jewish businesses (factories) and homes where trustees or interim administrators have been appointed shall be examined and confirmed by the latter. Payments for taxes, levies, fees and other liabilities to the state, self-governing unions and public insurance institutions shall be carried out directly by the institutes (Section 73 (1)).

§ 75.

Details of the method of payment of deposits and accounts (Sections 73 and 74) shall be determined by the Central Economic Office.

Part Five.
Criminal and final provisions.

§ 76.

Violation of the provisions of Sections 62 to 65 and Sections 67 to 75 is punishable as a serious pension infraction pursuant to the provisions of Act No. 7/1924 Sb.z. and n. as amended by this Act amending and supplementing this Act.

TITLE IV.
Other property restrictions.

Part One.
State contribution to pensions from public insurance.

§ 77.

(1) Jews are not entitled to the payment of a state contribution under Section 123 of Act No. 221/1924 Sb.z. and n. as amended by Article I of Decree-Law no. 112/1934 Sb.z. and n., also pursuant to § 18a of Act no. 242/1922 Sb.z. and n. as amended by Article I of Act no. 200/1936 Sb.z. and finally, pursuant to § 176 of Act no. 26/1929 Sb.z. and n. as amended by Article I of Act no. 117/1934 Sb.z. and n.
(2) Insured persons covered by para. 1 shall be obliged to report this fact to the relevant public insurance holder no later than 60 days after the date of entry into force of this Regulation.
(3) Failure to fulfill the obligation referred to in para. 2, punishes as an offense to the district (state police) office with a fine of 500 Ks to 50,000 Ks, which in the case of unenforceability to be closed from 5 days to 30 days.

Part Two.
Ineligibility to hold certain objects.

§ 78.

(1) Jews shall not be in possession of paintings, statues, busts of prominent national and state actors. Nor may they have national emblems, flags and flags.
(2) Jews are prohibited from holding photographic equipment, binoculars, nor are they prohibited from holding records with national songs (melodies).
(3) Infringement of para. 1 and 2 authorizes district (state police) authorities as a financial penalty from 100 Ks to 10,000 Ks, which in the event of unenforceability to be closed from 1 day to 15 days.

Part Three.
About statements.

§ 79.

(1) The landlord shall be entitled to terminate the lease agreement for Jewish persons and Jewish associations with a two-week notice period. Denunciation can be made at any time.
(2) The right to terminate the lease agreement pursuant to para. 1 a temporary trustee also has a non-Jewish person applying for rent.
(3) The interim administrator may set lower rents than the Jewish tenant has paid only with the permission of the Central Economic Office.
(4) For reasons of public interest, the Central Economic Office may also order the Jew—the owner of the house or Jewish persons who, by whatever title, uses the flat in it, to empty it, with a two-week period. Such an order is an execution title pursuant to § 90, para. 2 of Decree-Law no. 8/1928 Sb.z. and n.
(5) The Central Economic Office may prohibit Jews from renting apartments in certain houses or in certain parts of a municipality (town).
(6) 1 and 2 may be used in the rooms (flats) of Jews-doctors as long as they are authorized to practice as a medical practitioner only with the permission of the Central Economic Office.
(7) The Central Economic Office may determine the rental buildings, houses, streets, parts of the municipality (town) in which the provisions of para. 1 and 2.

§ 80.

Renting a room (flat) according to § 79, par. 3 and 5 without the permission of the Central Economic Office is invalid.

Part Four.
Cancellation of lease contracts.

§ 81.

The State Land Office may annul, in the acreage, the contractual, lease-rent contracts by which the Gentiles put their agricultural property (§ 3, para. 2, Act No. 46/1940 Sl.z.) into the agenda, lease-rent to Jews or Jewish associations, namely even before the expiry of the contractual rental and rental period. These contracts can be canceled at any time, but only if the notice period of at least 30 days is maintained, while the contractual contracts only at the end of the marketing year.

§ 82.

The tenant, in the possession of the tenant, shall not be entitled to compensation of loss and loss of profit on the grounds that the agenda, in the case of the tenant, shall be prematurely canceled pursuant to § 81.

§ 83.

(1) The State Land Office shall deliver the area pursuant to Section 81 to the owner of the property (his authorized representative) and to the planner, or to the lessee.
(2) The area of the State Land Office, issued pursuant to Section 81 and bearing an enforceability clause, shall be an enforceable title of a judicial execution.

PART THREE.

Exclusion from public life.

TITLE I

Exclusion from public office.

§ 84.

(1) The public functions of Jews and Jewish mixers (§ 12) shall expire at the latest 2 months after the entry into force of this Regulation.
(2) Termination of function under para. 1 has the effect of giving up the function.

§ 85.

The membership of Jews and Jewish Mixtures in the corporations referred to in § 13 shall expire at the latest 2 months after the entry into force of this Regulation.

§ 86.

The provisions of § 84 shall also apply to the termination of functions pursuant to § 14.

TITLE II.

Dismissal of public utilities, compensation and alteration of some provisions on remuneration and care pay.

Part One.

Dismissal from public services.

§ 87.

(1) Jews excluded under § 15 from public or other public services must be released from them.
(2) 1 shall also apply to Jewish mixers, referred to in § 2, point. a), lift—as they are officers and non-commissioned officers (§ 15, paragraph 2)—and under point. b), and about the non-Jewish spouses of the Jews.

§ 88.

(1) Dismissal pursuant to Section 87 shall not prevent the establishment or termination of disciplinary proceedings against a dismissed employee for an act committed before dismissal.
(2) 1 shall also apply if the disciplinary continuation was discontinued due to the dismissal of the employee pursuant to Government Decree no. 74/1939 Sl.z. In this case, the disciplinary continuation should be restarted even if it has been stopped.

(3) In the case of a disciplinary conviction, the loss of severance pay may also be declared as a disciplinary punishment (§ 89 et seq.)

Part Two.
Compensation for redundant employees.

§ 89.

(1) Employees dismissed from public or public services (§ 87) who report less than 10 years of actual service counted as retirement benefits shall receive an allowance of 8% of the pension base for each full year of that service.
(2) A genuine service shall be understood only as a public service or other service actually performed, counted by the appreciation of premium reserves.

§ 90.

(1) Employees who have shown at least 10 years of actual service counted as retired may choose:
(a) or severance pay;
(b) or entitlement to rest pay.
(2) The choice under para. 1 shall be made in writing to the office responsible for remuneration within three months of the date of dismissal. If the election has not been made within that period, the right to the salary pursuant to para. 1, point (a) b).

§ 91.

(1) Employees who have chosen severance pay pursuant to § 90, para. 1, point (a) (a) shall receive, for the first 10 years, a genuine service counting for the retirement rate of 8%, for each additional full year of that service of 6% of the pension base. This severance pay may not exceed twice the pension base.
(2) The provisions of § 89, para. 2 shall apply.

§ 92.

(1) Entitlement to the payment of rest pay according to § 90, para. 1, point (a) (b) arises on the first day of the month following the employee's 60th year of age. Entitlement to the payment of rest pay shall arise even before the age of 60 if the employee is permanently incapable of earning any illness for which he has not intentionally caused himself; the payment of the rest of the salaries shall take place from the first day of the month following the demonstration of this incapacity by the attestation of the official doctor.
(2) From the date of dismissal until the date of entitlement to the payment of the rest pay, the employee is obliged to pay a maintenance allowance of 3% of the last pension base annually. The maintenance allowance must be paid in advance on a half-yearly basis on behalf of the authority responsible for the assessment of the rest pay. If the employee is late in paying the maintenance allowance for more than one year, the entitlements under para. First
(3) Restful salaries shall be calculated in accordance with the regulations in force from the pension base held by the employee on the day of dismissal and on the basis

of the eligible working time on that day, with a 30% reduction in retirement. This reduction must not drop the retirement below 6,600 Ks per year.

(4) The provision on reduction of retirement income pursuant to par. 3 does not apply to non-Jewish spouses released under § 87, Para. 2.

§ 93.

(1) Provisional salaries of survivors of employees who have chosen to be entitled to remuneration according to § 90, para. 1, point (a) (b) and have died before the age of 60, shall be measured according to the applicable pension regulations. Entitlement to them arises only if the employee fulfills the obligation imposed in § 90, para. 2. Provisional salaries shall be calculated from the pension base held by the staff member (spouse or father) on the day of dismissal and on the basis of the eligible time on that day, subject to the provisions of Article 95.

(2) Provisional salaries for staff who have died in active service under the effect of this Regulation shall also be measured in accordance with par. First

(3) Death in cases of para. 1 and 2 are reduced by half.

Part Three.

Amendment of certain provisions on rest and care salaries.

§ 94.

The retired beneficiaries of the state's restive salaries of Jews are reduced by 30%. By this reduction, the earnings must not fall below 6,600 Ks per year.

§ 95.

(1) The widow's and orphan's pension received by Jews is reduced by 30%. This reduction must not reduce the widow's pension to below 6,000 Ks, orphan's pension to below 3,000 Ks per year.

(2) Education allowances shall be calculated from the reduced widow's pension.

§ 96.

(1) The remuneration allowances for survivors of Jewish employees who have died in retirement under the effect of this Regulation shall be measured in accordance with the regulations in force, subject to the provisions of Section 95.

(2) Deaths from retired Jews shall be assessed from the retired reduced under Sections 92 and 94.

Part Four.

General provisions.

§ 97.

(1) The severance pay shall be paid within a maximum of four periods, within three, six, nine and twelve months of the dismissal; severance grants not exceeding 2,000 Ks

shall be paid at the same time; severance payments exceeding this amount shall be paid in such a way that the installments will be at least 2000 Ks.

(2) The provision of severance pay excludes the issue of a transfer amount under the rules on public insurance and returning pension posts.

§ 98.

Article 28 para. 1, second sentence of Government Decree no. 380/1938 Sb.z. and n. and § 12 para. 2 to 6 of Act no. 40/1941 Sl.z. they shall not apply to the beneficiaries of the national rest and maintenance salaries provided for in this Regulation.

§ 99.

(1) State employees pursuant to this Regulation are employees of the state, institutes, enterprises, funds and facilities of the state or administered by the state, to which the Act no. 103/1926 Sb.z. and n. and legislation based on it.

(2) The provisions of this Part also apply to:

(a) teachers covered by the Teaching Act No. 104/1926 Sb.z. and n.,

(b) non-state professors of secondary schools, teacher training institutes and other higher vocational schools;

(c) persons to whom Act No. 70/1930 Sb.z. and n. and for other recipients of the rest and maintenance salaries of the Jews paid by the Railway Administration, the contractual reservations contrary to this Regulation being lifted,

(d) survivors of persons referred to in (a); a) to c), as they do not fall under the provisions of para. 1.

§ 100.

Not all provisions on the minimum amount of rest and care allowance apply to the persons covered this Regulation, except where applicable the minimum annual amount is determined to be lower than 6,600 Ks for rest pay and for care salaries lower than 6,000 Ks per year.

TITLE III.

Exclusion from medical practice and authorization of civil engineers.

§ 101.

(1) The rights of Jewish physicians and veterinarians to practice medical, post-veterinary practice shall expire no later than 3 months after the entry into force of this Regulation.

(2) 1 also applies to civil engineers.

(3) 1 and 2 may prolong the government for a necessary period of time, generally for individual occupations or in individual cases.

TITLE IV.
Termination of medical concessions and transfer of pharmacies.

§ 102.

(1) Rights or concessions to a public pharmacy with real, radical or personal rights, whose owner (co-owner) or concessionaire (co-concessionaire) is a Jew, shall be withdrawn on the day the relevant Commissioner takes over the relevant pharmacy. The appointment of a Commissioner-General shall be published in the Official Newspaper.
(2) Rights or concessions to a public pharmacy with real, radical or personal rights, whose owner (co-owner) or concessionaire (co-concessionaire) is not a Jew, but in the business management of the relevant pharmacy is in any social relation with the Jew, are also subject to § 102 to 109.
(3) Public pharmacies with real, radical or personal rights, which are administered by an orphan's, widow's or any other right, are also subject to the provisions of Sections 102 to 109, since the holders of these rights are Jews.

§ 103.

(1) Until the Government Commissioner appointed by the Ministry of the Interior takes over the pharmacy, which is subject to the provisions of Section 102, the existing holder of rights to the relevant pharmacy must procure the necessary supplies of medicines, pharmaceuticals and all materials of all kinds and ensure the uninterrupted operation of the pharmacy.
(2) Since the entry into force of this Regulation, existing holders of rights to pharmacies to which this Regulation applies may dispose of these rights only with the consent of the Ministry of the Interior. Dispositions without this consent are legally ineffective.
(3) The Government Commissioner shall, on behalf of the previous rightsholder, keep the relevant pharmacy until the granting of the revoked right or concession to the new concessionaire or until its liquidation (Section 104 (2)).

§ 104.

(1) For a pharmacy withdrawn pursuant to Section 102 (hereinafter referred to as "withdrawn pharmacy"), the Ministry of the Interior may, at its discretion, award a concession to a new applicant as a personal right to a public pharmacy. In exceptional cases, the Ministry of the Interior may also grant such a concession to a tenderer who does not fulfill the prerequisites for a medical diploma.
(2) The withdrawn pharmacies, for which the Ministry of the Interior does not intend to grant a new applicant a concession, shall be liquidated.

§ 105.

(1) The owner shall be entitled to financial compensation from the Liquidation Medical Fund for the deprived right to a public pharmacy with real or radical right (Section 108). The amount of monetary compensation is determined by 10% of the annual

average by the competent tax office of steady turnover achieved in the relevant pharmacy in 1936, 1937 and 1938. No correction of the turnover declaration carried out after January 1, 1939 is taken into account.

(2) No personal compensation shall be payable for the withdrawal of the concession to a public pharmacy with the right to personal assistance.

§ 106.

(1) When granting a concession to a public pharmacy with a personal right to a new concessionaire pursuant to Section 104, para. 1, the latter is obliged to pay an allotment contribution to the Liquidation Medical Fund. The amount of the allocation is determined at 25% of the annual average turnover, determined pursuant to § 105, para. 1.

(2) The new concessionaire may pay the allotment contribution to the Liquidation Medical Fund in installments so that the first third of the contribution must be paid as soon as the personal right to the public pharmacy is granted; Payments should always be submitted by the 15th of the month following the end of the six-month period. If the repayment term is not maintained, 5% interest on late payment shall be imposed, which, together with the unpaid installment, shall be enforceable by the Liquidation Medical Fund by execution pursuant to Part Two of Government Regulation no. 8/1928 Sb.z. and n. The feasibility of the assessment is confirmed by the Ministry of the Interior.

(3) If the concessionaire dies before payment of the allotment allowance and the pharmacy will therefore be managed by an orphan or widow's law, the obligation to pay further to the orphans or widows shall not pass, but pharmacy. Late interest is not prescribed.

§ 107.

(1) The new concessionaire is obliged to take over all stocks of official and unofficial medicines and pharmaceuticals, for the operation of pharmacies of essential and indispensable special medicines, as well as the equipment of the withdrawn pharmacy, namely: stocks at purchase price and facilities at estimated cost. Acquisition and pricing of supplies and equipment, as well as determination of which medicines and medicines are essential for the resettlement of a pharmacy and which special medicines are indispensable, shall be carried out by a commission appointed by the Ministry of the Interior. Appeals against the decisions of this commission are admissible within 15 days to the Ministry of the Interior.

(2) The new concessionaire shall pay the inventory and equipment price to the Liquidation Medical Fund in 12 equal half-yearly installments at 5% interest. If the repayment term is not maintained, the provisions of § 106, para. 2, penultimate sentence.

§ 108.

(1) The aim of the uniform execution of monetary dispositions in respect of withdrawn pharmacies pursuant to this Regulation is to serve the "Liquidated Medical Fund" established by the Ministry of the Interior (Section 7 of Act No. 145/1939 Coll.).

Members of the Hlinka Guard marching in. (*Holocaust Education & Archive Research*)

Men of the Hlinka Guard cut the beard of a Jewish man during a deportation action in Stropkov. (*Holocaust Education & Archive Research*)

Hlinka Guard force Jews on to rail cars in Zilina. (*Holocaust Education & Archive Research*)

The Hlinka Guard oversees a deportation action in Stropkov. (*Holocaust Education & Archive Research*)

Right: Hlinka Guard at the Novaky Camp. (*Holocaust Education & Archive Research*)

Below: President Dr. Jozef Tiso awarding men of the *Waffen*-SS for putting down the Slovak uprising in the foreground, soldiers of the 5th Field Company of the Hlinka Guard in the background. (*Slovak National Archive*)

Hlinka Youth Day in Bratislava, August 6, 1940. (*Slovak National Archive*)

Vlca (Wolf Cub). (*Slovak National Archive*)

Hlinka Youth Parade in Trencin, 1939. (*Slovak National Archive*)

Hlinka Youth peeling potatoes. (*Slovak National Archive*)

Left: Hlinka Youth Chief Commander Alojz Macek visiting Hlinka Youth camp in Orava, August 23, 1941. (*Slovak National Archive*)

Below: Labor Camp in Novaky for the Jews, 1941. (*Military History Archive, Bratislava*)

Deportation of Jews. (*Slovak National Archive*)

Postcard issued to commemorate the death of Andrej Hlinka, 1938. (*Small Carpathian Museum, Perinok*)

Left: The second commander of the Hlinka Guard: Alexander Mach. (*Slovak National Archive*)

Below: The first transport of Jews to the Nazi concentration camp in Auschwitz, March 25, 1942. (*Archive of the SNP Museum in Banska Bystrica*)

Above: Hlinka Guard officers force Slovak Jews on to train, 1942. (*Slovak National Archive*)

Right: "We're United! Our Goal: New Slovakia! 1938–1939." Poster. (*Museum of the Slovak National Councils*)

Jews from the city of Dunajska Streda, Slovakia, being deported to Auschwitz, June 1944. (*Slovak National Archive*)

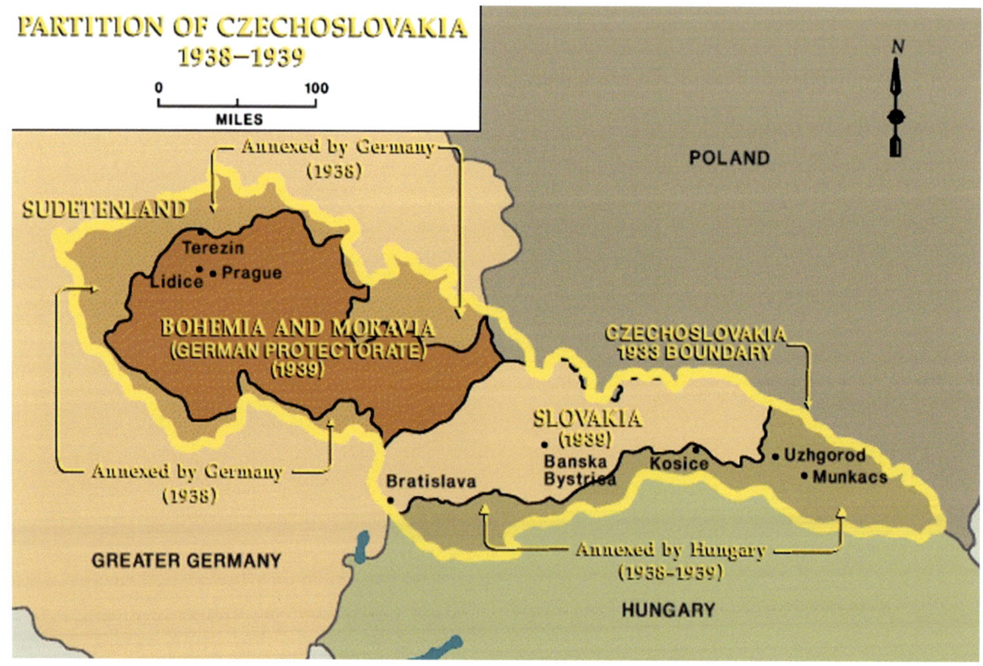

Partition of Czechoslovakia, 1938–1939. (*U.S. Holocaust Memorial Museum*)

Jewish inmates at forced labor in the Vyhne concentration camp in Slovakia, 1941–44. (*Slovak National Archive*)

The "autonomist flag," 1938–45 party flag of the Ludaks and their organizations: Hlinka Guard and Hlinka Youth. (*Slovak National Archive*)

Above left: Vojtech Tuka in uniform. (*Slovak National Archive*)

Above middle: Hlinka Guard uniforms 1939–1945. (*Military History Archive, Bratislava*)

Above right: Left to right: Leader of the Hlinka Guard and minister of interior, Alexander Mach and Otomar Kubala, vice leader of the Hlinka Guard, and a school principal. (*Slovak National Archive*)

Slovak president Dr. Jozef Tiso on an official state visit to Germany, escorted by Joachim von Ribbentrop. (*German National Archives*)

Above left: Slovak Hlinka Guard leaders Alexander Mach (left) and Karol Murgaš (right) in black uniforms with *Reichsleiter* Dr. Robert Ley (middle) in Čadca, during his visit to Slovakia. (*Slovak National Archive*)

Above right: Slovak Jews with Star of David displayed on outer clothing. (*Slovak National Archive*)

2731 was deported to Auschwitz in an RSHA (Main Reich Security Office) transport from Bratislava on March 28, 1942. The fate of female prisoner number 2731 is unknown. (*Auschwitz Memorial and Museum*)

Above left: Vojtech Tuka marches alongside Keitel and von Ribbentrop in 1940 Berlin. (*Slovak National Archive*)

Above right: "*Nebuď služobníkom žida: kto sa so židom spolcuje, ten so židom skapína*" translates to "do not be a servant to the Jew: he who associates with a Jew will sink down to his level." (*Slovak National Archive*)

Above left: President Jozef Tiso decorating German soldiers for suppressing the Slovak National Uprising in Banská Bystrica, November 31, 1944. (*Slovak Military History Archive*)

Above right: Selection on the ramp at Auschwitz II-Birkenau, 1944. (*Auschwitz Album*)

View of buildings in the Sered' concentration camp in Slovakia, 1941–44. (*Slovak National Archive*)

Jews prior to being deported from Slovakia along with their personal effects, 1942. (*Yad Vashem Photo Archive*)

Slovak militia standing next to Jews, before the latter were deported from Slovakia along with their personal effects, 1942. (*Yad Vashem Photo Archive*)

Above left: Five of the 997 girls transported to Auschwitz. (*Slovak National Archive*)

Above right: A 1938 portrait of Jozef Tiso. (*Slovak National Archive*)

(2) The Liquidated Medical Fund shall keep a separate "liquidation account" for each withdrawal pharmacy and for new concessions granted instead of withdrawn pharmacies.

(3) The liquidation account of the withdrawn pharmacy shall receive the following income:

(a) the price for the supplies and equipment of the withdrawn pharmacy from the new concessionaire at the relevant interest, as well as interest on late payment;

(b) monetary compensation for the right withdrawn to a public pharmacy with a right or realist from the allotment account.

(4) The Liquidation Medical Fund shall pay the receivables of creditors against the former holder of the right to it from the liquidation account of the withdrawn pharmacy, up to the amount of income in points a) and b), para. 3. Any balance of income on the winding-up account shall be paid to the former holder of the rights to the withdrawn pharmacy to which the winding-up account relates.

(5) When paying receivables, it is necessary to pay first of all taxes and public benefits, receivables of pension institution and other public social insurance institutions, financial penalties according to § 21, salaries (wages) of employees or receivables of the lessor stocks of all kinds and debts, secured in public books in pharmacies with real or radical rights.

(6) Since the sums paid into the liquidation account in favor of the former holder of the rights to the withdrawn pharmacy would not be sufficient for full payment in para. 5 of those claims, the creditors mentioned there, as well as any other creditors referred to therein, refer to the proceedings against the original debtor. The State, the Liquidation Medical Fund and the new concessionaire do not assume any liability for the exchanges, debts and obligations of former holders of rights to withdrawn pharmacies.

(7) The allotment account shall be allocated to the allotment account from the new concessionaire for the concession granted to a public pharmacy with a personal right and any interest on late payment.

(8) The following shall be paid from the allotment account:

(a) compensation for the withdrawal of the right to a public pharmacy with a right or a realization in the liquidation account in favor of the former rightsholder of the withdrawn pharmacy;

(b) remuneration and overheads of the Liquidation Medical Fund.

(9) The surplus allocation account shall be used for the construction of state hospitals.

§ 109.

The withdrawal of rights or concessions to a public pharmacy with a real, radical or personal right pursuant to § 102 shall automatically terminate the possible rental ratio of the lessor of the withdrawn pharmacy. Claims for damages due to premature termination of the contract to the contracting party—the Jew is not.

PART FOUR.

Transfer of property.

TITLE I

Inventory.

§ 110.

(1) Jews, non-Jewish spouses of Jews and Jewish associations are required to declare all their property in the Czech Republic and abroad, as well as its value at the beginning of the day on which this Regulation enters into force.

(2) Foreign Jews residing in the Czech Republic are obliged to declare only property (with value) located in the Czech Republic.

(3) Any person subject to the reporting obligation under para. 1 and 2, shall recognize its assets separately. The property of non-beneficiaries is required to be reported by their legal representatives.

(4) The questionnaire shall be submitted in quadruplicate on an official fact sheet issued by the State Statistical Office. This form will be purchased by parties at municipal (district) notary offices - in Bratislava at the Police Directorate.

§ 111.

(1) The value of each component of assets shall be shown in the statement according to the current price it has on the date this Regulation enters into force.

(2) Items serving personal needs and items of furnishings of the flat and inventory, as their current price does not individually exceed the amount of 3,000 Ks, should be listed in the statement in bulk.

§ 112.

(1) The statement of property shall be filed by 1 October 1941 with the municipal (district) notary office competent according to residence (registered office) and in Bratislava with the Police Directorate. For a person who is not resident in the Slovak Republic, the place of administration is the Police Headquarters in Bratislava.

(2) The authority competent under para. 1, the report shall indicate the incorrect or incomplete statement as such and shall notify the author. Within the period referred to in 1, the submitter may complete, correct or submit a new statement.

(3) A person who fails to comply within the time limit pursuant to para. 1 reporting duty, the Central Economic Office appoints a curator (§ 16 of the birth no. 8/1928 Coll. And n.), Who finds and reports the property. The remuneration of the curator shall be determined by the Central Economic Office on the expense of the reported person property.

§ 113.

(1) Persons (associations of persons) obliged to report according to § 110 para. 1 and 2, the curator (§ 112, para. 3), shall report to the competent authority (§ 112, para. 1) within 15 days any change (increment or decrease) of property that occurs on or

after the date of this regulation shall enter into force if this amendment exceeds the framework of regular management or regular business relations, it will make it more difficult to acquire assets in the value of more than 5,000 Ks; if one has no assets.

(2) Reports according to para. 1 shall be administered in quadruplicate on the prescribed official form.

§ 114.

(1) A crime is committed and punished by a lawyer within 5 years, who fails to prove in good time (§ 112 and § 113) his property, or who submits to the financial statements materially false or incomplete.

(2) A criminal authority commits and is punished by a lawsuit within 5 years by the responsible body of the Jewish Association (§ 110, paragraph 1), which does not report the assets of the association in good time (Sections 112 and 113) or,

(3) The offense is committed and punished by imprisonment for up to 2 years, who commits the act referred to in para. 1.

(4) The offense is committed, unless it is a more serious criminal offense, and is punished by imprisonment of up to 1 year, who in any way helps the person whose property falls under the reporting duty to conceal or hide such property.

(5) The provisions of Section 92 of the Criminal Code may not be applied to the sentence and the sentence may not be imposed conditionally.

(6) When convicted of a crime under para. 1, the court declares that the convict's property is forfeited to the State. The court will deliver the judgment to the competent district office which will seize the seizure. Otherwise, all the assets used to commit or commit the acts referred to in par. 1 to 4, or which were provided as a reward for assistance in or for their commission, the court is to confiscate in accordance with Section 61 of the Criminal Code.

(7) Continuation for actions under para. 1, 2 and 4 falls within the jurisdiction of the regional court, for acts under para. 3—within the jurisdiction of the district court.

TITLE II.

Purchase of real estate at the execution auction by Jews purchased .

§ 115.

A gentile (both natural and legal person)—hereinafter referred to as "applicant"—whose real estate was bought by a Jew at an execution auction is entitled to buy this property back at a redemption price.

§ 116.

The provision of § 115 shall not apply if on the date of entry into force of this regulation

(a) the property right has already been vested in favor of a gentile (natural or legal person),

(b) the application for the deposit of the right to property in favor of a gentile (natural or legal person) is filed with the court and will not be subsequently rejected;

(c) the non-library owner of such property is a Gentile (natural or legal person).

§ 117.

(1) The redemption price (§ 115) is equal to the price at which the Jew bought the property at auction.

(2) If the Jew bought the property at auction before October 30, 1918, the redemption price pursuant to par. 1 shall be increased if, and to the extent that, the claims of non-Jewish mortgage lenders are satisfied, but at most fourfold.

(3) Where investments have been made on real estate after the auction, the value of these shall be added to the redemption price (paragraphs 1 and 2) in an amount that objectively increased the value of the real estate at the date of estimation (§ 124, paragraph 4); the amount actually invested.

§ 118.

(1) If the applicant has died or has not exercised the right of redemption in time (§ 119), this may be exercised within a period of three months by persons who would inherit the property from the applicant.

(2) If the persons in para. 1, moreover, the right of redemption may be exercised separately or jointly.

§ 119.

(1) The right of redemption shall be exercised by written request within 6 months of the date of entry into force of this Regulation. In the event that an application for the transfer of property rights in favor of the Gentile, filed on the date of entry into force of this Regulation, was later refused (Section 116 (b)), from the date on which the refusal became final.

(2) The application shall be submitted to the district court in whose territory the property is located, in as many copies as there are landlords, and in addition one copy: for the court, for the tax office and for the State Land Office.

§ 120.

(1) The application shall contain:

(a) the designation of the court;

(b) the designation of the parties by name, profession or occupation, residence or stay;

(c) marking the real estate with land-book data,

(d) identification of the files on the auction which is the basis of the purchase, according to the file number and the court,

(e) an indication of the facts relevant to the buying-in conditions and an indication of the evidence thereon;

(f) a proposal to authorize redemption.

(2) At the same time, the application must be deposited in the court deposit for the purchase price in the amount of a quarter of the price for which the Jewish—Jewish association—purchased the property at auction and attach the confirmation thereof.

§ 121.

Delayed application or application to which no confirmation of the advance payment pursuant to § 120, para. 2, shall be refused on its own initiative.

§ 122.

(1) The redemption application shall be recorded in the Land Register.

(2) If the court does not reject the application, it shall notify all landlords, the relevant tax office and the State Land Office of the application by delivering one copy of the application.

(3) If the notice to the landlord could not be delivered, or if within 30 days of the dispatch there was no confirmation of delivery, the court shall appoint the curator and shall notify the curator of the notification and other resolutions.

§ 123.

The right to increase the feed-in tariff by the value of investments may be exercised by any landlord interested in a written application, which must be submitted within 30 days of the delivery of the notification (§ 122).

§ 124.

(1) After the expiry of the 30-day period (Section 122 (3)), the court shall set a deadline for summoning the applicant and all landlords to find out the factual circumstances, whether the terms of the redemption are set and to stabilize the redemption price.

(2) If the applicant or landlord who submitted an application for an increase in the feed-in tariff (§ 122) does not arrive on the date, it must be considered that he / she withdrew his / her application. Otherwise, the absence of a landlord does not hinder the negotiation.

(3) The conditions and factual circumstances, whether the conditions for the purchase and the existence of investments, must be proved according to the rules of undisputed continuation.

(4) The value of the investments and the value of the burdens specified in Section 191 of the Enforcement Act inserted after the auction must be ascertained in accordance with the regulations of the estimation order (Act No. 100/1933 Coll., Et al.).

§ 125.

(1) According to the results of the evidence, the court shall order or refuse the buy-out request or authorize the buy-out and deliver the order to the applicant, all landlords, the relevant tax office and the State Land-use Office.

(2) The resolution authorizing redemption shall contain:

(a) the designation of the court;

(b) designation of the applicant and landlord owner and their representatives by name, occupation (occupation), residence (stay),

(c) marking the purchased property with land-book data,

(d) a statement that the purchase is authorized;

(e) the redemption price (Section 117 (1) and (3)),

(f) a decision to continue spending;

(g) justification;
(h) the date of the resolution.
(3) Against the resolution rendered pursuant to para. 1, recursion is allowed. If the second stool court has changed the order of the first stool court, further recourse to the third stool court is permitted.

§ 126.

(1) The resolution authorizing the buyout shall have the effect of the execution auction without preserving the services entered after the auction on the day of its delivery; therefore, the provisions of Sections 180 to 184 of the Enforcement Act must be applied by analogy.
(2) After the resolution authorizing the buyout is valid, the order shall be negotiated in accordance with the provisions of Sections 188 to 199 of the Enforcement Act.
(3) In the order on the court, the court shall determine the increase in the feed-in tariff pursuant to Section 117, para. 2.

§ 127.

The applicant shall deposit the remainder of the redemption price with 5% interest from the date of the resolution pursuant to Section 125 within five years from the date of the resolution.

§ 128.

After the entire redemption price has been paid, the court will order its payment according to the schedule resolution.

§ 129.

(1) If the applicant has not paid the redemption price or has withdrawn from the redemption within five years, the court shall notify the State Land Register thereof office.
(2) The State Land Office shall have the right to take over the property within 30 days from the delivery of the notice according to the state of continuation at the time of exercising this right.
(3) This right to take over shall be exercised by the State Land Office by depositing the redemption price in a court deposit and notifying the court which authorized the redemption.

§ 130.

If the State Land Office has not taken over the property, the court will cancel the continuation and order the deletion of the purchase note in the land register.

§ 131.

(1) If the continuation has been canceled or the property has been taken over by the State Land Office, the applicant must immediately hand over the property to the landlord owner State Land Office.

(2) For the period in which the applicant held the property, the landlord must to the owner of the land office to issue a net return on real estate.

§ 132.

The advance payment (Section 120 (2)) is at the same time an advance on expenses that annoy the applicant, the income which the applicant is obliged to issue (Section 131 (2)) and taxes and public property benefits payable after the day of issuing the resolution permitting the purchase, which the applicant bears pursuant to Section 184 of the Enforcement Act.

§ 133.

(1) If the applicant has paid the redemption price, or if the State Land Office took over the property in the event of non-payment, continued spending together with the curator's expenses, in addition to the parties' own expenses (of the applicant and landlords) and the expenses of their attorneys, they are preferred items in the feed-in tariff.
(2) If the applicant has not paid the redemption price, or if he has withdrawn from his application and the State Land Office has not taken over the property, all the costs of continuation shall be borne by the applicant.

§ 134.

(1) If the application was submitted by a person referred to in Article 118 and failed to prove that he was the only person eligible for the purchase, the court shall only proceed after the expiry of the time limit pursuant to Article 118, para. 1.
(2) Where applications have been submitted separately by several persons, the continuation shall be combined.
(3) If more persons have fulfilled the purchase conditions and no share agreement has been reached between them, the purchased property shall be allocated in equal shares.
(4) If one of the applicants withdrew from the application or failed to fulfill the conditions of purchase, his rights and obligations shall pass on to other persons, while the court shall give the other persons a reasonable period of time to fulfill their obligations.

§ 135.

If the applicant has withdrawn from the application or has not paid the redemption price in time, the amount he has paid on the redemption price after payment of the proceeds, expenses, taxes and public benefits referred to in § 132 shall be returned to him.

§ 136.

(1) If the persons referred to in § 115 and § 118 within the period pursuant to § 119, para. 1, do not exercise the right to repurchase, it passes to the State Land Office, which may exercise it or under this Title (§ 115 to § 140) for another three months, or under § 150.
(2) Acquisition of real estate by the State Land Office pursuant to this Title shall have the legal effect of acquisition under Section 150.

§ 137.

The exercise of the right of redemption under Sections 115 to 136 and 150 excludes the exercise of the right of execution and any other right of redemption.

§ 138.

Unless otherwise provided in this Title (Sections 115 to 140), similar provisions of the Enforcement Act shall apply.

§ 139.

Pursuant to Sections 115 and 118, the right of redemption is granted only to citizens of the Slovak Republic.

§ 140.

(1) The value of the object of continuation pursuant to Sections 115 to 139 shall be the price at which the Jew purchased the property at auction.
(2) If the buy-out was permitted under the buy-out right pursuant to Section 115:
(a) the rate of the transfer fee is reduced to 1% at the value up to 10,000 Ks and to 2% at the value up to 20,000 Ks,
(b) the applicant is exempted from the guarantee of the municipal benefit from the increase in the value of the property.

TITLE III.

Obligation to recover the profits acquired by the sale of real estate purchased at the execution auction.

§ 141.

(1) A Jew is obliged to make a profit (§ 146), at the request of a gentile, acquired by the sale of a property purchased at an execution auction against a gentile.
(2) 1 also applies to the Jewish Association.
(3) If the property was sold by the heirs of the Jew, the obligation under para. 1.
(4) 3 does not apply to non-Jewish heirs.

§ 142.

(1) If a Jew (§ 141, para. 1) has died, they are jointly and severally obliged to make a profit to his heirs up to the amount of the estate.
(2) If the Jewish association ceased to exist (Section 141, paragraph 2), they are jointly and severally obliged to make a profit of the person (the association of persons) to whom the assets of the ceased Jewish association passed to the amount of the assumed value.
(3) The obligation to make a profit according to para. 1 and 2 does not apply to non-Jews and non-Jewish associations.

§ 143.

(1) If a gentile who would have been entitled under the previous provisions to make a profit has died, heirs may apply for a profit.
(2) 1 does not apply if the person to inherit is a Jew.

§ 144.

The claim for profit must be brought within six months of the entry into force of this Regulation by an action which, irrespective of the value of the dispute, is a matter for the district court in whose territory the property purchased by the Jews is auctioned.

§ 145.

(1) Where a property is subject to redemption under Title II. (Sections 115 to 140), A gentile cannot apply for a profit under this title (Sections 141 to 149). In this case, and also if the persons referred to in Sections 141 and 143 do not or cannot exercise the right of extradition profit, this passes to the state.
(2) The entitlement of the state to make a profit shall be exercised pursuant to Section 144 within one year of the entry into force of this Regulation.

§ 146.

(1) Profit (§ 141) shall be understood as the difference between the price at which the Jew (Jewish association) bought the property at auction and the price at which the property was sold.
(2) If investments have been made in the real estate between the auction and the sale, the profit determined according to par. 1 to reduce by the amount by which the investment objectively increased the value of the property at the date of its sale, but not more than the amount actually invested.
(3) Prices before 30 October 1918 should be adjusted four times.

§ 147.

Only nationals of the Slovak Republic are entitled to a profit under this Title (Sections 141 to 149).

§ 148.

Profit distribution according to § 142, para. 1 does not create a claim under § 179 of the Act. Art. XI / 1918 to repay or to proportionally reduce inheritance benefits (turnover tax and transfer fee).

§ 149.

The provisions of this title (Sections 141 to 149) shall not apply if 32 years have elapsed between the sale by which the Jew made a profit and the claim by the Non-Jew.

TITLE IV.
Execution of land reform on Jewish agricultural property.

§ 150.

(1) Agricultural properties owned by Jews and Jewish associations shall become the property of the Slovak State on the date determined by the State Land Office by a decree in the Official Newspaper. These properties shall be additionally provided with compensation, the amount of which shall be determined pursuant to Section 156 and paid pursuant to Section 159 by the State Land Office.
(2) 1 shall not apply to immovable property:
(a) which is disposed of with the consent of the State Land Office (Section 26 of Act No. 46/1940 Coll.), if the application for consent was submitted by 30 May 1941,
(b) which are subject to redemption under Title II. (Sections 115 to 140), if their persons referred to in Sections 115 and 118
(c) which by the date determined by the State Land Office pursuant to para. 1 shall be sold by court sales while maintaining the provisions of Sections 16 to 18 of Act No. 46/1940 Coll., If the auction is not canceled pursuant to § 179 of the Enforcement Act, or if it is not declared invalid pursuant to §§ 185 or 187 of the Enforcement Act.

§ 151.

(1) Agricultural property according to § 150 is all property except:
(a) residential buildings, if these are not part of the agricultural unit;
(b) building plots in built-up parts of municipalities (towns), if these plots are not part of the agricultural unit,
(c) industrial, commercial enterprises (plants);
(d) gardens of an area not exceeding 1,000 square feet relating to real estate referred to in (a); and (c).
(2) Industrial and commercial enterprises (plants) according to para. 1, point (a) (c) are not: distilleries, bricks, sawmills, mills and quarries, if they are part of an agricultural unit.
(3) In disputed cases, whether the property is agricultural or not, the President of the State Land Office shall decide in agreement with the Chairman of the Central Economic Office.

§ 152.

(1) The courts shall, at the request of the State Land Office, enter in the land register the right to property owned by the State for the Slovak State (State Land Office) pursuant to § 150, or on the basis of the land office shall indicate in the application.
(2) The court may submit a request from the State Land Office filed pursuant to par. 1, refuse solely on grounds of lack of jurisdiction and refuse solely because it contradicts the ground book condition.
(3) Against the ruling of the court ordering the deposit of property rights pursuant to para. 1, the complaint is not admissible.

§ 153.

(1) At the request of the State Land Office, a person whose real estate has become the property of the State pursuant to Section 150 shall be obliged to hand it over to the State (State Land Office), to the person designated by the State Land Office; if it fails to do so, the court shall, at the request of the State Land Office, state the State (State Land Office), and the person designated by the State Land Office shall hold the property pursuant to Section 180, Para. 2 of the Enforcement Act.

(2) While the State Land Office, the person designated by the State Land Office, does not take possession of the property, the person whose real estate has become the property of the State pursuant to Section 150 is obliged to manage the property under the principles of sound management no. 240/1940 Sl.z. and to pay all the public taxes, levies, charges and their accessories which annoy her, the owner of the real estate and the real estate itself, as well as the allowance under § 166.

§ 154.

(1) If a property that has become the state property pursuant to Section 150, the rights and obligations of the sponsor shall remain unchanged at the time of ownership transfer or lease, the tenant shall remain unchanged to the state until the State Land Office abolishes the lease. The rental fee payable after the date of transfer of ownership to the state is obliged to pay the rental tenant to the State Land Office.

(2) The State Land Office may cancel the rent, rent-rent ratio by giving notice even before the expiry of the contractual rent, rent-rent period; they may be terminated at any time, subject to a period of notice of at least 30 days, but only at the end of the marketing year. The State Land Office shall give notice of notice.

(3) If the issuer, the tenant of the tenant does not pay taxes or other public receivables, this is the reason for the cancellation of the nominal, tenant rent ratio.

(4) The assignee of the tenant shall not be entitled to compensation of loss and loss of profit due to the fact that the tenancy of the tenant shall be in accordance with par. 2 canceled.

(5) Area of the State Land Office issued pursuant to para. 2 and with an enforceability clause, it is an enforceable title of a judicial execution.

§ 155.

The State Land Office may dispose of immovable property that has become the property of the state pursuant to § 150, pursuant to Act no. 46/1940 Sl.z. or according to directives issued by the government.

§ 156.

(1) The amount of compensation (§ 150) shall be determined by the State Land Office in respect of:

(a) to the real value of the property on 30 May 1941, after deduction of the tare amounts which will continue to be preserved;

(b) to the real value of investments according to the time of taking over the property (§ 153, paragraph 1),
(c) for the allotment price, the price for which the State Land Office will sell the property,
(d) directed by the State Land Office,
(e) for a contribution to the Land Reform Fund (Section 7 (3) of Act No. 46/1940 Coll., as amended by Section 3 of Act No. 176/1940 Coll.),
(f) the price at which the Jew (Jewish association) acquired the property;
(g) the claims of mortgage creditors.
(2) If the real estate is bound by the services, shall be subject to other easements, not expressed in numbers, which will not be preserved, the State Land Office in the area referred to in para. 1, determines pursuant to § 24 of Government Decree no. 100/1933 Sb.z. and n. the capital that corresponds to their value.

§ 157.

The contribution of title pursuant to § 152 shall have the same legal effect on creditors who are entitled to preferential satisfaction on the schedule of the auction purchase price, on mortgage creditors, other materially entitled and third parties, § 150 without leaving ground book tare. However, the State Land Office may stipulate that some land book debts will remain unaffected by the transfer of ownership under § 150 to the amount that they would have been satisfied under the Schedule Resolution had they not been retained.

§ 158.

(1) The district court shall allocate the compensation determined pursuant to § 156 at the request of the State Land Office, supported by an assessment, pursuant to §§ 188 to 199 of the Enforcement Act, with the derogations referred to in para. 3 to 6.
(2) The schedule according to para. 1 is the district court with jurisdiction over the property for which compensation is to be allocated.
(3) The priority item in the schedule of compensation is also the hectare allowance referred to in Section 166, in the amount in which it will be applied by the State Land Office, in order of public debts.
(4) The unused part of the compensation shall be paid and ordered by the court on those public taxes, levies, fees and their accessories—irrespective of whether they are harassing the property or not—which owed by a person who was the owner of the real estate until the transition pursuant to § 150 and who was not satisfied either in the order of preference or in the order of mortgage lenders and who became due by the date of the schedule hearing.
(5) If the summons on the day of the hearing on the order of the landlord lender or the person who was the owner of the property until the transfer of ownership under § 150 could not be served, or within 15 days of dispatch, and other resolutions shall be delivered to the curator. The curator represents the participant for whom he was appointed until he or she takes care of his representation. The curator's remuneration is the preferred item in the compensation schedule.

(6) The court shall be obliged to deliver to the State Land Office a valid resolution with the legality clause.

§ 159.

The State Land Office is obliged within 30 days from the delivery of the schedule resolution (Section 158, paragraph 6):

(a) receivables sorted in the schedule resolution in the priority and land-book order, which will not be retained and taken over, as well as receivables sorted according to § 158, para. 4 or pay directly to the beneficiaries or deposit in court,

(b) to ensure that the rest of the compensation after deduction for the compensation of employees pursuant to § 62 of Act no. 46/1940 Sl.z. was entered in the substitute book (b. born 241/1940 Sl.z.).

§ 160.

In the judicial continuation referred to in Sections 158 and 159, the State Land Office has the same rights as the enforcing creditor in the execution continuation.

§ 161.

If the State Land Office submits to the court that the obligation referred to in § 159 has been complied with, the court shall erase from its obligation all encumbered or recorded real estate items and notes except those that will be retained and taken over and executed pursuant to Sections 200 to 202 of the Enforcement Act. payment of the amount of compensation deposited by the State Land Office in the court deposit to those entitled for whom it was paid.

§ 162.

(1) The living and dead inventory and other items (real estate accessories) necessary for the operation of agriculture on real estate that has become the property of the state pursuant to § 150 may be redeemed by the State Land Office, except if these items belong to the Non-Jews.

(2) If there is no agreement on the amount of the redemption price, the State Land Office shall determine the redemption price.

(3) If the items purchased under para. 1, belonged to the owner of the property, the purchase price is part of the compensation for the property.

(4) If the items purchased under para. 1, belonged to a person other than the owner of the property, the purchase price is paid to the owner of the property.

(5) If the State Land Office finds out by a request to the competent district court, tax office, district office, or other office, that the purchased goods are subject to the rights of third parties, or if he finds that there are other grounds for payment, instead of paying, he shall place the redemption price in the district court's deposit with the relevant application.

(6) Area of the State Land Office issued pursuant to para. 1, with an enforceability clause, is an enforceable title of a judicial execution.

§ 163.

(1) The State Land Office shall be called upon pursuant to Section 153, Para. 1 and the notice issued pursuant to § 156 shall be delivered only to the person whose real estate became the property of the state pursuant to § 150; 2 shall be delivered only to the tenderer, to the lessee, and shall be delivered only to the owner of the item.
(2) If the State Land Office of the persons referred to in par. 1 of the notice, the petition cannot be delivered, or if within 15 days of the dispatch there is no confirmation of delivery, it shall appoint the curator for the purpose of representation before the State Land Office.

§ 164.

(1) As soon as the transfer of ownership of property pursuant to Section 150 occurs, the courts shall annul the internal report, except for the internal report ordered pursuant to the Decree with the power of Act no. 240/1940 Sl.z. and auction continuation, except for cases referred to in § 150, para. 2, para. c).
(2) The State Land Office is entitled to request that the auction be declared invalid on the grounds that the auction conditions pursuant to Section 185 of the Enforcement Act have not been met.
(3) If an auction is canceled pursuant to Section 179 of the Enforcement Act or declared invalid pursuant to Section 185 or Section 187 of the Enforcement Act (Section 150 (2) (c)), a new auction may not be ordered. If the auction is declared invalid pursuant to Section 185 of the Enforcement Act, the remainder of the proceeds, the remainder of the sums paid for the auction purchase price after deduction of the auction expenses, shall be returned by the court to the auction buyer.

§ 165.

(1) A creditor who has a lien or execution lien, a recorded lien, or a noted enforceability of the lien, shall be filed with the State Land Office within 8 days of its delivery, in writing, its collateralized receivable actually exists and in what amount, in principal, interest and spending.
(2) For non-legal persons, persons residing outside the territory of the Slovak Republic and legal persons, it is obliged to file a certificate pursuant to para. 1 their legal representative, their representative.
(3) The person referred to in para. 1 and 2, which certificate according to para. 1, within 8 days of receipt of the request, will not, or will give a false certificate, impose on the proposal of the State Land Office district (state police) office in the amount of a fine of 100 Ks to 100,000 Ks.

§ 166.

Until agricultural real estate has not become the property of the state according to § 150, para. 1, or until the State Land Office has consented to their sale pursuant to Section 26 of Act No. 46/1940 Coll., Levies and collects the said office annually from the owner of 20 Ks from one hectare as a contribution to the Fund, established pursuant to

§ 50 of Act no. 46/1940 Sl.z. The contribution is paid annually in advance for the whole calendar year. Forest seizures shall be taken over

The Ministry of Economy—since it has not done so—into its own expert report, which will last until the transfer pursuant to § 150, para. 1 or pursuant to § 26 of Act no. 46/1940 Sl.z.

TITLE V.

Transfer of Jewish enterprises.

§ 167.

(1) The following are to be considered as Jewish enterprises:

(a) individual businesses, if these are Jews;

(b) enterprises of Jewish associations.

(2) A secondary establishment of a Jewish enterprise shall be considered a Jewish enterprise.

(3) The Jewish or non-Jewish nature of undertakings under this Title (Sections 167 to 190 shall be determined by the Central Economic Office in doubtful cases).

§ 168.

(1) Jewish owners are obliged to mark their businesses (predominantly) with the inscription "Jewish Enterprise" in prominent places.

(2) Jewish enterprises under interim administration shall be marked "Enterprise under interim administration."

(3) Prescribed inscriptions according to para. 1 and 2 are issued by the Central Economic Office.

§ 169.

(1) Unexecuted or temporarily revoked trade licenses of Jews and Jewish associations shall expire on the date of entry into force of this Regulation.

(2) 2 shall apply to the rights of Jewish seasonal undertakings only if they have not been in operation in the last season.

§ 170.

In order to exclude Jews and Jewish associations from Slovak economic and social life, the Central Economic Office may order:

(a) liquidation of the Jewish enterprise,

(b) transfer of a business of a Jew or a Jewish association to a gentile or to a non-Jewish association in which the Jew does not participate for the liquidation value of the business

(§ 171, paragraph 1),

(c) the transfer of a Jew's business to a non-Jewish association in which the Jew-transferor participates for the general value of the business (Sections 171 (2) and 172),

(d) transfer of the participation of a Jew or Jewish association in commercial companies (shares, ordinary deposits, factory or other shares) to a non-Jew or non-Jewish association for the fair value of the participation (Sections 171, 3 and 172) except (a) e), and only after the prior approval of a commission established by the Slovak National Bank pursuant to Government Regulation no. 113/1939 of the Slovak Republic, whose member in such cases is also a representative of the Central Economic Office,

(e) transfer of the participation of a Jew or Jewish association in public commercial or limited partnerships to a Non-Jew who enters the company as a new or additional associate, for the ordinary (municipal) value of participation (Sections 171 (4) and 172).

§ 171.

(1) The liquidation value of a Jewish enterprise [Section 170, lit. (b)] shall be determined by the Central Economic Office; prior to its designation, the Slovak Revision and Confidentiality Company is to express its opinion within the forfeiture period determined by the Central Economic Office.

(2) The general value of a Jewish enterprise [Section 170, lit. (c)] shall be determined by the Central Economic Office so that from the liquidation value stabilized in accordance with par. 1 deducts debts established under § 172 and debts recognized by the consignee, even if they have not been registered.

(3) The general value of the participation of Jews, and of Jewish associations in commercial companies [Section 170 (a)]. (d)] shall be determined by the Central Economic Office or, having regard to the stock exchange, nominal or selling price of the participation, or the relevant fraction of the municipal value of the undertaking, as determined in the manner referred to in paragraph 1 (a). 2.

(4) The general value of the participation of the Jews, of the Jewish associations in public commercial or limited partnerships [§ 170, lit. (e)] shall be determined by the Central Economic Office by the appropriate fraction of the general value of the undertaking, as determined in accordance with paragraph 1 (a). 2.

§ 172.

In order to ascertain the state of property of a Jewish enterprise, the Central Economic Office—or at the behest of an interim administrator—may invite creditors by means of a notice published in the Official Newspaper to file their claims against the transferor within 15 days. (c) or (e) in the event that the transfer is actually affected, in the event of the transfer of their satisfaction from the assets of the undertaking. Obligations on taxes, fees and other state receivables must be ascertained by inquiring at the appropriate tax authority. The question replaces sending a copy of the decree for the Official Journal.

§ 173.

If it is found that the assets of a Jewish enterprise have been deliberately diminished against the principles of sound management, the Central Economic Office may order its supplementation from other assets of the transferor, preferably from the assets of members of the Jewish Association.

§ 174.

(1) In the case of liquidation of an enterprise [Section 170, lit. (a)] The Central Economic Office shall determine the condition and manner of liquidation and may derogate from the rules in force on the continuation of liquidation. Decisions on winding-up and its conditions are published in the Official Newspaper at the expense of the business owner.

(2) Upon expiry of the liquidation period, the trade license of a Jew, or a Jewish association, expires.

§ 175.

(1) In the case of the transfer of an enterprise pursuant to Section 170 (a) b) the debtor's debts are not transferred to the receiver except in the case of their takeover (§ 176, paragraph 4). Creditors against whom the debts have not been taken over will be satisfied in accordance with § 176 of the liquidation value. The obligations of the transferor towards creditors shall remain unaffected.

(2) In the case of the transfer of an enterprise pursuant to Section 170 (a), c):

(a) the debtor's debts are transferred to the non-Jewish association only if: and since they were registered pursuant to § 172;

(b) the Central Economic Office shall determine the ratio between the shareholders;

(c) The obligations of the transferor vis-à-vis creditors shall remain unaffected.

(3) In the case of transfer of participation pursuant to Section 170 (a) d):

(a) the ratio of the receiver of the company to the creditors remains unchanged;

(b) in the case of a public company or limited partnership, the Central Economic Office shall determine the ratio between the shareholders.

(4) In the case of transfer of participation pursuant to Section 170 (a) e):

(a) the ratio of the company to the creditors remains unchanged, with the limitation that creditors will only be satisfied if they have submitted their claims under § 172,

(b) The Central Economic Office shall determine the ratio between the shareholders, and the position of the former non-Jewish shareholders shall not deteriorate.

§ 176.

(1) In the case of the transfer of an enterprise pursuant to Section 170 (a). (b) within 120 days of receipt of the decision to transfer the undertaking, the transferor shall deposit an amount corresponding to the undertaking's liquidation value in a court deposit at the district court competent for the place of the undertaking.

(2) The court shall distribute the amount (paragraph 1) to the creditors of the transferor. To this end, it shall, without delay, upon receipt of the decision to transfer the business by decree to the CCP, invite creditors within 15 days to file their claims, stating their amount, their accessories, the facts on which they are based and evidence, including non-mortgage creditors under the consequences of their dissatisfaction from the scheduled amount. If a dispute is raised on the request, the court of procedure and the file number should also be mentioned. The court shall deliver the decree to the competent tax office.

(3) In the decree, the court shall simultaneously set a deadline for the allocation of the liquidation value. The deadline should be set so that the schedule hearing can take place no later than 45 days after the publication of the decree. Mortgage requirements secured on immovable property belonging to the enterprise will mainly satisfy the liquidation value of the acquired property according to the land book order, according to the execution rules. If there is no agreement between the creditors who have other than mortgage claims against the transferor, the court shall determine the order and manner of satisfaction according to the principles of execution. if the requirements cannot be fully satisfied from the liquidation value, the court proceeds according to the principles of bankruptcy.

(4) Within the period referred to in para. 1, there is no need to deposit part of the amount attributable to the undertaking's debts recognized by the court and taken over by the beneficiary. The receiver of the non-Jewish mortgage requirements may assume the debts with the consent of the mortgage lender; in Jewish mortgage requirements shall be entitled to take over the debts without such consent. With the consent of the creditor, the borrower may also take over non-mortgage debts of the undertaking.

(5) The Central Economic Office may authorize a period of up to 5 years and determine the amount of the installments to deposit the part of the amount that would be incurred by Jewish creditors. Authorization of installments may require the Central Economic Office to provide an adequate guarantee.

(6) Even when the loan is terminated to the transferee, the mortgage lender must maintain the conditions applicable to the transferor. A transfer under this Regulation cannot justify the termination of the loan, even if the contrary had been agreed.

(7) Upon the decision of the Central Economic Office on the transfer of an undertaking, the transferor shall immediately transfer the undertaking to the transferee.

(8) After having deposited an amount corresponding to the determined value of the property belonging to the enterprise, the court shall, after taking over the debts owed to it, inject ownership rights from the Office in favor of the recipient, while erasing any outstanding debts.

§ 177.

Of the amount that would have been transferred to the transferor after satisfying the creditors under § 176, the competent court would remit 20% of the State to the benefit of the general treasury.

§ 178.

(1) In the case of the transfer of an enterprise pursuant to Section 170 (a). (c) the Central Economic Office shall determine the conditions and method of payment of the municipal value of the enterprise (Section 171 (2)).

(2) In the case of the transfer of participation in commercial companies pursuant to Section 170, Letter (d) and (e), the Central Economic Office shall determine the manner and conditions of payment of the municipal value of participation (Article 171 (3) and (4)).

§ 179.

(1) If the transferor does not have the capacity to transfer a trade under the applicable legal regulations, the Central Economic Office may grant partial or complete disqualification under the applicable regulations, but it is not bound by the prescribed continuation.

(2) On the basis of a decision of the Central Economic Office on ordering the transfer of an enterprise, the competent trade licensing office shall grant a trade license to the transferee without payment of the incorporation fee without further continuation. The transferee may transfer a trade to the granting of a trade license on the basis of a decision of the Central Economic Office on the transfer order.

(3) The Regulation on the transfer of participation shall replace the authorization pursuant to the Decree with the power of Act no. 359/1940 Sl.z.

(4) By issuing a decision of the Central Economic Office on ordering the transfer of a business, the trade license of a Jew, or a Jewish association, ceases to exist.

§ 180.

(1) The Central Economic Office shall be entitled to lease business premises affected by the continuation pursuant to this Title (Sections 167 to 190) within 15 days of the expiry of the liquidation period, but no later than 15 days after the liquidation decision has been issued (§ 170). If such rooms have already been rented without the approval of the Central Economic Office within the said time limits, the Central Economic Office may cancel the lease contracts. The annulment notice is an enforceable title pursuant to § 90, par. 2 of Decree-Law no. 8/1928 Sb.z. and n.

(2) To continue under para. 1, the provisions of §§ 2 and 3 of Act No. 335/1939 Sl.z.

§ 181.

(1) The recipient, as well as the non-Jewish association (Section 170), shall conduct the business with the care of a proper trader.

(2) Until the liquidation, fair value (municipal) value of the enterprise is settled, the shares in the business companies will continue to be settled until the other obligations resulting from the transfer are fulfilled:

(a) the undertaking may not be destroyed without the authorization of the Central Economic Office;

(b) the undertaking is subject to control by the Central Economic Office;

(c) an interim administration may be imposed on an undertaking if its management would breach the duties of a diligent trader.

(3) If the conditions as to the liquidation of the liquidation, hitherto fair (municipal) value of the enterprise, the participation in the companies without proper justification are not met in good time, the transfer decision may be revoked and the enterprise, transfer to another bidder, where the original recipient is responsible for the actual damage and is obliged to pay the costs of the continuation.

(4) The Central Economic Office may, within two years after the transfer order pursuant to Section 170, Letter (a) of Act no. (b) to (e) to impose an interim administration

on the proposal of the relevant tax administration if the business owner would not properly pay taxes and other public requirements. Expenditure connected with interim administration is not a deductible item with the owner under the Direct Tax Act.

(5) The assets of the undertakings referred to in para. 4 may not be carried out within two years of the transfer order for the purpose of securing non-prescribed and unpaid taxes, as well as other public requirements.

§ 182.

(1) In the case of the property of a Jew or of a Jewish association which serves wholly or mainly for the operation of an enterprise, the Central Economic Office may order the transfer of the property of Jews and Jewish associations to the enterprise even if the owner of the property is not the owner.

(2) If the immovable property of a Jew or a Jewish association is to be transferred with the enterprise, the Central Economic Office may ask the court to record the intended transfer in the land register.

§ 183.

The Central Economic Office may ask the courts to make estimates, to conspire to the parties (the landlord, the transferor) and witnesses in a similar application of the law applicable to the provision of legal aid.

§ 184.

The provisions on court holidays shall not apply to the continuation of proceedings under this Title (Sections 167 to 190).

§ 185.

The Central Economic Office may order the compulsory reporting of all the facts necessary for the implementation of this Title (Sections 167 to 190). The data thus established may only be used for the purposes of this Title.

§ 186.

Spending of administrative or judicial continuation—in addition to legal representation—also taxes, fees and other state benefits are the preferred item in the schedule (§ 176).

§ 187.

(1) The basis of the transfer fee and turnover tax shall be the value determined by the Central Economic Office.

(2) Access of new or further shareholder [Section 170, lit. e)], as well as an increase in the participation of the existing non-Jewish partner already existing public company or limited partnership [§ 170, point. d)], shall not be considered as a new partnership agreement and shall be subject only to the value of the transferred participation determined by the Central Economic Office.

§ 188.

(1) Failure to maintain an order pursuant to Section 173 regarding the addition of the assets of a Jewish enterprise, as well as the provisions of Section 168, para. 1 and 2, § 176, para. 7, § 181, para. 1a 2, and finally not maintaining the order under § 185 punishment as an offense district (state police) office by closing from 10 days to 6 months and a fine of 1,000 Ks to 500,000 Ks. The unenforceable pecuniary penalty should be converted into a closure from 10 days to 6 months.
(2) By the punishment referred to in para. 1 shall also be punished:
(a) A Jew who independently carries out a trade without a trade license;
(b) A Jew who trades door-to-door without a door-to-door book,
(c) sole traders who misuse their right to cover the unauthorized resumption of the trade of a Jew, as well as a Jew who instigates or suffers for the right to be misused to cover his unlawful domination of trades.

§ 189.

For Jewish enterprises under temporary administration, the Central Economic Office may, by decree in the Official Newspaper, ease restrictions on Jewish enterprises.

§ 190.

Anyone who knowingly misrepresents or uses such facts to elicit a permit or decision under this Title (Sections 167 to 190) shall be punished—unless it is a more severe criminal offense—by a district court for imprisonment of up to one year and a fine of 100 Ks to 200,000 Ks. The unenforceable pecuniary punishment should be converted into a prison from 1 day to 6 months.

TITLE VI.

Transfer of other real estate.

§ 191.

(1) The immovable property of Jews and Jewish associations shall become the day determined by the Government in a decree in the Slovak Code by the ownership of the Slovak State (Central Economic Office).
(2) 1 shall not apply to immovable property which must be regarded as agricultural property (§ 151) or the property of undertakings (§167 to § 190) and pharmacies (§102 to § 109).

§ 192.

(1) The courts shall, at the request of the Central Economic Office, enter in the land register the ownership right to real estate, which became pursuant to Section 191, para. 1 by the State, for the Slovak State (Central Economic Office) or on the basis of a document issued on the alienation [§ 199, para. 1, point (a) (b)] for persons identified by the Central Economic Office in the application.

(2) The court may submit a request submitted by the Central Economic Office pursuant to para. 1, refuse solely on grounds of lack of jurisdiction and refuse solely because it contradicts the ground book condition.
(3) Against the ruling of the court ordering the deposit of property rights pursuant to para. 2, the complaint is not admissible.

§ 193.

(1) Interim administrators of real estate referred to in § 191, para. 1, they shall carry out the interim administration for the Slovak State even after the decree (§ 191, para. 1) has been issued until the next decree of the Central Economic Office.
(2) The net proceeds of the interim administration (para. 1) shall be for the benefit of the Fund for the Support of Jewish Immigration.

§ 194.

Persons (associations of persons) whose real estate has become pursuant to Section 191, para. 1 at the invitation of the Central Economic Office to hand over the real estate of the State (Central Economic Office); if they fail to do so, the competent court shall, upon the proposal of the Central Economic Office, place the State (Central Economic Office) in possession of the property pursuant to Section 180, para. 2 of the Enforcement Act.

§ 195.

(1) If the real estate, which according to § 191, para. 1, becomes the property of the Slovak state, is in the lease (agenda), the rights and obligations of the lessee (the issuer) towards the state remain unchanged as it lasted against the previous landlord with the limitation referred to in para. 2 and 3.
(2) If the tenant—assignee—(para. 1) is a Jew or a Jewish association, the Central Economic Office may cancel the rent (expense) ratio by notice. The notice of termination, at least 14 days, shall be set by the Central Economic Office.
(3) Failure to pay taxes, fees and other public receivables by the lessee—the issuer—is the reason for the cancellation of the rent—expense ratio.
(4) The lessee—the assignee—is not entitled to compensation for damages and lost profits due to the fact that the rent—bonus—ratio was according to para. 2 or 3 canceled.
(5) Area of the Central Economic Office issued pursuant to para. 2 and with an enforceability clause is an enforceable title of a judicial execution.

§ 196.

Real estate that has become the property of the state (§ 191, para. 1) shall be compensated; the amount and the conditions for payment of the compensation shall be determined by the Central Economic Office in the form of an assessment taking into account the fair (municipal) value and the claims of non-Jewish mortgage lenders, according to guidelines issued by the Government.

§ 197.

(1) If the immovable property (Section 191 (1)) is bound by other services, numerically unexpressed, which will not be preserved, the Central Economic Office shall determine in the notice referred to in Article 196 the capital corresponding to their consideration pursuant to Section 24 Government Decree no. 100/1933 Sb.z. and n.

(2) If real estate (Section 191 (1)) is subject to liens, the mortgage lender shall maintain the conditions applicable to the transferor when the loan is terminated to the transferee. A transfer under this Title (Sections 191 to 204) cannot be a reason for the termination of the loan, even if the contrary had been agreed.

§ 198.

The Central Economic Office may order the compulsory reporting of all facts necessary for the implementation of the provisions of this Title (§191 to § 204). The data thus established may only be used for the purposes of implementing the provisions of this Title.

§ 199.

(1) The Slovak State (Central Economic Office) of real estate, which according to § 191, para. 1 may become its property, may:

(a) hold in possession;

(b) alienate non-Jewish natural or legal persons for transfer value;

(c) to lease to non-Jewish domestic natural or legal persons.

(2) The transfer value and rent (paragraph 1 (b) and (c)) shall be determined by the Central Economic Office, taking into account local circumstances, in accordance with guidelines issued by the Government.

(3) Conditions and method of detention in state ownership [para. 1, point (a) a)], alienation [para. 1, point (a) b)] and rental [para. 1, point (a) c)], as well as the method of payment and management of transfer value and rent pursuant to para. 1 shall be determined by the Central Economic Office in general by a notice in the Official Newspaper and, in individual cases, by an assessment, in accordance with directives issued by the Government.

§ 200.

(1) The compensation referred to in Article 196 shall be deposited by the Slovak State (Central Economic Office) in the court deposit with the district court in the territory of which the property is situated (Article 191, paragraph 1). provisions §§ 189 to 199 of the Act no. Art. LX / 1881 and § 35 of Act no. Art. LIII / 1912 with the derogations referred to in para. 2 to 4.

(2) The unpaid part of the compensation shall be refunded and ordered by the court on those public taxes, levies, fees and their accessories—irrespective of whether they are harassing the property or not—which are owed by the person who was the owner of the property under Section 191, para. 1 and which were not satisfied either in the order of preference or in the order of mortgage lenders and which became due by the date of the schedule hearing. The rest of the compensation will be paid by the court of the Fund for the Support of Jewish Immigration.

(3) If the summons on the day of the hearing on the order of the landlord creditor or the person who owned the property could not be served, or if no confirmation of service was received within 15 days of the dispatch, the court shall appoint the curator. The curator represents the participant for whom he was appointed until he or she takes care of his representation. The remuneration of this curator is the preferred item in the compensation schedule.
(4) The court shall be obliged to deliver to the Central Economic Office a schedule resolution with the final clause.

§ 201.

After the compensation has been deposited in the court deposit (§ 200) and the timetable order has become final, the court will erase all deposited and recorded debit items on the property as it has not been preserved.

§ 202.

If the Central Economic Office acreage according to § 192, par. 1 cannot deliver persons (associations of persons) whose real estate has become pursuant to § 191, par. 1, or, within 15 days of dispatch, no acknowledgment of delivery, shall make substitute service by publishing the notice in the Official Newspaper.

§ 203.

(1) After the Decree pursuant to Section 191, Para. 1, the courts are required to annul, on their own initiative, the pledge, the internal administration and the auction continuation of those properties which, under that provision, have become the property of the State.
(2) However, if the property has already been sold off on the day of transfer of ownership to the State (Section 191 (1)), but the auction buyer is not yet registered as the owner in the land register, if the auction is canceled under Section 179 of the Enforcement Act, or is declared invalid pursuant to Section 185 or 187 of the Enforcement Act; The Central Economic Office is entitled to request that the auction be declared invalid for the non-fulfillment of the auction conditions by the auction buyer pursuant to Section 185 of the Enforcement Act.
(3) If the auction is canceled pursuant to Section 179 of the Enforcement Act, or if it is declared invalid pursuant to § 185 or § 187 of the Enforcement Act (paragraph 2), a new auction may not be ordered. If the auction was declared invalid pursuant to Section 185 of the Enforcement Act, the rest of the remainder of the composite purchase price, after deduction of the auction spend, will be returned by the court to the auction buyer.

§ 204.

(1) Failure to maintain an order pursuant to Section 198 of the Penalty as an offense by a district (state police) office by closing from 10 days to 6 months and with a fine of 1,000 Ks to 500,000 Ks. The unenforceable pecuniary penalty should be converted into a closure between 10 days and 6 months.
(2) An attempt is punishable.

TITLE VII.

Purchase of agricultural inventory.

§ 205.

In addition to the cases referred to in Section 162, the State Land Office may purchase live and dead agricultural inventory which is used for the management of agricultural property and which is the property of the Jews or Jewish associations.

§ 206.

The provisions of Section 162 shall apply mutatis mutandis to redemption pursuant to Section 205.

TITLE VIII.

Transfer of other movables.

§ 207.

(1) The Central Economic Office may order a compulsory sale for the proper (municipal) value of the movables of Jews and Jewish associations to domestic non-Jewish natural or legal persons.
(2) The Central Economic Office may arrange for seizures of the items referred to in para. 1.
(3) 1 does not apply to:
(a) articles intended directly for worship or house worship, prayer books, equipment belonging to worship rooms, graves and crypts, including those for immediate burial;
(b) religious relics, family portraits,
(c) orders, merit coins and other badges of honor,
(d) articles necessary for the pursuit of a profession or trade;
(e) household and kitchen furniture, household utensils, containers, cooking and eating utensils, stoves, stoves, clothes items necessary and necessary bed linen;
(f) medicines and other things and auxiliary means necessary in case of illness or physical defect,
(g) food, italics and lighting equipment needed for one month;
(h) living and dead stock used for the management of agricultural property (Sections 162 and 205), since these belong to Jews or Jewish associations.

§ 208.

(1) The proper (municipal) value of the objects referred to in § 207 shall be determined by the Central Economic Office, after hearing the expert, taking into account the purchase price and wear. The value of each subject must be determined separately.
(2) The applicant shall, at the request of the Central Economic Office, deposit an appropriate advance on the expenses of the estimated continuation, which shall in any case be borne by the applicant.

§ 209.

(1) The Central Economic Office shall issue a bill of compulsory sale and deliver it to the District Court and the tax office in whose district the object of forced sale is located.
(2) In the notice (paragraph 1), the Central Economic Office shall determine the conditions and method of payment of the ordinary (municipal) value and may allow a period of payment of the regular (municipal) value in installments scheduled for a maximum of 5 years. Authorization of installments may require the Central Economic Office to provide an adequate guarantee.

§ 210.

(1) In the case of a forced sale pursuant to Section 207, the transferor shall be obliged to deposit the ordinary (municipal) value in the court deposit at the district court in whose district the object of the forced sale is located.
(2) The court shall allocate the amount determined pursuant to Section 208 to the creditors of the transferor. To this end, upon receipt of the notice of forced sale of the items referred to in Article 207, it shall, by decree in the Central Custodian of the Creditor, call upon the lodged their claims stating their amount, accessories, the facts on which they are based, the evidence, and whether they have any right on the subject of the forced sale under the consequences of their disqualification from the scheduled amount (Section 36 of Act No. 23/1928 Coll.) and others). The court shall also send a copy of the decree to the competent tax authority.
(3) In the decree, the court shall simultaneously set a deadline for the distribution of the ordinary (municipal) value.
(4) Of the amount allocated, the costs of the decree (paragraph 2) and of the continuation of court proceedings pursuant to this Title (Sections 207 to 214) shall be paid first and the pledged as well as enforceable claims of the creditors of the transferor shall be reported in due time per § 37 of Act no. 23/1928 Sb.z. and n.

§ 211.

By taking over the forced sale assessment, the transferee acquires the right to take possession of the objects and becomes the owner of them. This measure, with an enforceability clause, is the enforceable title of the judicial execution.

§ 212.

If the transferee fails to meet the conditions for payment of the proper (municipal) value in time (Section 208, paragraph 2), the Central Economic Office may withdraw the items and transfer it to another bidder. The original consignee is obliged to reimburse the Central Economic Authorities for the amount of wear and tear of the objects and to be liable for the damage incurred.

§ 213.

(1) If an object of title is in favor of a gentile—a non-Jewish association—a forced sale (§ 207) shall be ordered only if the recipient already proves that he has agreed with the

owner at the request for forced sale or on taking over the outstanding purchase price or that the outstanding purchase price with accessories has paid him. The owner is obliged to accept this payment.

(2) The reservation of the property right of a Jew (Jewish association) is not an obstacle to forced selling.

(3) Enforcement and other liens shall not constitute an obstacle to forced selling pursuant to Section 207 and shall be satisfied from the ordinary (municipal) value (Section 210 (4)).

(4) Upon delivery of the forced sale notice (Section 209, para. 1), the execution court (tax office) shall postpone the auction continuation from its authority.

§ 214.

From the funds (Section 210 (4)) the court will make a 50% contribution to the Fund for the Eviction of Jews; the remainder will be credited to a tied account of a Jew (Jewish association).

PART FIVE.

Fund for the support of Jewish emigration.

§ 215.

A Fund for the Support of Jewish Emigration (hereinafter referred to as "the Fund") has been set up at the Central Economic Office. The administration of the Fund shall be governed by the statute which it shall submit to the Government for approval within 30 days of the entry into force of this Regulation.

PART SIX.

Property management.

TITLE I

About temporary administrators for houses.

§ 216.

(1) For serious economic or social reasons, the Central Economic Office may impose an interim administration on the domestic property of Jews, Jewish associations, Jewish bases and funds, to which the State Land Office may not request internal administration.

(2) The interim administration may not be imposed on domestic property which is subject to court-enforced administration. In the case of a court internal report, the interim administration referred to in para. 1.

§ 217.

The temporary administrator may be a morally well-preserved Slovak national who is at least 24 years old and has the necessary knowledge and experience.

§ 218.

(1) The interim administrator shall exercise, on behalf of the owner and on his behalf, all rights and obligations except the right to alienate the property. It shall be liable for any damage that would result from a failure to fulfill its obligations under the administration. When administering, the interim administrator shall be bound by the instructions of the Central Economic Office.
(2) Before taking office, the temporary administrator shall make a promise in the hands of an authorized representative of the Central Economic Office.
(3) The interim administrator shall be obliged to maintain official secrecy about the facts of which he / she learned during the performance of the interim administration.
(4) The interim administrator shall be obliged to carry out the report in person, to keep accounts and to submit reports and explanations to the Central Economic Office; candidates may request the interim administrator to write off the billing for the whole of the previous year; the interim administrator is obliged to issue it by the end of January each year at the latest. Within 15 days of the date of issue of the depreciation, candidates may lodge an objection with the Central Economic Authority against the statement of account, as decided by the Central Economic Office definitively. The costs associated with the examination of the bill shall be borne by the applicant.
(5) The interim administrator shall be entitled to reimbursement of cash expenses and remuneration against the owner. The amount of remuneration shall be determined by the Central Economic Office. The decision of the Central Economic Office on the determination of remuneration is an enforceable title pursuant to § 90, para. 2 of Decree-Law no. 8/1928 Sb.z. and n. The remuneration paid is not a deductible item under the Direct Tax Act.
(6) The interim administrator may use the rooms (flat) in the managed house only with the permission of the Central Economic Office and under the conditions specified by it.
(7) The Central Economic Office may at any time transfer the change in the person of the temporary administrator or cancel the temporary administration.

§ 219.

(1) The interim administrator may only, with the permission of the Central Economic Office, take measures that do not belong to ordinary management, in particular to encumber the property and to give permission to deposit the lien instead of the landlord owner.
(2) The Central Economic Office shall supervise the management of the interim administrator and shall take care of the elimination of defects and irregularities in the performance of the interim administration.
(3) Public proceeds and benefits, insurance premiums, wages, social insurance contributions, interest and annuities on mortgage and other tare payments shall be paid in the first instance from the proceeds of the interim administration. The details of the management and management of the proceeds shall be determined by the Central Economic Office.

§ 220.

The imposition and cancellation of the interim administration shall be recorded in the land register. This note has the effects of a court internal report.

§ 221.

(1) An interim administrator who grossly violates his / her duties shall be punished by a district (state police) offense for fines from 100 Ks to 100,000 Ks, which in case of unenforceability is to be closed from 1 day to 3 months.
(2) Conditional suspension of the sentence is excluded.

TITLE II.

About trustees and interim administrators in industrial, trade and craft enterprises.

Part One.

General provisions.

§ 222.

The Central Economic Office may appoint a trustee or interim administrator at any time.

§ 223.

(1) A trustee—a temporary administrator—may be a morally well-preserved Slovak citizen who is at least 24 years old and, if possible, the relevant professional education and knowledge.
(2) A trustee—a temporary administrator—shall have the status of a public authority in the performance of his duties. This function does not establish a service relationship with either the enterprise or the State.
(3) Prior to taking up his duties, the trustee—interim administrator—shall pledge to the representative or representative of the Central Economic Office.
(4) The Central Economic Office may at any time transfer or change or cancel the person of the trustee, interim administrator or the trust or interim administration.

§ 224.

(1) The trustee—the interim administrator—shall also maintain the adjustments and orders issued by the Central Economic Office in general or in individual cases.
(2) The trustee—the interim administrator—also supervises the maintenance of the provisions of Part IV., Title V. (Sections 167 to 190).
(3) The trustee—the interim administrator—shall be obliged to maintain official secrecy about the facts of which he became aware in the course of the trust—interim administration.

§ 225.

The trustee—the interim administrator—shall be entitled to reimbursement of cash expenses and remuneration, the amount of which shall be determined by the Central Economic Office to the debit of the undertaking. Unpaid cash outflows and unpaid remuneration are recoverable under Section 90, Para. 2 of Decree-Law no. 8/1928 Sb.z. and n. by decision of the Central Economic Office.

Part Two.
About confidants.

§ 226.

(1) A trustee may not use a designation other than "trustee."

(2) The trustee has a control function; supervises the management of the business and makes suggestions for the removal of defects if the business is not managed with the care of a proper trader. To this end, it may consult all books, records and other aids relating to the conduct of the business; however, it may neither accept nor make any payments to the undertaking.

(3) Professional and interest organizations (trade associations, trade committees and their associations, chambers of commerce and industry, Central Association of Slovak Industry, etc.) are obliged to provide free advice to the trustee within their competence and information if requested.

Part Three.
About the interim report.

§ 227.

(1) The interim administrator shall, on behalf of the holder of the undertaking, take all measures necessary to maintain the proper and accurate functioning of the undertaking. The management of the company and everything connected with it passes to it. He shall be liable for any damage that would result from the neglect of his obligations.

(2) The interim administrator shall represent the undertaking in his report entrusted to the courts and authorities.

(3) The interim administrator shall be obliged to carry out the report in person and to keep the accounts of the Central Economic Office within the time limits specified by these offices and to provide him with the necessary reports and explanations at any time.

§ 228.

(1) The interim administrator needs the authorization of the Central Economic Office if he wishes to take measures which are not ordinary management, as well as all other measures of particular importance.

(2) The Central Economic Office shall supervise how the interim administrator manages and shall, ex officio, ensure that the defects and irregularities found in management are eliminated.

(3) The interim administrator shall pay all the expenses of the interim administration as well as the expenses connected with the proper operation of the enterprise; in particular—public taxes and levies, wages, social insurance contributions, interest and annuities on mortgage requirements, insurance premiums, etc.

(4) The net proceeds of the interim administration of the enterprise shall be handed over to the holder of the enterprise to its tied account (Article 64). However, the holder of an

undertaking shall, if so, decided by the Central Economic Office, deposit the cash necessary for the operation of the undertaking and pay its deficit. The area of the Central Economic Office is an enforceable title pursuant to § 90, para. 2 of Decree-Law no. 8/1928 Sb.z. and n.

§ 229.

The Enforcement Report may only penalize the net proceeds which, according to § 228, para. 4 effect the business owner.

§ 230.

(1) The introduction and cancellation of the interim administration shall be recorded in the relevant public book if they are part of the real estate business. The introduction of the interim administration has the effect that the interim administration may be kept against anyone who has acquired rights to the enterprise following the comment.
(2) If the company holder's company is registered in the company register, it shall mark on the proposal of the Central Economic Office the imposition, the cancellation of the interim administration and the name of the interim administrator.

Part Four.
Criminal and final provisions.

§ 231.

(1) A trustee or temporary administrator who grossly violates the obligations imposed on him by the provisions of Sections 222 to 230 or does not maintain the regulation or the order of the Central Economic Office (Section 224 (1)), up to 3 months and a fine of 100 Ks to 100,000 Ks. The unenforceable pecuniary penalty will be converted to a close from 1 day to 3 months.
(2) Conditional suspension of the sentence is excluded.

§ 232.

The provisions of Government Decree no. 137/1939 Sl.z. in the wording of the Decree with the power of Act no. 327/1939 Sl.z. do not apply to trustees and temporary administrators in Jewish enterprises.

PART SEVEN.

Meeting the costs of revision, control and liquidation and the general value of Jewish and aristocratic businesses, as well as Jewish property.

§ 233.

(1) The costs of reviewing, controlling and stabilizing the liquidation value of Jewish enterprises, as well as the costs of controlling enterprises transferred pursuant to Section 170 or referred to in Section 181, Para. 4, shall be borne by the business owner.
(2) The costs of the revision as well as the control of the temporary administration of the Jewish property and Jewish associations shall be borne by the owner of the household property.

(3) The costs of stabilizing the municipal value of the subject of legal acts pursuant to Section 53 shall be borne by the persons specified therein.

§ 234.

(1) The amount of costs (§ 233) shall be determined by the Central Economic Office.
(2) The decision of the Central Economic Office, by which it determines the costs, is an enforcement order pursuant to § 90, para. 2 of Decree-Law no. 8/1928 Sb.z. and n.

§ 235.

The costs referred to in § 233 are not a deductible item under the Direct Tax Act.

PART EIGHT.
Special rules in tax and fee matters.
TITLE I
Tax legislation.

§ 236.

(1) 1, para. 3 of Part Two of Act No. 266/1936 Sb.z. and n. as amended by Article 29 of Decree-Law no. 160/1939 Sl.z. it does not apply to Jewish taxpayers and Jewish associations since 1940.
(2) For the general income tax prescribed with respect to the provision of para. 1 of the income of former Jewish enterprises, neither the non-Jewish owners of these enterprises nor the assets of the non-Jewish enterprises are liable.

§ 237.

(1) Official decisions and measures of the tax authorities (commissions) in matters of direct taxes and turnover taxes, issued after 1 January 1930 until 31 December 1940, concerning taxpayers of Jews, non-Jewish spouses of Jews and Jewish associations, whether they have entered into force or not, review and, according to the results of the review, revoke, replace or amend others without giving reasons. Tax reductions at bankruptcy and settlement may also be abolished.
(2) 1 also applies to property benefit and property gain, as it is depreciation of grace or relief according to § 5 of the Act no. 6/1924 Sb.z. and n.

§ 238.

(1) Limitation periods specified in Sections 277 and 280 of the Act on Direct Taxes, in Section 45, Para. 1 to 4 of the Law on turnover tax, which have expired after 1 January 1930 to 31 December 1940 or are in progress with tax entities referred to in § 237, para. 1 shall be renewed and shall begin on 1 January 1941.
(2) Renewal of the limitation periods under para. Paragraph 1 (1) shall also apply to tax legislation which has not yet entered into force, provided that the limitation period is appealed in the appeal.

§ 239.

(1) The provisions of § 238, para. 1 shall apply mutatis mutandis to the renewal of the limitation periods determined for the introduction of criminal proceedings pursuant to Sections 206 and 208, para. 2 of the Act on Direct Taxes and § 45, para. 8 to 10 of the Turnover Tax Act.
(2) The provisions of § 202, para. 2, para. b) and § 204 of the Act on Direct Taxes and § 44, para. 1, no. 3 of the Act on Turnover Tax, Effective Regret for Criminal Sequences introduced under para. 1, are suspended.

§ 240.

(1) The right of the state to recover due taxes with surcharges and accessories for tax years 1927 and following from the tax entities referred to in § 237, para. 1, until the deadline specified in Section 281 of the Direct Tax Act and Section 45, Para. 5 of the Law on turnover tax has expired or is in progress, is renewed and the limitation period begins to run for it again on 1 January 1941.
(2) The right of the state to recover a benefit from an asset and an increase in an asset under Act no. 309/1920 Sb.z. and n. from tax entities referred to in § 237, para. 1, provided that until 31 December 1940 the limitation period laid down in Article 5 of Act No. 31/1878 r.z. has expired or is in progress, is renewed and the limitation period begins to run for it on 1 January 1941.
(3) For tax entities referred to in § 237, para. 1, the provisions of § 276, para. 3 and § 283, para. 2 of the Direct Tax Act.

§ 241.

(1) For arrears of direct taxes with surcharges and accessories, turnover and luxury taxes with accessories, property and accrued property benefits and fines and penalties with accessories - Jews and Jewish associations, whether or not arrears from the time before or after the entry into force of this Regulation, personally and with all their property, spouses and relatives or relatives up to the second stage, who are living or at the time when the tax or benefit becomes chargeable, will commit the offense for which or a fine assessed, lived with the taxpayer in the same household and are persons referred to in § 237 para. 1. Where one of several guarantors has paid the outstanding balance (part thereof), he shall be entitled to compensation against those guarantors in respect of the part which is proportional to the other guarantors by number.
(2) For tax entities referred to in § 237, para. 1, the provisions of § 264, para. 1, no. 3 a 5 a ods. 3 of the Direct Tax Act.

TITLE II.

Fee regulations.

§ 242.

(1) All administrative acts (excavations), decisions, measures in matters of fees, issued by the tax authorities after January 1, 1919 and concerning entities referred to in § 237,

para. 1, may, regardless of their legality, review and revoke; the payment obligation of these entities may be determined by a new continuation.

(2) The provisions of § 237, para. 1, last sentence, shall apply mutatis mutandis to charges.

§ 243.

Limitation periods for extinction, additional extinction, retirement penalties and the recovery of fees, as set out in the Fees Act, as these are the entities referred to in Section 237, Para. 1, do not apply.

§ 244.

(1) For legal acts concluded between entities referred to in § 237, para. 1. The following legal presumptions shall apply irrespective of the time when the charge becomes chargeable:

(a) a property transfer for remuneration shall be deemed to be a gift if it has been entered into between the Jews by spouses or relatives of a straight branch without limitation and in the branch up to the second stage included, even if only one of these Contracting Parties is a Jew;

(b) a dowry, irrespective of the person providing it, shall be regarded as an unconditional gift.

(2) Contrary to the presumption referred to in para. 1, point (a) (a) shall be recognized only if the purchaser is able to demonstrate reliably that he has had the means to settle the purchase price and that he has actually paid it, and if the seller demonstrates that the purchase price has affected his property. The proof of payment of the purchase price in the contract of sale itself is not sufficient proof. The existence and amount in the contract of liabilities assumed must be proved by credible documents; In the same way, it must be demonstrated that the liabilities assumed (liabilities) were paid to the purchasers if they were to be recognized as payments for the purchase price.

(3) If the dowry was returned to the provider because the marriage ceased to exist and the provider proves that it has affected his property, the presumption of the gift pursuant to para. 1, point (a) (b) is refuted.

§ 245.

(1) Charges for arrears, penalties and fines, regardless of whether they originate from the time before or after the entry into force of this Regulation, are personally guaranteed by the entities referred to in § 237, para. 1, which acquired property from the taxpayer of the Jew (§ 237, para. 1) as a gift or an act disguising the gift, up to the value of the property thus acquired. Between the spouses and relatives and sister-in-law up to the second stage, the transfer of property for remuneration is regarded as a gift or an act disguising the gift; the opposite of this presumption can only be proven in the manner specified in § 244 para. Second

(2) The provisions of § 36 of the legal article XI / 1918 on liability in kind shall apply to the persons referred to in § 237, par. 1 without limitation but without prejudice to the rights acquired by the Non-Jews.

TITLE III.

Common provisions.

§ 246.

Taxes, fees, fines and penalties, which are subject to the provisions of Sections 236 to 245, may be secured by the financial administration on the property of the taxpayer (Jew) concerned or of a Jewish association. Such detention shall be carried out on the basis of an enforceable detention order issued pursuant to Section 284, Para. 1 of the Act on Direct Taxes, in which it is not necessary to state the reasons why the Office considers the recovery to be endangered.

§ 247.

Measures pursuant to Section 237 shall be the competent authority which issued the measure or decision in the last instance.

§ 248.

For the purpose of continuing with the implementation of the provisions of Sections 236 to 245 as regards taxpayers (taxpayers) pursuant to Section 237, Para. 1, the legal provisions on banking and business secrecy are suspended.

§ 249.

Public authorities, institutes, public notaries and natural and legal persons are obliged to co-operate in the execution of this section (Sections 236 to 249) and to handle the requests of the tax authorities with the highest speed.

PART NINE.

Common provisions.

§ 250.

Scope of certain terms used in the Regulation.

(1) Where the legal situation of the Jews, which remains in force, still refers to the term "Jew," from the date of entry into force of this Regulation, the term "Jew" must be understood in accordance with § 1.

(2) Where the term "Gentile" (non-Jewish) is used in this Regulation, it is to be understood, except in the case of § 9, that a Jewish spouse is also involved.

§ 251.

Specific provisions on the effectiveness of this Regulation as regards some people.

(1) Persons who are only subsequently found to be Jews, or who become Jewish, or who become Jews only after the entry into force of this Regulation, shall only take effect from the date on which they were lawfully determined to be Jews. blends, from the day they became.

(2) Where a time limit is specified for the fulfillment of an obligation under this Regulation, it shall be calculated in the cases referred to in para. 1 from the days of the facts mentioned there.

(3) The effects of the provisions relating to the non-Jewish spouses of Jews shall affect them in cases of marriage with a Jew after the date of entry into force of this Regulation - from the date of the marriage. The provision of para. 2 applies here as well.

§ 252.

(1) Decisions (measures, etc.) issued pursuant to this Regulation shall not be appealed to the Supreme Administrative Court—except in the cases referred to in §§ 3, 5 and 167, para. Third

(2) In those cases where a complaint against the Supreme Administrative Court is excluded, it is not possible to seek redress before the state courts pursuant to Section 66 of Act no. 185/1939 Sl.z.

§ 253.

Statements of service.

If a private employment relationship is terminated with respect to the provisions of this Regulation—except in the cases pursuant to Part 1, Title X, Part 2 (Sections 43 to 48)—they shall apply to it and to the provisional provisions of Government Regulation No. 65/1939 Sl.z.

§ 254.

Official performance benefits.

(1) In the case of exemptions pursuant to Article 255, the fee for official services (Article 1 of Act No. 340/1940 Coll.) Shall be collected at the following rates:

(a) for the granting of exemption from the provisions of § 1 in the amount from 1,000 Ks to 500,000 Ks,

(b) for granting exemption from the provisions of § 2 in the amount from 500 Ks to 100.000 Ks,

(c) for granting exemption from individual or several provisions of the Regulation in the amount from 10 Ks to 300.000 Ks,

(d) A fee of 10 Ks (birth no. 260/1940 Coll. Part A, item 2) shall be levied for the certificate issued pursuant to § 3.

(2) Otherwise, the provisions of Act no. 340/1940 Sl.z. and Government Decree no. 360/1940 Sl.z.

PART TEN.

Exemptions and exemptions.

§ 255.

(1) The President of the Republic may grant exemptions from the provisions of this Regulation.

(2) Exemptions may be total or partial and may be subject to conditions.

(3) Exemptions may be withdrawn at any time.

§ 256.

Exemptions granted under Government Decree No. 63/1939 Sl.z. or under other laws governing the legal status or legal situation of the Jews shall be exempted from similar provisions under this Regulation. The provisions of § 255, par. 3 shall apply mutatis mutandis to these exceptions.

PART ONE.

Transitional provisions.

§ 257.

Releasing housewives from Jewish households.

With domestic helpers who cannot be employed under Article 41, the service relationship must be canceled by October 31, 1941 at the latest.

§ 258.

Time limit for submitting applications for permission to employ Jews.

(1) Any employer who employs a Jew on the date this Regulation enters into force shall, before 1 October 1941, submit an application for a work permit pursuant to Section 43, disregarding applications submitted until the entry into force of this Regulation.

(2) Until the application pursuant to par. 1 submitted after the entry into force of this regulation, a Jew may remain in his previous job.

(3) The provisions of paragraph 1 shall not apply in cases where an application for a work permit has already been granted before the entry into force of this Regulation or in which the application has been rejected by the Central Economic Authority, whether or not the period of notice has expired.

§ 259.

Deadline for the submission of licenses, withdrawals and forfeiture receivers and weapons.

(1) Weapons' certificates, fishing licenses, driving licenses, passports, passports and temporary passports issued by Jews before the entry into force of this Regulation shall cease to be valid and their owners—by the district (state police) competent for the place of residence, within 8 days after the entry into force of this Regulation, in the case of travel—even temporary—passports, the nearest return from abroad.

(2) Jews (non-Jewish members of the Jewish household) are to hand over the concessions for the possession of a radio receiver, or a radio transmitter, within 8 days of the date of entry into force of this Regulation at the postal office which issued them. Radio receivers and radio transmitters that Jews (non-Jewish members of a Jewish household) had forfeited to the state. This also applies to radio receivers that have been confiscated so far administratively. The seizure will be carried out by the district (state police) authorities.

(3) Also, any weapons owned by the Jews shall be forfeited to the State. This also applies to weapons seized up to now administratively. The seizure will be carried out by the district (state police) authorities.

(4) Failure to fulfill the obligations referred to in para. 1 to 3, is enforceable as an offense district (state police) authorities with a fine of 100 Ks to 10,000 Ks, which in the case of unenforceability to be closed from one day to 15 days.

§ 260.

Special time limit for opening escrow accounts, safekeeping and passbooks.

Persons who are Jews pursuant to § 1 but have not yet been required to open escrow accounts (§ 64 et seq.) And escrow (§ 68 et seq.) Within 8 days of the entry into force of this Regulation. Within the same period, they are obliged to deposit their cash on passbooks (§§ 62 et seq.).

§ 261.

Special provision on civil servants.

(1) Jews excluded from public or other public services pursuant to Section 15 shall be released within two months of the date of entry into force of this Regulation.

(2) In the case of the exclusion of Jewish mixers referred to in Section 2 (a). a) lift—as they are officers and non-commissioned officers (§ 15, para. 2) also in § 2 let. (b), and of the non-Jewish spouses of Jews, the release shall take place within 6 months of the date of entry into force of this Regulation.

(3) In the interest of the service, the Government may extend the time limits specified in para. 1 and 2.

§ 262.

(1) If someone has been dismissed from public or other public services because they were subject to the provisions of § 1 of Government Regulation no. 63/1939 Sl.z. and Government Decree no. 74/1939 Sl.z. 143/1941 Sl.z., however, under this Regulation, he is not a Jew or a Jewish mixer referred to in § 2 (a). a), as well as officers and non-commissioned officers (§ 15, par. 2), also in § 2, point. (b) shall be deemed to reimburse any severance pay, if any, re-admitted to the service with the rights he had on dismissal, the time from dismissal until his resumption of service being calculated neither for the increase in service nor for the retirement allowance nor for its assessment. However, if transfer to retirement could be envisaged, he / she shall be remunerated as if he / she was retired on the date of his release.

(2) Beneficiaries of state rest or care salaries, which were subject to the provisions of § 1 of Decree-Law no. 63/1939 Sl.z. and Regulation No. 143/1941 Sl.z. (Sections 11 and 12 of the latter Regulation), but pursuant to this Regulation, they are not Jews or Jewish mixers referred to in Section 2 (a). a), as well as officers and non-commissioned officers (§ 15, par. 2), also in § 2, point. (b) are entitled, from the first day of the month following the date of entry into force of this Regulation, to rest, reinsurance benefits, to those they enjoyed on the date of entry into force of Regulation No. 143/1941 Sl.z.

§ 263.

Forfeiture of objects referred to in § 74.

The subjects mentioned in § 78, par. 1 and 2 are forfeited to the State. Jews are obliged to hand them over to the District (State Police) Office within 8 days of the entry into force of this Regulation.

§ 264.

Special provision for inventory.

Statement of assets according to § 112, par. 1, Jews who have fulfilled the reporting duty under § 3, par. 1 have completed the reporting obligation under § 3, para. 1 č. 203/1940 Sl.z.

§ 265.

Special time limits for the purchase of real estate.

Regarding real estate that could be redeemed under Act no. 213/1940 Sl.z. as amended by Regulation No. 52/1940 Sl.z .:

(a) in the case of § 116, the date shall be 11 September 1940,

(b) right of redemption pursuant to Section 119, Para. 1, the first sentence shall apply until 10 September 1941, including.

§ 266.

Exclusion of the right to recovery of profits under § 144.

Claims under § 144 may not be asserted by those persons who could have already claimed it under Regulation No. 313/1940 Sl.z.

§ 267.

Transitional provisions for the implementation of land reform.

(1) The provisions of Act no. 46/1940 Coll., The legislation amending this Act and the legislation issued pursuant to it, because they contradict this regulation, do not apply to the cases regulated in this regulation.

(2) Even after the immovable property has been transferred to the state property, the expert report of the Ministry of Economy pursuant to Section 166, last sentence, shall remain subject to a person designated by the State Land Office.

(3). 326/1940 Sl.z.z.so calculate periods from the note of intended takeover, these periods must be calculated for real estate covered by § 150 to § 166, from the date determined by the decree pursuant to § 150.

PART TWELVE.

Final provisions.

§ 268.

(1) All legislation is repealed as it governs the conditions and matters governed by this Regulation; In particular, the following are repealed: 63/1939 Coll., In addition to §

8, Government Decree no. 137/1939 Sl.z. as amended by Decree-Law No. 327/1939 Sl.z. and no. 197/1940 Coll., Government Regulation no. 145/1939 Sl.z., Government Regulation no. 184/1939 Coll., Government Regulation no. 230/1939 Coll., In addition to § 4, also § 23 of Act no. 46/1940 Sl.z. as amended by Regulation No. 56/1941 Coll., Decree with the power of Act no. 130/1940 Coll., As it concerns Jews, Regulation no. 203/1940 Coll., Act no. 213/1940 Sl.z. as amended by Regulation No. 52/1940 Coll., Regulation no. 215/1940 Coll., Regulation no. 216/1940 Coll., Regulation no. 234/1940 Coll., Regulation no. 255/1940 Coll., Regulation no. 256/1940 Sl.z. as amended by Regulation No. 305/1940 Coll., Except § 7, par. 3, Reg. 257/1940 Sl.z. as amended by Regulation No. 44/1941 Coll., Regulation no. 291/1940 Coll., Regulation no. 303/1940 Sl.z. as amended by Regulation no. 53/1941 Sl.z. and no. 129/1941 Coll., Regulation no. 313/1940 Coll., Regulation no. 314/1940 Coll., Regulation no. 315/1940 Coll., Regulation no. 23/1941 Coll., Regulation no. 57/1941 Coll., Regulation no. 84/1941 Coll., Regulation no. 93/1941 Coll., Regulation no. 143/1941 Coll., Regulation no. 153/1941 Coll., Regulation no. 186/1941 Sl.z. and Regulation No. 194/1941 Sl.z.

(2) For persons who were Jews according to § 1 par. 1 of Government Decree No. 63/1939 Coll., But they are not pursuant to this Regulation, the relevant restrictions on the existing legislation governing the legal status and legal situation of the Jews—as they are not based on a decision of an office, court or body of a public corporation. Such persons, if they remain Jewish mixers (§ 2), will remain subject to the restrictions that affect Jewish mixers under this Regulation.

§ 269.

Continuations initiated under existing legislation, regulating the legal status and legal situation of Jews, if they are Jews, then Jewish mixes shall be completed in accordance with the provisions of this Regulation.

(1) Continuations which have been initiated under existing legislation governing the legal status and legal situation of Jews, if they are Jews, then Jewish, are to be completed in accordance with the provisions of this Regulation.

(2) Continuations under Act no. 113/1940 Coll., In which, by the date of entry into force of this Regulation, decisions on irrigation or authorization pursuant to Section 2 of the said Act on the Transfer of Business have already been issued, shall be completed by the Central Economic Office pursuant to the regulations of this Regulation; however, according to the provisions of Act no. 113/1940 Sl.z.

(3) The provisions of § 179, par. 2. Paragraphs 2 to 4 shall also apply to business transfer permits and to irrigation decisions issued pursuant to §§ 2 and 4, par. 2 of Act no. 113/1940 Sl.z.

(4) Acts transferred in matters of Act no. 113/1940 Coll., In which, however, by the date of entry into force of this Regulation, no decision on the irrigation has been issued, or in which the license pursuant to § 2 of Act No. 113/1940 Coll. 113/1940 Sl.z. they shall not be binding on the Central Economic Office.

§ 270.

(1) This Regulation shall enter into force on the day of its publication; it will be done by all members government: Dr. Tuka, Sivák, Mach, Dr. Pružinský, Dr. Fritz, Dr. Medrický, Stano, Čatloš.

Čl.1 Valid from 24.6.1942
Čl.2 Valid from 5.3.1943
Čl.3 Valid from 5.3.1943
Čl.4 Valid from 5.3.1943

The Jewish Code marked a breakthrough in the status of the Jewish population. The *Gardista* daily was eager to announce that the Jewish Code had been adopted and explained to its readers its basic provisions. It pointed out that by enacting the law, the desire of the whole Slovak national community, which was always manifested to the greatest extent among the workers, was fulfilled. As written:

> Even after the historic Salzburg agreement, the whole Slovak public was most pleased to accept the 14th point of the Slovak National Socialist Program, which spoke about the final and uncompromising solution of the Jewish question in Slovakia. However, a final and uncompromising solution could come and will only be possible if this burning issue is resolved on a racist basis in accordance with the Nuremberg Laws. Finally, there is a definitive settlement—without exception, without the so-called indispensable—with the most disruptive element in our state. As our security authorities and the Guard have found, the Jews have always been mixed up in any subversive, whether propaganda or other activity. Thus, it is time to purify our social and economic life definitively.

Following the Hlinka Guard regulations, the guardsmen were supposed to follow the Jewish Law Regulations published in the *Gardista*, because only in this way would cooperation be possible to define this plea from the public.

Part of the racist measures against the Jews was their eviction from the main streets or streets and squares named after Hlinka or Hitler. The Hlinka Guard was involved in the process of identifying the streets and squares from which the Jews were to move. By December 1940, the Hlinka Guard had ordered the local headquarters to write lists of streets from which Jews should move out. The Jews were forbidden to live at the Hlinka and Hitler Square in Bratislava since November 4, 1940, but a new legal regulation was expected that would extend the possibilities of evicting Jews from several locations. At similar levels, commissions were mostly designated at local levels, with Hlinka Guard commanders in charge.

The summer of 1941 was active in issuing anti-Jewish orders and orders from the Hlinka Guard to address the Jewish issue. In addition to the regulations, the Hlinka Guard headquarters were tasked with writing lists of all working Jews, to prevent further spread of the subversive activity of the Jews. Supposedly, the Hlinka Guard had several reports of provocative behavior of Jews, which in the Slovak community was supposed to have caused outrage. Therefore, the Hlinka Guard ordered local headquarters to divide Jews into three groups in the lists, namely:

First: Jews who are particularly harmful and dangerous by their provocative action, and Jews are lazy.
Second: Jews who live on their own capital.
Third: Jews who were excluded from working possibilities.

Selected Jews were to be called for a number of public works, such as repairing roads, water supplies, sewerage, regulation, etc. Work camps were to be set up as soon as possible. The Ministry of the Interior, by circulars of August 16, 1941, asked the county and district authorities to announce the possibility of building dislocation centers and labor camps for Jews in their districts. The Hlinka Guard was to be involved more than a month in advance to assist in the establishment and guarding. By order of July 1, 1941, the Hlinka Guard ordered the district commanders to expeditiously send to Hlinka Guard headquarters lists of guards, officers, and reserve soldiers who could voluntarily report to the Jewish labor camps during the on-call alert period. Middle-aged guards, energetic, radical, and uncompromising anti-Jewish foundations, and certificates in the Hlinka Guard came into consideration.

The Hlinka Guard was aware that many regulations of anti-Jewish legislation might seem to the Slovaks to be contrary to Christian morality. It therefore proposed to organize a series of lectures for guards on topics such as "Judaism as a plague on the body of the nation in the past" or "The importance of removing Jews from Slovakia" at which the local headquarters cultural officers stressed that all other issues were not as important as a definitive solution to the Jewish question and that the Hlinka Guard had the greatest credit for solving this issue. According to the order:

> The implementation of regulations was an important point in the Hlinka Guard program and the National Socialism program. They were to be reminded that the Hlinka Guard is aware of the isolated, humanly unpleasant cases of this final solution. They know that some cases individually assessed are painful to individuals. But they are also aware that they do everything they do out of love for the nation, and that is more than the interests of Jews around the world. Therefore, Hlinka Guard takes full responsibility for this solution and cannot be diverted from anyone who has begun by anyone and no sentimentality. The removal of the Jews from Slovakia is a necessity in the interests of the nation, state and its future, and this fact will lead Hlinka Guard uncompromisingly until the last Jew leaves the territory of Slovakia.

14

The Hlinka Guard and the Ultimate Solution to the Jewish Question

From November 4 to 7, 1938, between 4,000 and 7,600 Jews were deported, in a chaotic, pogrom-like operation in which Hlinka Guard, *Freiwillige Schutzstaffel*, and the German Party participated. The victims were rounded up, loaded onto buses, and dropped off past the new border with Hungary. About 260 were foreigners, such as Austrian Jews who had escaped into Czechoslovakia following the annexation of Austria by Germany. The bulk of the deportees were Jews with Polish citizenship, who were effectively stateless because they had lost their Polish nationality by living abroad. Young children, the elderly, and pregnant women were among those deported. Deportees faced bullying and intimidation from the Hlinka Guard and were warned that their presence in Slovakia was not desired and that they would face criminal charges if they attempted to return.

Most of the deportees, not just Slovak Jews, but also Polish citizens and stateless people, ignored the warning and made their way back home, which was unauthorized but quietly tolerated. In many places, the Hlinka Guard's zealous enthusiasm was such that they continued the action after the order was rescinded. The Jews of Vranov nad Topľou were expelled on November 7. Four Jews who tried to return to Banská Bystrica were deported again, but 70 percent of the 292 Jews deported from Michalovce had returned by November 19. Meanwhile, Jews with a net worth of over 500,000 Czech Republic Korunas were arrested to prevent the flight of capital. Jews with foreign citizenship, except German, Hungarian, and Romanian nationality were exempt from deportation. Hungary refused to admit the deported Jews, so Tiso canceled the operation on November 7, 1938.

Deportees were confined in makeshift tent camps at Miloslavov near Bratislava and Veľký Kýr near Nitra on the new Slovak–Hungarian border during the winter. The camps were located in the neutral zone of 3 km between the countries; there was an additional 1.5-km demilitarized zone on the Slovak side. Neither country accepted responsibility for them nor guarded them, blaming the other country for the situation. Miloslavov was located on a road near Štvrtok na Ostrove, 250 meters from the new border. At both camps, there were initially no shelters, and especially children and elderly became ill due to the wet winter weather. At Miloslavov, the temperatures for the first week got as low as 23 degrees Fahrenheit before the deportees obtained any shelters.

Heinrich Schwartz, a representative of the Orthodox Religious Communities, and Marie Schmolka, director of Hebrew Immigrant Aid Society Prague, were allowed to visit Miloslavov in late November. With the aid of Jewish organizations, the refugees obtained food, shelter, and more clothing. According to a November 29 letter from the president of Orthodox Religious Communities, the population of Veľký Kýr was 344 (132 men, seventy-three women, and 139 children) and Miloslavov had more than 300, including 120 men, seventy-seven women, and 105 children. Of the detainees at Miloslavov, most (197) were stateless, although many of these had lived in the country for many years. Seven of the deportees had Slovak citizenship, thirty were from Carpathian Ruthenia, twenty-eight originated in the local area, twenty-two were from Poland, and thirty-eight from Germany. Another camp, at Šamorín, had 190 people: 108 men, forty women, and forty-two children.

In the letter, the community leader begged for the Slovak Jews to be allowed to go home and the other Jews to be released so that they could wind up their affairs and leave the country. He promised that the Jews not from Slovakia would live in centers or with relatives and that all expenses would be borne by the Orthodox community. At the same time, local officials worried that the tent camps would become a haven for infectious diseases, which could spread to neighboring Slovak communities. On November 30, a quarantine was imposed in Miloslavov, which also prevented aid from Jewish organizations in Bratislava. The poor conditions in the camps were condemned by the United Kingdom and France and worsened Slovakia's image abroad.

By early December, the Hungarian authorities also expelled several hundred Jews with foreign citizenship, although Czechoslovak Jews from southern Slovakia were treated as Hungarian citizens. On December 8, 1938, Slovak authorities issued a directive that the deportation of Jews would not be done as a whole, but on a case-by-case basis and in line with Czechoslovak law. Jews from other countries, such as Poland or the Czech lands, were to be returned home, while stateless Jews were imprisoned in camps along the border. Although these orders did not say so explicitly, they implied that most of the deported Jews with Czechoslovak citizenship would be allowed to return home. After this, the remaining deportees were mostly stateless. At Veľký Kýr, this was implemented beginning on December 12. On December 19, 118 deportees at Miloslavov were moved to Kühmeyer Inn on the outskirts of Bratislava and from there to a former ammunition factory in Patrónka, where they remained until the 1942 deportations. According to Slovak National Archives documents, many of the Jews from Miloslavov were able to emigrate and the rest were deported overnight to Hungary in January 1939, in order to minimize publicity. On February 21, 1939, 158 Jews were released from Veľký Kýr, but it is unclear when the camp was shut down.

Along with Germany's arrest and expulsion of about 17,000 Polish Jews living in Nazi Germany in October 1938 and Hungary's expulsion of Jews from the areas it annexed in 1938, the Slovak deportations were the first in central Europe. There were also expulsions after the *Anschluss*, the annexation of the Sudetenland, and *Kristallnacht*. Frightened, many Slovak Jews tried to transfer their property abroad and attempt emigration. Over the winter, many refugee Jews from Germany and Austria managed to leave the country. Between December 1938 and February 1939, more than 2.25 million Korunas were transferred illegally to the Czech lands, the Netherlands, and the United Kingdom; additional amounts were transferred legally. The deportations reduced British investment, increasing dependence on German capital. They also served as a rehearsal for the 1942 deportations, in which two-thirds of Slovak Jews were deported to ghettos and extermination camps in occupied Poland.

By early 1939, the British consulate in Bratislava was receiving forty visa applications daily. Interest in emigration among Jews surged after the invasion of Poland, as Jewish refugees from Poland told of atrocities there. Although the Slovak government encouraged Jews to emigrate, it refused to allow the export of foreign currency, ensuring that most attempts remained unsuccessful. No country was eager to accept Jewish refugees, and the tight limits on legal emigration to Palestine prevented Jews from seeking refuge there. In 1940, Bratislava became a hub for organizing illegal immigration to Palestine. By early 1941, further emigration was impossible. Even Jews who received valid United States visas were not allowed transit visas through Nazi Germany. The total number of Slovak Jewish emigrants has been estimated at 5,000 to 6,000.

Jews serving in the army were segregated in a labor unit in April 1939 and were stripped of their rank at the end of the year. From 1940, male Jews and Romani people were obliged to work for the national defense on manual labor on construction projects for two months every year. All recruits considered Jewish or Romani were allocated to the Sixth Labor Battalion, which worked at military construction sites at Sabinov, Liptovský Svätý Peter, Láb, Svätý Jur, and Zohor the following year. Although the Ministry of Defense was pressured by the Ministry of the Interior to release the Jews for deportation in 1942, it refused. The battalion was disbanded in 1943, and the Jewish laborers were sent to a number of work camps.

The first labor centers were established in early 1941 offering retraining courses for Jews forced into unemployment; 13,612 Jews had applied for the courses by February, far exceeding the program's capacity. On July 4, the Slovak government issued a decree conscripting all Jewish men aged eighteen to sixty for labor. By September, 5,500 Jews were performing manual labor for private companies at about eighty small labor centers, most of which were dissolved in the final months of 1941 as part of the preparation for deportation. Construction began on three larger camps—Sereď, Nováky, and Vyhne—in September of that year.

Initially, anti-Semitic laws defined Jews by religion rather than ancestry. Jews who were baptized before 1918 were considered Christian. The partial reliance on religious criteria was at the request of the Catholic Church, which opposed racism.

Local authorities had imposed anti-Jewish measures on their own. The head of the Šariš-Zemplín region ordered local Jews to wear a yellow band around their left arm from April 5, 1941, leading to attacks. As the focus shifted to restricting Jews' civil rights rather than depriving them of their property, Department 14 of the Ministry of the Interior was formed to enforce anti-Jewish measures.

The passage of the Jewish Code of September 9, 1941 required that all Jews over six years old wear a yellow star. The racial definition of Jews was criticized by the Catholic Church, and converts were eventually exempted from some of the requirements. The Hlinka Guard and *Freiwillige Schutzstaffel* increased assaults on Jews, engaged in anti-Semitic demonstrations on a daily basis, and denounced insufficiently anti-Semitic non-Jews as "White Jews." The law enabled the Central Economic Office to force Jews to change their residence. This provision was put into effect on October 4, 1941, when 10,000 of 15,000 Jews in Bratislava, who were not employed or intermarried, were ordered to move to fourteen towns. The relocation was paid for and carried out by the Department of Special Tasks. Although the Jews were ordered to leave by December 31, 1941, fewer than 7,000 people had moved by March 1942.

Slovakia was the first Axis partner to consent to the deportation of its Jewish residents in the framework of the "Final Solution." According to a census of December 15, 1940, there were 88,951 Jews in Slovakia. The Slovak government enthusiastically embraced the idea of deporting their Jews. They had promised to supply Germany with 120,000 workers.

The National Defense Law 20/1940 exempted Jews from military service in the new Slovak State but required them instead to do manual labor at military work camps. Such Jews, who were called "*Robotnik Zid*" or work Jews, and wore distinctive blue uniforms and berets. They were assigned to the Sixth Labor Battalion which consisted of five companies, three of which were exclusively made up of Jews. New Jewish recruits were assembled in Cemerne, in eastern Slovakia, where they underwent basic military training using shovels instead of rifles. By October 1941, there were actually 80,000 Slovak workers in Germany. At that point, the Slovak government offered to substitute 10,000–20,000 Slovak Jews in place of the missing promised workers.

At first, the Germans did not respond to the offer, but shortly after the Wannsee Conference on January 20, 1942, Slovak leaders negotiated the terms of an agreement whereby the Slovak government would pay Germany 500 Reichsmarks for every deported Jew. The expulsion of the Jews of Slovakia to the district of Lublin began on March 25, 1942 and ended on June 14, 1942. Nearly 40,000 Jews were deported in thirty-eight transports. Only a few of the deportees survived. However, only a small proportion of the Slovak Jews were sent directly to the death camps. Most were sent first to ghettos which served as interim stops before the final deportation to the death camps.

When the mass deportation of Slovak Jewry began in the spring of 1942 the position of the work Jews improved *vis-à-vis* the civilian Jewish population. The

Jewish labor companies fell under the authority of the Ministry of Defense which was often in conflict with the Ministry for Internal Affairs that was responsible for the deportation actions. For their part, the Germans agreed that the Jews would not be returned to Slovakia and that Germany would make no claims on the property abandoned by the Jews. The initial agreement had been for 20,000 young, strong Jews, but before their deportation had even started, Himmler proposed that Slovakia be made free of Jews.

Sereď Concentration Camp

The Sereď labor and concentration camp operated under the wartime Slovak state administration from September 1941 to March 1945, with a short break after the outbreak of the Slovak National Uprising against German occupation that lasted from late August to September 1944. The camp was established in the existing buildings of a former military engineering unit's headquarters in Sereď. The Sereď camp was designated for the growing number of socially excluded and impoverished Jews from Slovakia, who had been stripped of their civil rights and their property through a government decree in 1939.

The Sereď camp was an outgrowth of existing temporary forced labor units which were created after 1939, in what was then the territory of Slovakia, in order to inter not only Jews, but also Roma individuals, and Slovaks who were deemed politically unreliable. Under the wartime Slovak state, concentration camps were an integral component of the Final Solution to the Jewish question in Slovakia. The totalitarian regime dominated by the Hlinka Slovak People's Party established labor centers and then labor camps, including the one in Sereď, as part of a wider plan for the persecution and exploitation of Jewish citizens. The Sereď camp commander was a "deserving" member of the Hlinka Guard, a paramilitary organization of the party which guarded the camp during this time. The Jewish Police and the Jewish Board also participated in the camp's administration. On the one hand, the Sereď camp functioned as an economic unit where labor represented partial protection and an opportunity to avoiding deportation; on the other, it served as a temporary detention center for Jews, who were deported from there to other concentration camps outside Slovakia. Between March and October 1942 alone, at least 4,463 persons were deported from Sereď.

After the National Uprising against the German occupation in 1944, the Sereď camp was reopened under the command of SS-*Hauptsturmführer* Alois Brunner, a close associate of Adolf Eichmann's, who had previously organized the deportations of Greek and French Jews to Nazi concentration and extermination camps. His aim was to achieve the so-called Final Solution to the Jewish question in Slovakia.

Under Brunner's leadership, conditions within the camp became significantly worse: Jewish as well as non-Jewish inmates were tortured and murdered or deported to other Nazi camps located in Third Reich-controlled territory. From September 1944 to March 1945, eleven transports from the Sereď concentration camp and several transports from Prešov carried the remaining Jewish prisoners out of Slovakia. Some were sent to Auschwitz; others to Sachsenhausen, Ravensbrück, or Terezin. Approximately 13,500 people were deported.

Nováky Concentration Camp

The first Jews were brought to Nováky in late 1941, but the camp expanded greatly in 1942, when the Germans began the mass deportation of Slovak Jews. Nováky was created due to the efforts of the Slovak Jewish Center, which had petitioned the Slovak government to establish camps where Jews could work and be spared from deportation. Nováky, one of the largest labor camps in Slovakia, held 1,600 Jewish prisoners. Most were skilled craftsmen and carpenters who worked in workshops.

As the Final Solution took shape, the resulting increase in deportation of Slovak Jews led to transformations in the utilization of the Slovak labor camps. The first Jews were brought to Nováky in late 1941, but the camp began operating in earnest in mid-1942, when the Germans began the mass deportation of Slovak Jewry. The products produced there were high-quality and made the camp an economic success. Nováky was run by a council representing a Jewish community that managed to manipulate the Slovak camp commandant, who was a drunk. The conditions at the camp were not bad. Food rations were adequate, the prisoners ran their own school, medical clinics, and welfare institutions, and cultural activities such as drama, religious studies, and sports were allowed. In fact, the camp even had a swimming pool. An underground was also in existence at Nováky.

Vyhne Concentration Camp

The labor camp at Vyhne was established in early 1940 to house 326 Jewish refugees from Prague who had been imprisoned in Sosnowiec, Poland. The group was brought to Slovakia by the Slovak Jewish Center. Ultimately, most of the 326 successfully reached Palestine. In March 1942, the Germans began the mass deportation of Slovak Jewry. At that point, the Jewish Center asked the Slovak government to establish camps where Jews could work and be spared from deportation. Soon Vyhne was also turned into a Jewish work center. The Jews at these camps showed the Germans how valuable they were as workers. In Vyhne, they developed a productive textile industry. In addition, the conditions at the camp were not bad. The prisoners received adequate food rations, the children there had a school, and the inmates were even allowed to leave the camp from time to time. The commandant was a member of the Hlinka Guard.

The beating and physical abuse of Jews was relatively common, as was the humiliation associated with cutting chin or hair, shown in suggestive photographs that have been preserved in small numbers to this day. They searched for hidden valuables, robbed them of personal needs, entertained with extortion, who promised to help or meet relatives, of course for money, or raped the concentrated Jewish women. On the other hand, there were occasions when in return for the young Jewess giving her body to the guard, he did not hesitate to equip her and her husband with a pass that saved them from being transported.

Despite the fact that robbing and rape had actually happened, Mach declared that "the transports and centers are under the supervision of the Guardsmen who take care of them. It is very well looked after for health, supply and other such matters, so there is absolutely no way of saying that the Jews are being treated abruptly and no longer inhumane."

In the context of Mach's statement, it is interesting to observe how some guardsmen treated Jews in labor camps in Vyhne, Sereď, and Nováky, and in labor centers. Of the Jewish Code, all Jews aged sixteen to sixty, who did not do work under Section 38 of the Armed Forces Act, were required to do the work assigned to them by the Ministry of the Interior. For this reason, labor camps for Jews began to be set up, which were supervised directly under the Hlinka Guard.

The Hlinka Guard thus again, as in several previous cases, assisted the state apparatus in the implementation of restrictive regulations, which was certainly a pleasure for many guard members. One group may have seen their guardian duty in guarding the camps, but a large group of guards used their function to enrich themselves and supply themselves with various commodities available to some Jews.

One of the overseers of the labor camp in Nováky, guard Stefan Antala, even criticized the camp commander for allegedly breaking rules about fraternizing with Jews. The subject of the dispute was the birthday of the camp commander Jozef Polhor, in which guardsmen and Jews entertained themselves. Several Jewish women were also present at the party, who were supposed to take care of those present. The positive attitude of some guards to alcohol and entertainment seems to have overshadowed their declared perception of a solution to the Jewish question.

The Nazis did not have a high opinion of the Hlinka Guard's co-operation in the implementation of anti-Jewish regulations. In its regular reports, the SD often criticized Hlinka Guards for not being primarily ideological, but focusing on self-enrichment. Among other things, they wrote:

> Jews' strong corruption and bribery have also hit Hlinka Guard leaders. By paying a certain amount of the Jews' money to the respective Hlinka Guard sites, it was possible to postpone the displacement or to give way to another form. Since the leaders themselves did not act consistently on the Jewish question, it is difficult to expect such behavior from subordinates.

By bribes, the Jews were able to achieve the concession of Hlinka Guard members assisting in transports or searches. It was even found that members of the transport crew staying during the coffee breaks were sitting at a table with the Jews they were supervising and had received money from. When they arrived at the collection camp, all valuables and money were taken away, but only a part of them was handed over to their superiors.

In addition to the guard service in labor camps or concentration centers, the guardsmen also participated in the search of forests, secluded houses, cottages, and even flats for actions and raids and searched houses of people sheltering Jews. Guardsmen, as companions to the security forces, were supposed to search out all the forests, cottages, kennels, bricks, quarries, and other places where "Jews or anti-state elements" could hide.

The guardsmen were also enthused by the fact that at the concentration camps were instructors. SS non-commissioned officers, who had already had experience of similar events outside Slovakia, became a model for many guardsmen. On the other hand, the Jews, who had experience in both labor camps and transports, claimed that in many cases the guards began to behave brutally during the transports, even though they were relatively milder as labor camp guards. In the initial period, however, the deportations took place without a legal basis, even though in the initial phase Mach claimed that "we are proceeding exactly according to the law." It was not until May 15, 1942 that the removal of Jews was legalized. The Assembly of the Slovak Republic passed the following Constitutional Act:

68th Constitutional Act of May 15, 1942 on the Eviction of Jews.

§ 1.

Jews can be evicted from the territory of the Slovak Republic.

§ 2.

(1) The provision of § 1 does not apply:

(a) to persons who, at the latest on March 14, 1939, became members of a Christian religion,

(b) to persons who have a valid marriage with a Gentile, before 14 September 1941.

(2) Persons to whom the President of the Republic has granted or will be granted an exemption pursuant to Section 255 of Regulation No. 198/1941 Sl. z., furthermore doctors, pharmacists, veterinarians, engineers and other persons, if the competent ministry deems it necessary to keep them in public, technical or economic life.

(3) The exemption from expulsion (paragraphs 1 and 2) shall also apply to the spouse, minor children and, in the case of par. 1, par. (a) to the parents of the exempt persons.

§ 3.

(1) Expatriate Jews and Jews who have left or leave the territory of the state lose their citizenship of the Slovak Republic.

(2) Assets of persons referred to in para. 1 is forfeited to the State. The State guarantees the creditors only up to the value of the assets taken over.

§ 4.

(1) The movable property of persons referred to in § 2 shall be kept and owned by them. The right to repayment of movables withdrawn from their possession before May 16, 1942 under their previous regulations cannot be brought before the courts.
(2) Special rules shall apply to live and dead agricultural inventory.

§ 5.

(1) In order to implement the provisions of § 1 and § 3, in particular to liquidate the personal and property legal situation of expatriate Jews as well as Jews who have left the territory of the Slovak Republic, the Government shall issue the necessary regulations by decree even if the Constitution requires regulation.
(2) Regulations issued pursuant to para. 1 are valid, signed by the Prime Minister and all its members, and are declared in the Slovak Terminology.

§ 6.

Regulations on the legal status of Jews, as long as they limit the personal and property circumstances of a non-Jewish spouse of a Jew, cease to be effective on the day this Act is promulgated.

§ 7.

This constitutional law shall apply and shall enter into force on the date of promulgation. Members of the government: Dr. Tiso, Dr. Sokol, Dr. Tuka, Mach, Sivák, Dr. Pružinský, Dr. Medrický, Minister Stan Fritz, Chatlos.

First Transports: 1942

Date	Source	Destination	Number of Deportees
March 25–26	Poprad	Auschwitz	997
March 27	Žilina	Majdanek	1,000
March 27–28	Patrónka	Auschwitz	1,002
March 28–30	Sered	Majdanek	1,000
March 30–31	Nováky	Majdanek	1,003
April 1–2	Patrónka	Auschwitz	965
April 2–3	Poprad	Auschwitz	997
April 5	Žilina	Majdanek	1,495
			TOTAL: 8,459

The Hlinka Guards welcomed the beginning of the departure of the first Jews from Slovakia on March 27, 1942. Already a month before, even with the participation of number of Guards, the district authorities were to make an inventory of Jews aged sixteen to sixty years. This was to take place in front of the attendance commission, which was to feature the district Hlinka Guard commander. According to Nazi observers, the mass "baptism of Jews" began with the start of deportations.

Jews were more systematically concentrated from the beginning of March 1942. Under the regulations, they sent deportation notices to the Jews only four hours before they were to depart to prevent them from escaping or hiding. Guard members were invited to perform guard services in concentration camps as well as during loading into transports. Following the Hlinka Guard regulations, they were not be tempted by sentimentality or sensitivity. To ensure the deportations, the commanders were to choose only the best and with the "firm backbone of the Guards" to avoid any suspicion, in the event of shame on the goodwill of the Hlinka Guard. According to the Hlinka Guard, it was evident that the Jews would do their utmost to evade this order and try to escape by suicide or something else. The guards had to create patrols to observe the movement of Jews in the villages, their behavior, travel, contact with Aryans, and anything that would interfere with the smooth concentration of Jews.

The aim of the Hlinka Guard was to export all Jews from Slovak territory without the possibility of their return, so guardsmen should not have to look at individual cases in terms of their pain but in terms of national interests. According to Mach, referring to human feelings, there would be "unprecedented brutality against those who fought against the Bolshevik revolution and the Jew." For this reason, anyone who was sentimentality or expressed human compassion could not be a guard in the concentration center. As in the case of labor camps, radically anti-Jewish guards were to be chosen.

The original deportation plan, approved in February 1942 by the German and Slovak governments, entailed the deportation of 7,000 single women aged sixteen to thirty-five to Auschwitz and 13,000 single men aged sixteen to forty-five to Majdanek as forced laborers. The cover name for the operation was *Aktion* (Action) David. The SS officer and Jewish adviser Dieter Wisliceny and Slovak officials promised that deportees would not be mistreated and would be allowed to return home after a fixed period. Initially, many Jews believed that it was better to report for deportation than risk reprisals against their families for failing to do so. However, 3,000 of the 7,000 women who were supposed to be deported refused to report as ordered. Methods of escape included sham marriages, being sent away to live with relatives, or being hidden temporarily by non-Jews. The Hlinka Guard struggled to meet its targets. As a result, only 3,800 women and 4,500 men were deported during the initial phase of deportations. Nevertheless, they opened a new chapter in the history of the Holocaust because the Slovak women were the first Jewish prisoners in Auschwitz. Their arrival precipitated the conversion of the camp into an extermination camp.

Department 14, a subsidiary of Slovakia's Central Economic Office, organized the transports, while the Slovak Transport Ministry provided the cattle cars. Members of the Hlinka Guard, the *Freiwillige Schutzstaffel*, and the *gendarmerie* were in charge of rounding up the Jews, guarding the transit centers, and eventually loading them into overcrowded cattle cars for deportation. Transports were timed to reach the Slovak border at Čadca at 4:28 a.m.; they left Patrónka, Poprad, and Nováky in the evening, and Žilina at 3:20 a.m. In Zwardon at 8:30 a.m., the Hlinka Guard turned the transports over to the German Schutzpolizei (Security Police). The transports would arrive in Auschwitz the same afternoon and at Majdanek the next morning.

With Poland under Hitler's regime, parents thought it best to send their Jewish daughters to safety in Slovakia, which was not yet occupied by Nazi Germany. But it turned out Slovakia was not safe at all.

"You will not need those anymore," a member of the paramilitary Hlinka Guards said to the young Jewish women when he took their earrings and gold chains. They were lying on straw in one of the houses in Poprad, waiting for the train that would take them to a forced labor camp. They were not aware of the fact that they would in fact go to Auschwitz in a few days. "At that point we still thought it was just a joke," Laura Špániková, who was twenty years old back then, remembers. Witnesses said that rumor had it that the transports would take people to work in Slovak factories. The father of the then-eighteen-year-old Edita Grosmanova thought so too. When her mother wanted her to escape from the forced labor camp to Hungary, he refused saying, "it is a bad law, but it is the law." Grosmanova was taken to a school where the women met an SS officer and a doctor. She also remembers people were not scared back then, they were singing and joking while waiting in the school.

On March 25, 1942, the first transport train left Poprad at 8 p.m. Before its departure, Wisliceny spoke to the deportees on the platform, saying that they would be allowed to return home after they finished the work that Germany had planned for them. The first deportees were unaware of what lay ahead and tried to be optimistic. According to survivors, songs in Hebrew and Slovak were sung as the first two transports of women to Auschwitz left the platforms.

"The first scary feelings came when we were taken to the cattle cars," Grosmanova said. The train car was dark, the only light sifted through the cracks between the boards. Tens of women only had two buckets available. One for their physiological needs, another one with drinking water. It was hard for them to tell how long they travelled. "We were hungry and cold. It was a terribly cold March," one of the women from the transport said.

A total 997 young women, 297 of them teenagers, found themselves on the first transport to Auschwitz, ordered by the Reich Security Services. They arrived at the camp, their destination a shock to all of them. "We arrived in Auschwitz, an empty place!" one survivor says. "There was nothing there. Nothing! Just snow-filled fields with nothing visible for miles but some boxes with lights." The Nazis intended to deport 999 Jewish women, but their list contained duplicates, resulting in only 997 women actually deported.

Obsessed with occult mysticism, the leaders of the Third Reich were not beyond using whatever practices they could to secure victory. Himmler was an avid astrologer; Goebbels was fascinated by Nostradamus. The number 999 was used by Nostradamus who wrote: "At the judgement, although there be 999 who condemn a man, he shall be saved if one plead for him." Perhaps this use of pagan mythology is why the number of 999 girls was chosen.

It was the men's prison camp where the girls were housed for the next five months. Stripped naked, shorn like sheep, and tattooed like cattle, they had large, awkward four-digit numbers, starting with 1,000, inked onto the outside of their forearms. The Slovak women were the first Jewish prisoners in Auschwitz. Their arrival advanced the conversion of the camp into an extermination camp. Most of the Slovak Jewish women deported to Auschwitz in 1942 who survived the war were from the first two transports in March, because they were younger and stronger. Those from eastern Slovakia were especially likely to be young, because most Jews from that area were Haredim (a member of any of various Orthodox Jewish sects characterized by strict adherence to the traditional form of Jewish law) and tended to marry young: more than half were aged twenty-one or younger. The women deported from Bratislava were older on average because they married later in life and some did not marry at all; only 40 percent were twenty-one or younger.

The segregation of Jews from economic and social life, and their exclusion from a long list of professions led the authorities to send the now unemployed and impoverished Jews to forced labor camps. In 1941, the Ministry of Interior ordered the Jewish Center to organize forced Jewish labor in work centers and work commandos. Unemployed Jews, most of whom were merchants, intellectuals, or students between the ages of eighteen and sixty, were forced to report for work details. The Jewish Center (Jewish institution established by the Slovak government in 1940 to run Jewish affairs) set up vocational training courses to impart basic skills in agriculture and industry to those Jews who had to report for forced labor, while at the same time searching for work for them. Forced Jewish labor was employed in the construction of railways, the paving of roads, the diversion of rivers and other manual labors. In September 1941, there were some eighty centers for forced labor in Slovakia, employing 5,440 Jewish men. At the end of 1941, many of these centers closed, and the Jews were concentrated in three labor camps located within Slovakian borders—Sereď, Nováky, and Vyhne.

SS leader Reinhard Heydrich visited Bratislava on April 10, 1942. He and Vojtech Tuka agreed that further deportations would target whole families and eventually remove all Jews from Slovakia. Ostensibly, the change was to avoid separating families, but it also solved the problem of caring for the children and elderly family members of able-bodied deportees. The family transports began on April 11 and took their victims to the Lublin district.

This change disrupted the SS's plans in the Lublin district. Instead of able-bodied male Slovak Jews being deported to Majdanek, the SS needed to prepare space for

Slovak Jewish families in the region's overcrowded ghettos. The transports from Slovakia were the largest and longest of all the deportations of Jews to the Lublin District.

The trains went through two railway distribution points, in Nałęczów and Lublin, where they were met by a ranking SS officer. In Lublin, there was usually a selection and able-bodied men were selected for labor at Majdanek, while the remainder were sent to ghettos along the rail lines. For the trains that went through Nałęczów, the Jews were dispatched to locations seeking forced labor, usually without separating families. Most of the trains brought their victims, 30,000 in total, to ghettos whose inhabitants had been recently deported to the Bełżec or Sobibór death camps, as part of a "revolving door" policy in which foreign Jews were brought in to replace those murdered. The final transports to the Lublin district occurred during the first half of June 1942; ten transports stopped briefly at Majdanek, where able-bodied men (generally those aged fifteen to fifty) were selected for labor; the trains continued to Sobibór, where the remaining victims were murdered.

The family transports were marked by scenes that horrified many non-Jewish Slovaks, such as Hlinka Guard men chasing and assaulting Jews in the streets and stealing the last of their possessions. The victims were given only four hours warning to prevent them from escaping. Beatings and forcible beard shaving were commonplace, as was subjecting Jews to invasive searches to uncover hidden valuables. Although some guards and local officials accepted bribes to keep Jews off the transports, the victim would typically be deported on the next train. Others took advantage of their power to rape Jewish women. Official exemptions were supposed to keep Jews from being deported, but local authorities sometimes deported exemption holders.

Most groups stayed only briefly in the Lublin ghettos before they were deported again to the death camps, while a few remained in the ghettos for months or years. Several thousand of the deportees ended up in the forced-labor camps in the Lublin area, such as Poniatowa, Końskowola, and Krychów. Unusually, the deportees in the Lublin area were quickly able to establish contact with the Jews remaining in Slovakia, which led to extensive aid efforts. However, the fate of the Jews deported from Slovakia was ultimately sealed within the framework of Operation Reinhard, along with that of the Polish Jews. Of the estimated 8,500 men who were deported directly to Majdanek, only 883 were still alive by July 1943. Another few thousand Slovak Jews were deported to Majdanek following the liquidation of ghettos in the Lublin district, but most of them were murdered immediately. The remaining Slovak Jews at Majdanek were shot during Operation Harvest Festival; the only significant group of Slovak Jews to remain in Lublin district was a group of about 100 at the Luftwaffe camp in Dęblin-Irena.

Transports to Lublin

Date	Source	Destination	Number of Deportees
April 11–13	Trnava	Lubartów/Majdanek	1,040
April 14–15	Nitra	Lubartów/Majdanek	1,038
April 16–17	Nitra	Rejowiec/Majdanek	1,048
April 20	Nitra	Rejowiec	1,030
April 21–22	Topoľčany	Sereď	1,001
April 27	Nové Mesto, Piešťany, and Hlohovec	Opole	1,382
May 5–7	Trebišov	Lubartów/Majdanek	1,040
May 6–8	Michalovce	Łuków	1,038
May 7–9	Michalovce	Łuków	1,040
May 8	Michalovce	Międzyrzec Podlaski	1,025
May 11	Humenné	Chełm	1,009
May 12	Žilina	Chełm	1,002
May 13	Prešov	Dęblin–Irena	1,040
May 14	Prešov	Dęblin–Irena	1,040
May 17–20	Bardejov	Końskowola	1,028
May 18	Bardejov	Opole	1,015
May 19	Vranov	Opole	1,005
May 20	Medzilaborce	Końskowola	1,630
May 23 or 27	Sabinov/Prešov	Rejowiec	1,630
May 24–25	Poprad	Rejowiec	1,000
May 24 or 28	Stropkov	Rejowiec	1,022
May 25 or 26–May 29	Spišská Nová Ve	Izbica/Majdanek	1,052
May 29–30	Poprad	Izbica/Majdanek	1,000
May 30	Žilina	Opole	1,000
May 30–June 1	Poprad	Sobibór/Majdanek	1,000
June 2	Liptovský Svätý Mikuláš	Sobibór/Majdanek	1,014
June 5	Bratislava/Žilina	Sobibór/Majdanek	1,000
June 7	Bratislava/Žilina	Sobibór/Majdanek	1,000
June 8	Žilina	Sobibór/Majdanek	1,001
June 9	Zvolen/Kremnica	Sobibór/Majdanek	1,019
June 11	Nováky	Sobibór/Majdanek	1,000
June 12	Sereď/Žilina	Sobibór/Majdanek	1,000
June 12–13	Poprad	Sobibór/Majdanek	1,000
June 14	Nováky/Žilina	Sobibór/Majdanek	1,000
			TOTAL: 34,135

Transit Ghettos

Transit ghettos were established and located close to the main railway lines heading for the final destinations. The condition of life in these small provincial Polish towns was very primitive. There was lack of water and food, old and mostly wooden houses, demolished during the deportations of their owners to the death camps. These places were not prepared to absorb thousands of people at any given time. Therefore, the ghettos were overcrowded with ten to twenty people per room and with many starving and dying of malnutrition. The situation in Izbica or Piaski, one of the towns having a closed ghetto, can be compared with the Warsaw Ghetto, but in a micro-scale. Among the deportees were many doctors, but there was no real possibility in helping people due to the lack of hospitals and drugs. In the memoirs of the witnesses from Izbica, there is mention of many victims succumbing to the typhus epidemic.

Chełm Transit Ghetto

At the beginning of September 1939, Chełm was occupied by Nazi Germany, but on September 25, the Germans withdrew in advance of Soviet forces. The Ribbentrop–Molotov agreement held that Chełm should be under German control, and on October 9, the city was ceded back to Nazi Germany. During their brief period in Chełm, the Soviet authorities established a civil government under a Jewish major, who was a Soviet sympathizer. Fearing reprisal from the Polish residents in Chełm, hundreds of Jews fled together with the retreating Red Army. Immediately following the German occupation, the Jews who remained in Chełm were attacked and brutalized, in part because of their central role during the brief Communist occupation.

On December 1, 1939, over 1,000 Jews were murdered during the first deportation from Chełm. The commander of the German forces in Chełm ordered the leader of the Jewish community to concentrate 2,000 Jewish men between the ages of sixteen and sixty in the market square where some were murdered. The rest were taken to Hrubieszow. Some 1,000 Jewish men were murdered *en route*. About 400 were forced to swim across the icy Bug River, and most of them drowned. A few hundred of the deportees managed to survive and returned to Chełm.

In December 1939, a ten-member *Judenrat* (a council representing a Jewish community) was established in Chełm, and almost a year later, at the end of October 1940, the Chełm ghetto was established in a poverty-stricken neighborhood at the edge of the city. At this time, the Jews of Chełm were required to relocate to the area within the ghetto walls. A few months later, at the beginning of 1941, dozens of Jews were deported from Chełm and forcibly relocated to the Wlodawa ghetto. This process continued until the end of March 1941. During this period, the Germans confiscated the property of the Jews of Chełm, demanding that they report for forced labor, and from time to time requiring large monetary payments to ensure the "safety" of the community. In May 1941, some 2,000 Slovakian Jews were deported to Chełm. From the end of 1941, exit from the ghetto was banned. German and Polish policemen were placed as guards at the ghetto's gates, and a Jewish Order Police of 150 men was established to maintain control inside the ghetto. Stricken by hunger and overcrowding, a typhus epidemic claimed many lives. Many Jews attempted to smuggle food from outside the ghetto; some were apprehended and summarily executed for their actions by the Germans.

During the ghetto period, the Germans continued to fill work quotas for forced labor companies from the Jewish population. For some of those conscripted, forced labor meant relocation to distant labor camps. At the same time, Jews from nearby towns in the Lublin district were concentrated in the Chełm ghetto. They arrived with no belongings, following forced marches where they had been tortured by the Germans, and forced to watch the execution of hundreds of their fellows.

Dęblin-Irena Transit Ghetto

Dęblin-Irena was a Nazi ghetto for Jews in Irena, a Polish town located in Puławy County in the Lublin District of the General Governorate. Initially, it was an open ghetto; many Jews worked on labor projects for various local firms, especially the railway and the Luftwaffe. Beginning in May 1941, the ghetto became a collection center with Jews sent there from the Opole and Warsaw ghettos. Until late 1942, Jews earned wages as forced laborers. Many were conscripted to work for German companies such as Schwartz and Hochtief. These firms were hired to do construction on the military bases in the town; Schultz was under contract for construction on the Austrian Eastern Railway. Dęblin Fortress, which had been taken over by the *Wehrmacht* and where around 200 Jews from the ghetto worked, was the site of Stalag 307, a Soviet prisoner-of-war camp from July 10, 1941. The Jews could favorably compare their situation to that of the Soviet prisoners. The municipality conscripted other Jews for tasks such as street cleaning or snow clearing; these workers were not paid. The Jews from Dęblin-Irena tried to take the best jobs, so 200 of the Slovak deportees ended up working for the municipality. Another 200 of the Slovaks worked for the Schultz firm following an expansion. Survivors recalled that although German soldiers supervising the forced laborers tended to treat them relatively well, some Polish supervisors beat Jews and the Ukrainian guards at the railway camp were especially harsh.

The first deportation was on May 6, 1942 and took around 2,500 Jews to Sobibór extermination camp. In October 1942, the ghetto was liquidated; about 2,500 Jews were deported to Treblinka extermination camp while some 1,400 Jews were retained as inmates of forced-labor camps in the town. Many of the Slovak Jews, not knowing what to expect, had lingered in the ghetto while packing their bags. About 215 to 500 Jews were shot while clearing the houses. Between 2,000 and 2,500 people were deported to Treblinka extermination camp; mostly the Slovaks.

Izbica Transit Ghetto

Created by Nazi Germany in Izbica in occupied Poland, the Izbica ghetto was a Jewish ghetto, serving as a transfer point for deportation of Jews from Poland,

Germany, Austria, and Czechoslovakia to Bełżec and Sobibór extermination camps. The ghetto was created in 1941, although the first transports of Jews from the German Reich started arriving there as early as 1940. Izbica was the largest transit ghetto in the Lublin reservation, with death rate almost equal to that of the Warsaw ghetto.

The Jews who lived in Izbica were kept separate from the new arrivals. They were housed on the other side of the railroad tracks. Also, the Jews shipped in from Germany and Austria were differentiated from Polish Jews by the color of the obligatory star of David signs, yellow for German, and blue for the Polish Jews. In order to make space for the incoming transports, 2,200 local Jews were sent to the Belzec death camp on March 24, 1942.

Between March and May 1942, approximately 12,000 to 15,000 new Jews were transported to Izbica from across Europe as part of secretive Operation Reinhard; among them engineers, doctors, economists, army generals, and professors from Vienna, The Hague, Heidelberg, and Breslau, including the vice-president of Prague. They were housed in a few wooden barracks which could accommodate about half of the prisoners, pressed against each other like sardines. The rest were forced to subsist outdoors. Jews stayed in the barracks usually for no more than four days, with almost nothing to eat. Many victims succumbed to typhus due to poor sanitary conditions in the ghetto. The foreigners, many of whom were proficient in German, had an easier time identifying with their Nazi oppressors than the Polish Jews from inside the ghetto. Denunciations were commonplace.

In the early stage of the ghetto existence, the Nazis destroyed the local Jewish cemetery. The tombstones were desecrated and used to build walls of a new prison. The entire ghetto in Izbica was liquidated beginning November 2, 1942, which led to a week of horrific killings at the cemetery. Several thousand Jews (estimated at 4,500) were massacred by the Sonderdienst battalion of Ukrainian Trawnikis in an assembly-line-style and dumped into hastily dug mass graves.

Końskowola Transit Ghetto

Końskowola is a small town near Pulawy, Lublin province, Poland. Before the outbreak of World War II, there were about 1,100 Jews in Końskowola. At the end of 1940, a ghetto was established there. On May 8, 1942, 1,600 of the 2,000 Jews in the ghetto (including refugees) were sent to Sobibór to be replaced by about 3,000 Jews from Slovakia and additional refugees. Many groups of Jews were relocated, including Jews expelled from Slovakia. On May 8, 1942, the Nazis rounded up all the Jews and transported them to the Nazi extermination camp Sobibór. Around 3,000 of them were sent to labor camps and in October 1942, 1,000 unproductive Jews, including women and children, were executed outside the town. The labor camps were liquidated in May 1943.

Lubartów Transit Ghetto

Established by Nazi Germany in occupied Poland, it existed officially from 1941 until October 1942. The Polish Jews of the town of Lubartów were confined there initially.

The ghetto inmates also included Jews deported from other cities in the vicinity including Lublin and Ciechanów and the rest of German occupied Europe for the total of 3,500 Jews in its initial stages including 2,000 Jews from Slovakia. In May 1942, additional transport from Slovakia with 2,421 Jews arrived.

The deportation of Jews to the nearby towns of Firlej, Ostrów Lubelski, and Kamionka, started at the beginning of November 1939. All of the Jews were told to leave. There were, though, a few who stayed to work for the German Army. They were exiled from Lubartów until September 1940. The ghetto area around the two marketplaces of Lubartów were still in existence when the Jews returned from slave labor projects. A communal kitchen was organized for the now poverty-stricken Jews. Deportations were also conducted into the Lubartów Ghetto. An example of this is the transport of 1,000 Jews from Ciechanów. In addition, by May 1942, some 2,421 Slovakian Jews had been deported to Lubartów.

The first deportation to a death camp aboard Holocaust trains took place on April 9, 1942, the last day of Passover. On the first day, 800 Jews who did not have work cards were ordered to go to the railway station, from which they were taken to Belzec extermination camp. The last one of the train deportations to Belzec was on October 11, 1942, with 3,000 Jews sent to their deaths. Some of these deportees were sent to Majdanek, with the others going to the death camp in Treblinka. Jews that were found to be hiding were shot. In total, the number of Jews found after last deportation numbered 300. After a while, the Jews that were found were instead deported to the Piaski ghetto.

Jews who worked for the German Army were shot on January 29, 1943. After the last deportations, the synagogues and cemeteries were destroyed. The gravestones were used in a pavement at a *Wehrmacht* base. Lubartów was declared Jew-free by the Nazis in February 1943.

Łuków Transit Ghetto

The town was a stopover on the way to the gas chambers for thousands of Jews from the neighboring villages, many Polish towns, and even from other countries. In December 1939, more than 2,500 Jews from Serock, Nasielsk, and Suwałki were displaced to Łuków, a year later almost 1,000 Jews from Mława, and in May 1942 more than 2,000 Jews from Slovakia.

The first mass executions of Łuków Jews started in March 1942. At that time, Germans shot forty-seven people. In the summer, the Jews were forbidden to leave the town. A regular action of liquidation of the Jewish community started on October 5, 1942. On that day, about 4,000 people were transported to the Treblinka extermination camp and about 500 were executed in the town. Another 2,000 people were transported to Treblinka on October 8. After this action, the area of ghetto was decreased and the Jews from the neighboring towns and villages were forced to come to Łuków. After that, between October 26 and 27 and between November 7 and 11, another 4,000 people were taken to Treblinka and a few hundred more Jews were executed at the magistrate court of the Łuków and in the Jewish cemetery. The Jews who survived were closed in the ghetto at the beginning of December and there were regular executions. The ghetto was finally liquidated on May 2, 1943, when SS troops deported about 4,000 people to Treblinka. From 1942 and 1943, around 14,000 Jews from the Łuków ghetto and the neighboring towns and villages were sent to the gas chambers in Treblinka, and approximately 2,000 Jews were executed in the town.

Międzyrzec Podlaski Transit Ghetto

At the end of September 1939, during the Soviet invasion of Poland, the Red Army occupied the city of Międzyrzec Podlaski. At the beginning of October, the Soviet Union handed over the city to Germany as part of the German–Soviet Frontier Treaty amended to the secret Hitler–Stalin Pact against Poland in 1939. Following the exchange, approximately 2,000 of the city's Jews left for the territories of Poland annexed by the Soviet Union. The Germans set up a transfer ghetto in the historic neighborhood of Szmulowizna. It held 20,000 Jewish prisoners at its peak. On August 25–26, 1942 some 11,000–12,000 Jews were rounded up by German Order Police battalions amid gunfire and screams and deported to the Treblinka extermination camp.

The next mass extermination action took place around October and November 1942. "Strip-search" of young Jewish women was introduced by *Oberleutnant* Hartwig Gnade before executions dubbed "mopping up" actions. His first sergeant later said: "I must say that First Lieutenant Gnade gave me the impression that the entire business afforded him a great deal of pleasure." The wave of mass killings lasting non-stop for several days were conducted by the Trawniki battalion of about 350–400 men, while the Germans from the parallel Reserve Police Battalion 101 of the *Ordnungspolizei* from Hamburg dealt with the thousands of ghetto inhabitants.

On July 17, 1943, the ghetto was liquidated, with all remaining Jews deported to Treblinka and Majdanek extermination camps; at which time the last 160–200 residents were shot, and the city was officially declared free of Jews.

Opole Transit Ghetto

On February 15, 1941, and February 26, 1941, two deportation transports with 2,003 Jewish men, women, and children on board left Vienna Aspang Station bound for Opole, a small town south of Lublin. Opole had a long-established Jewish community; when war broke out, about 4,000 Jews lived here, i.e. about 70 percent of the population, a proportion which rose further after the beginning of the war, as Jews from other parts of Poland were forcefully resettled here.

By March 1941, about 8,000 Jews were deported to the ghetto which had been set up in Opole. The new arrivals were either lodged with resident Jewish families, or in mass accommodation, as for example in a synagogue or in newly erected huts. Beyond Jews from Vienna, the deportees included at least a small set of Jews from Czechoslovakia.

In the ghetto itself no restriction was placed on the freedom of movement of the inmates, and there were no boundary lines, yet it was forbidden on the threat of severe punishment to leave Opole without official permission. Control of the ghetto was undertaken by the security service of the SS, the *gendarmerie*, and also, as may be concluded from witness testimonies, by German Army soldiers. The inhabitants of the ghetto were largely dependent on themselves as far as earning a living was concerned. From May 1941, about 800 men capable of work were deployed as forced laborers in Deblin. The liquidation of Opole ghetto began as early as the spring of 1942. A transport to Belzec extermination camp left on March 31, 1942, and deportations to Sobibór followed in May and October 1942.

Rejowiec Transit Ghetto

In February 1941, the German Police ordered Jews to take the Torah scrolls and holy books outside and set them on fire. The Jews were ordered to dance around the flames. Soon after the synagogue and the prayer house were destroyed and all the Jews were removed from the center of the town to the outskirts, later during 1941 the Germans deported 1,300 Jews from Lublin and Krakow into already overcrowded accommodation.

On the April 7, 1942, the Nazis gathered about 2,000 Jews and drove them like cattle to the railway station. Many elderly people and children who could not keep up were murdered on the way to the station. This transport went to the newly constructed death camp at Sobibór, which was some 70 km from Rejowiec. Once the Polish Jews had been transported to certain death, over 5,000 Czech and Slovak Jews filled their place, thus turning Rejowiec into another transit ghetto in the Lublin Region.

In the summer of 1942, German and Ukrainian policemen accused the local Jewish community of killing one of their officers, and in retaliation several dozen Jews were locked in their homes and massacred with grenades. One unknown survivor who was deported from Slovakia managed to write to their local *Judenrat* via the Polish Underground about one such deportation and experiences in various camps:

> Our transport consisting of about 1,000 Jews was deported from Sabinov via Zilna, Cadoa directly to Poland. At the boundary we were told to line up and counted by the SD Sicherheistdienst on the station, while the women were counted in the carriages. Then we continued our journey for 3 or 4 days until we reached Rejowiec, where we left the carriages. During the whole of this time we suffered from thirst as we were given water on two occasions only, and no food at all, but we had left provided with plenty of provisions. In Rejowiec we were received by the inspector of the waterworks in Chełm, the SA district commander of the district and 9 members of the Jewish Police in Rejowiec, with their senior and head, Kessler, the eldest of the Jewish community, who helped us.
>
> On the next day, May 27, two transports of a size similar to ours arrived from Stropkov and Humenńe, so that we were then altogether 3,000 Slovakian Jews. On Chol Hamoed Pessach the Rejowiec Jews were deported, so that we found only about 3,000 Rejowiec Jews still in the Ghetto, as well as 60 Jews from the Protectorate, and some women from Nitra. As lodgings we got the houses formerly belonging to Jews,

> but as there was a scarcity of lodgings, 20 to 25 people had to squeeze into a room of 3 by 4 meters. For eight days nobody watched or cared for us, and there was a terrible confusion. We were given no food and of the valuable provisions which we had got at Zilina, the best portion, mostly spices were taken away from us, and the remainder stored in the schools. After a fortnight, when the food was completely spoilt and unfit for consumption, it was given back to us.

After a while, the 3,000 Slovakian Jews were asked to apply for swamp-draining work, but only strong men, altogether 450 men, went to work. Fathers of more than three children were excluded. Those people received 250 grams of bread daily, a thin barley-groats soup for lunch, and a black coffee for supper. Another 500–600 young people were ordered to the nearby camps like Sawin, Sajocice, and Chełm, where there was a SA formation in charge, without consideration of their families. Those people were selected by the Jewish Security Police, who accepted bribes.

Nobody cared or provided for the remaining 2,000 Slovak Jews. But after three or four weeks, the Jewish Council in Chełm founded a communal kitchen, which provided the Jews with a plate of soup. Due to insufficient food and impossible sanitary conditions, many cases of typhus, dysentery, and other epidemics occurred and caused many deaths among the older people.

On August 9, 1942, German police suddenly ordered a general line-up, the entire Jewish population, including the Jews of the ghetto as well as the labor camp, all together about 2,700 people, had to line up on the main square before the school with their luggage. All those who had not been able to obey the order owing to illness or exhaustion were shot in their quarters. The inmates of the Jewish hospital met with the same fate. About 10 a.m., the older people, who were too tired to hold their bags any longer and had set them down to sit on them, were shot in the neck from behind by SS men. Thirty to forty persons were killed in this manner. Orders were then given to march, women walking in front. They were taken over at Rejowiec railway station by the so-called "Black Ukrainians." There they were squeezed into waiting cattle trucks, 120 to 150 persons per truck. The doors were then closed from the outside, and the trucks were left standing at the station until 8 p.m. Twenty-five men were once let out to gather the abandoned pieces of luggage and load them into the trucks. They were baited and maltreated by the Black Ukrainians. It was August and unbearably hot in the trucks, and they were without water or air, but just stood body to body without any room for the slightest movement. A total 150 people died there from suffocation. The trains were on their way to Sobibór. Of the group, about 1,200 men and women were kept there, of whom about 400 were Czechs, 200 Slovaks, the remainder Poles; living conditions were indescribable. Some 200 people each lived in brick barracks 60 meters by 4 meters, there were neither straw nor covers or rugs of any kind, no washing accommodation, only indescribable and incredible filth and vermin.

A moratorium on transports to the east was issued on June 19 due to military campaigns on the Eastern Front. The rest of the family transports (eight in total) were therefore directed to Auschwitz. The first arrived on July 4, which led to the initial selection on the ramp at Auschwitz II-Birkenau, which became a regular event. Most deportees, especially mothers with children, were not chosen for forced labor and instead were killed in gas chambers. By August 1, most of the Jews not exempt from deportation had already been deported or had fled to Hungary, leading to a six-week halt in the transports. An additional three trains departed for Auschwitz in September and October.

For the first three months after the arrival of the first transport in March, Slovak Jewish women were the only female Jewish prisoners in Auschwitz. In mid-August, most of the Slovak Jewish women at Auschwitz were transferred to Auschwitz II-Birkenau, which was still under construction. Conditions were much worse. Employed mostly on outdoor labor details, most of the women died within the first four months at Birkenau. Along with backbreaking physical labor and starvation, many died in epidemics of typhus or malaria and the mass executions ordered by the SS to contain the epidemics. To contain a typhus epidemic in October 1942, the SS murdered 6,000 prisoners—mostly Slovak Jewish women, including some who were healthy. Another selection on December 5 eliminated the last major group of Slovak Jewish women in Birkenau. Of the 404 men who were registered on June 19, only forty-five were still alive six weeks later. By the end of 1942, 92 percent of the deportees had died. This left only 500 or 600 Slovak Jews still alive at Auschwitz and its sub-camps—about half of whom had obtained privileged positions in administration which allowed them to obtain the necessities for survival.

Between March 25 and October 20, 1942, about 57,000 or 58,000 Jews (two-thirds of the population) were deported. The deportations disproportionately affected poor, rural, and Orthodox Jews; although the Šariš-Zemplín region in eastern Slovakia lost 85–90 percent of its Jewish population, Žilina reported that almost half of its Jews remained after the deportation. The deportees were held briefly in camps in Slovakia before deportation; 26,384 from Žilina, 7,500 from Patrónka, 7,000 from Poprad, 4,160 from Sereď, and 4,000 to 5,000 from Nováky. Eighteen trains with 18,746 victims went to Auschwitz, and another thirty-eight transports, with 39,000–40,000 deportees, went to ghettos and concentration and extermination camps in the Lublin district. Only a few hundred survived the war. Czech historian Daniel Putík estimates that only 1.5 percent (around 280 people) of those deported to Auschwitz in 1942 survived, while the death rate of those deported to the Lublin region approached 100 percent.

Starting in the spring of 1942 and continuing until October of that year, Slovak leaders consented to the deportations of about 57,000 Jews from Slovakia to the death and concentration camps at Sobibór, Majdanek, and Auschwitz. After these initial mass deportations, the Slovak leadership suspended the deportations. Until August 1944, Jews were relatively safe in Slovakia. However, in August 1944, the Germans took control of their Slovak ally, crushing the uprising staged by local resistance movements.

In October 1944, the Germans deported about half of the remaining Jews, about 12,600 people, from Slovakia to Auschwitz. These deportations were enabled by the geopolitical turmoil that the Nazis had provoked. On March 15, 1939, Czechoslovakia disappeared from the world map when the Nazis occupied the territory and divided it among three different states. The newly formed Slovakian state was highly authoritarian and dependent upon the Nazi state, and the pre-existing antisemitism intensified rapidly, culminating in the deportations. The spring of 1942 heralded the most difficult time for Jews.

Transports to Auschwitz

Date	Source	Women	Men		Killed in gas chambers
April 12–13	Sered	443	634		1,077
April 17	Žilina	27	973		1,000
April 19	Žilina	536	46		1,000
April 22–23	Poprad	457	543		1,000
April 24	Žilina	558	442		1,000
April 29	Žilina	300	423	300	1,054
June 19–20	Žilina	255	404	341	1,000
July 3–4	Žilina	108	264	628	1,000
July 10–11	Žilina	148	182	670	1,000
July 16–18	Žilina	178	327	459	1,000
July 24–25	Žilina	93	192	715	1,000
July 31–August 1	Žilina	75	165	608	848
September 19	Žilina	71	206	723	1,000
September 23	Žilina	67	294	639	1,000
October 20–21	Žilina	78	121	649	848 or 860
	TOTAL:	3,394	5,216	5,432	14,839

According to a census of December 15, 1940, there were about 88,951 Jews in Slovakia. Between March and October 1942, Slovak *gendarmes*, assisted by Slovak military personnel, units of the Slovak People's Party's Hlinka Guard, and members of the Slovak ethnic German paramilitary formation *Freiwillige Schutzstaffel*, concentrated some 57,000 Slovak Jews in indigenously established labor and concentration camps—mainly in the camps Sered, Nováky, and Vyhne. The Slovak authorities then transported the Jews to the border of the government general or the German Reich and turned them over to German SS and police. German authorities killed virtually all of these Jews in Auschwitz, Lublin/Majdanek, Sobibór, and other locations in German-occupied Poland.

As reports, in part passed on by the Catholic Papal Nuncio in Bratislava, reached the Tiso government that the German authorities were murdering the Slovak Jews in German-occupied Poland, the Slovak President hesitated, and then refused, to deport the remaining 24,000 Jews in Slovakia in the autumn of 1942. During the deportations, some 6,000 Slovak Jews escaped to Hungary.

Even after October 1942, a few thousand Jews remained in Slovakia, mostly protected by exceptions, 144 who were the target of the guardian interest. Although the guards criticized the granting of exceptions, many times they enriched themselves. For example, in an April 14 report, the SD openly criticized the Hlinka Guard's assistance in granting exemptions to Jews.

Radical Hlinka Guard members demanded in letters addressed to various institutions or periodicals to resolve the "Jewish problem," which was to end with the resumption of deportations. Mach's stated that the transports should be renewed for all Jews, regardless of whether or not they were baptized. Mach said:

> What a sign of Judaism has always been clear to us and it seems even more clear to us today, and therefore one of our first duties will be to deal with the others when we have removed 80% of Judaism. We all see what the 20,000 Jews still have here. Whether they are baptized or not baptized, whether or not they have the legitimacy—they all go for one purpose. But March will come, April will come, and the transports will go.

Alexander Mach was not only the commander-in-chief of the Hlinka Guard, but also the minister of the Interior. His statements on the resumption of deportations were taken very seriously. As minister of the Interior, he also issued regulations aimed at restoring deportations. In March 1943, with the participation of the Hlinka Guard security authorities were raided, detaining Jewish persons without work permits, with fake baptismal letters and permits throughout Slovakia. Catholic bishops ordered churches to read a shepherd's letter condemning discriminatory measures against Jews and minorities in Slovakia.

Despite the efforts of the guards, however, the deportations could not be resumed. This was also one of the reasons that later caused Mach's fall in the eyes of radical guards, who later scorned his softness about the ultimate solution to the Jewish question. In their regular situation reports, the Hlinka Guard district headquarters often dealt with the Jewish issue, proving that it was very alive even after the deportations stopped.

The guardsmen continued to enrich themselves at the expense of the remaining Jewish fellow citizens. The regulation on the control of anti-Jewish measures, which they often put into practice with zeal, remained in force. On the other hand, they carried out many actions against the Jews on their own. They tried to extract what they could from what was not yet stolen. An important source of income was the guarding of flats after the Jews had been transported. Although there was a record on the sealing of the apartment with the items found there, many guards often enrich themselves with petty things, from today's perspective, such as soap or objects of daily use.

15

The Slovak National Uprising

From the beginning of 1943, the situation on the Eastern Front started to deteriorate for the Third Reich and its allies. After months of fighting, the Battle of Stalingrad saw the defeat of Nazi forces. Also, the Slovak Rapid Brigade began to retreat from the front. In the process, they lost equipment and materials, effectively losing the character of their motorized unit. Slovak requests for replenishing their supplies, equipment, and horses were answered only by vague promises from the German forces. Desertions of Slovak soldiers to the Soviet side increased dramatically.

The minister of National Defence, General Čatloš, sought to withdraw Slovak forces from the Eastern Front and relocate them to other territories under the Reich's control the in spring 1943. The Germans refused his request and the Security Division was moved from Ukraine to Minsk in Belarus at the end of June 1943. Under the pressure from developments at the front, every soldier still able to fight was needed there. The defeat in the Battle of Kursk sealed the fate of the Reich. From that moment onwards, Germany and their allies would only withdraw, which was presented by the Nazi propaganda as a strategical retreat.

In July 1943, the Allied invasion of Sicily began. After some reorganization in August, the Rapid Brigade was renamed the 1st Infantry Division and the Security Division became 2nd Infantry Division. Desperate pleas by the Slovak Government to control their own forces were futile. Any suggestions for the divisions to only perform security tasks organized under united command, were perceived by the Germans as a sign of doubt about the final victory for Germany.

In October 1943, the 2nd Infantry Division was reorganized and moved to Italy. By the end of the month, more than 2,000 members of the 1st Infantry Division were captured near Melitopol in Ukraine, although a number of them voluntarily walked over to the Soviet side. The division continued disintegrating in the coming months until June 1, 1944, when it was renamed and reorganized as labor unit.

Various sources with information about the real situation on the fronts reached Slovakia. Returning soldiers brought home eyewitness accounts about the supposed successful campaign and strategic retreat of the German Army. Slovak laborers in Germany had already experienced the air raids on industrial targets firsthand. Via London and Moscow radio stations, the Allied representatives repeatedly affirmed their recognition of the Czechoslovak government-in-exile. It became widely known that Slovaks were part of the Czechoslovak units stationed in the Soviet Union and Great Britain. The surrender of Italy in September 1943 also resonated in the public consciousness.

By the end of 1943, the populist regime faced a major internal crisis. It was clear that the coming defeat of the Third Reich would signal an end for them too. Many staff members of the security apparatus as well as members of the Slovak Army realized this. The most active and influential was a group of officers surrounding four commanders: Ján Golian, Mikuláš Ferjenčík, Mirko Vesel, and Dezider Kišša-Kalina. They wanted to coordinate their insurgency with the leadership in exile, President Edvard Beneš and the minister of National Defence in London. In February 1944, they sent an optimistic report on unification of resistance to London. The resistance was also supported by a change in opinion of the Communist movement. While before the war, Moscow Communists condemned even social democrats as enemies, now they encouraged national fronts to unite with all anti-Nazi forces. By the end of 1943, Slovak Communists found a common ground with the representatives of civil resistance surrounding Jozef Lettrich and Ján Ursíny and together they formed the underground Slovak National Council.

Ján Golian was the military leader working on the plan for the uprising. The ideal scenario depended on a deployment of the Field Army, composed of two divisions, in Eastern Slovakia. These units were supposed to allow the Red Army to cross through the Carpathian passes near Bardejov and Medzilaborce. All other units in Slovakia were supposed to secure Central Slovakia, perform a coup, and then contact the Field Army and together with the Soviet forces defeat the Germans. If the Nazi forces would start to occupy Slovakia before this plan was put to action, an emergency plan was in place to start armed resistance immediately, regardless of the state of preparation.

On June 16, 1944, the Apollo Oil Refinery in Bratislava was targeted by a U.S. air raid. The protective arm of Germany was simply an empty phrase by then. The war had reached the Slovak territory. One manifestation of spreading opposition sentiments in the Slovak society was the growth of the partisan movement. Among the partisans were the opponents of the regime, persecuted individuals, former soldiers of the Slovak Army as well as soldiers from the Soviet Army who managed to escape from German captivity. The increase of the partisan activities was supported by Soviet airdrops in the summer of 1944.

As late as August 6, Deputy Prime Minister Alexander Mach told the *Guardsman* newspaper that although there were a few small foreign groups, they had been captured or banished and there was absolutely no need for public concern about partisan danger. The government, however, was greatly concerned about the reports of partisan actions, and deployed the army against them on August 10.

On August 11, 1944, the government declared martial law throughout Slovakia. That allowed them to give stricter sentences, including the death sentence, without a proper trial. The disintegrating regime, however, could not stop the growing partisan movement. By August, there were thousands of partisans in the mountains and their activities were focused on Central Slovakia. The activities of the individual partisan brigades were not yet coordinated with the military headquarters. Partisans led by Soviet officers barred tunnels, looted supply stores, and, by the end of the month, did not hesitate to capture several villages. In Sklabiňa, they publicly declared a new Czechoslovak Republic on August 21, 1944. Several days later, on August 26, 1944, they liberated political prisoners in Ružomberok and occupied the city. The resistance reached a boiling point in Central Slovakia. Partisans started openly attacking the civilian population of German nationality, the local populist functionaries as well as German officers. Sometimes, usually under the command of Soviet leaders, soldiers also joined the attacks. On August 28, 1944, a group of captured German soldiers was executed in Martin. The actions of Soviet partisans accelerated the decision of the Nazis to occupy the Slovak Republic.

Germany, monitoring the partisan activity in Slovakia, decided to act and sent its troops into Slovak territory on August 29, 1944. The resistance was forced to follow the emergency plan and on the same day Ján Golian sent out a coded message to all units to "Begin with evacuation!" which was a call for armed resistance. The next day, the Free Slovak Transmitter in Banská Bystrica also broadcasted the call to mobilization. Thus, the Slovak National Uprising began. The lack of coordination in the resistance soon became apparent and the German forces disarmed two East Slovak divisions as well as the Bratislava unit. The rebels controlled only the area of Central Slovakia with Banská Bystrica as their headquarters. The rebel Slovak National Council prohibited all activities of the Hlinka Guard and the Hlinka Youth organizations, and also dissolved the German and Hungarian national parties. The uprising was committed to the idea of a democratic Czechoslovak Republic, and the partisans were part of the Czechoslovak Army.

The rebel army and civilian population were supplied with funds and reserves accumulated in Central Slovakia from June 1944, redirected under various pretexts by the employees of state departments working for the resistance. One example was the Governor Imrich Karvaš of the Slovak National Bank, who also directed the highest supply authority. Financial support was provided by Baťa factories and some other companies. Significant contributions were also made by large estates and companies in the liberated territory, such as the Podbrezová Iron Works and ŽOS Zvolen locomotive repair company, who made three armored trains for the rebels. The First Czechoslovak Army in Slovakia initially comprised roughly 18,000 soldiers. After the mobilization on September 5, this number reached almost 50,000.

However, they were badly equipped and the equipment they had was often outdated. On top of that, they lacked combat experience. The first commander in this uneasy situation was General Ján Golian, one of the creators of the rebel military plan of action.

The German units attacked the liberated territory from several directions. There were 9,000 soldiers deployed in the West and a further 15,000 in the East. They were often supported by local German citizens. The insurgent army and partisans managed to deflect the Nazi attacks, but nevertheless suffered substantial losses. The Germans failed despite their own expectations of a lightning-fast success. On October 6, 1944, General Rudolf Viest flew in and became the official commander of the uprising. Although the rebel defenses were strengthened in September, they were not able to stop the German forces. The 2nd Czechoslovak Airborne Brigade and 1st Czechoslovak Fighter Regiment were sent help from the USSR. The United States also sent material aid. But the odds were stacked against the rebels. In October, the German occupying forces started a general offensive and the rebels succumbed to the pressure. On October 27, 1944, General Viest ordered a retreat from Banská Bystrica to Donovaly and shortly thereafter dissolved the rebel army, which joined the partisan groups to escape capture and to continue the guerrilla warfare.

16

Hlinka Guard Emergency Divisions

The constitution of Hlinka Guard Emergency Divisions brought an element of pride, but also of fear to Slovak society, as the direct fighting had moved to its land. For the Hlinka Guard, the outbreak of the uprising was a new life-giving event. The guards could once again dust off the old ideas of the mission of the protectors of Slovak life and property. They again found an enemy against which it was necessary to intervene. In 1938 and 1939, this enemy was Czechs, but in 1944, the majority of them were already displaced. Jews continually became the target of their interest and the name of the guard gradually became associated only with anti-Jewish activities.

The fact that the uprising was organized by an army with which the guard did not maintain enthusiastic contacts, despite frequent propaganda declarations of unity, added to its importance. In particular, the soldiers were angered by the fact that the guardsmen had only looted while they sacrificed their lives for the Slovak state. The army did not trust them, and the Germans considered them unreliable, as many of the mercenaries also joined the rebels. The guard, at the moment, seemed the best and the only option that would be acceptable to the Germans. In his speech of September 6, 1944, the president stated:

> The Hlinka Guard, which has been credited with the loyalty of the state, will play a decisive role in this struggle. The radical was also impressed by the fact that he declared himself faithful in persevering in the line of Slovak–German friendship. It was a satisfaction for them, especially from the mouth of a man who tried to postulate more conservative principles against national-socialist ideas presented after the Salzburg events of 1940, especially Mach or Tuk.

There was nothing in the way of guards to take the responsibility for the direction of the state. The argument for a more vigorous approach was to be the uprising, which, according to them, broke out as a result of not resolving the solution of the

Czech and Jewish issues. The guardsmen could again attack the Czechs and Jews, whom they accused of preparing the uprising. Action against the Czechs and the Czechoslovaks was also supported by official propaganda, which tried to legalize the German intervention in Slovakia:

> If today they shout that the Germans this or that, do not believe them! They began to provoke, to overturn the order, to assassinate peaceful people, to destroy property, and therefore they bear full responsibility for the Germans being here. They did not have to be here, no one would have called them … but the Czechoslovaks who were obsessed with their kindness had created a situation in Slovakia that inevitably led to the present situation.

"They owe them [the guard] thanks and the right reward," wrote *Gardista*. According to the guards, half of the partisans were from the Czechs and the other half waited for a suitable opportunity to fight against Slovak independence. Similar statements gave support to anti-Czech actions. The situation quickly consolidated after the arrival of the German Army and the guardsmen gratefully started repressive actions against the Czechs, arrested them and together with Czechoslovak activists were transported to Ilava. For example, in Trnava alone, the district office withdrew Slovak citizenship from approximately 150 Czechs, allegedly sixty-six in Trenčín and eight Czechs in Nové Mesto nad Váhom. Similar actions were also conducted against the Jews, or Bolsheviks, whose guards found mainly in military circles.

Contradictions also occurred in the leadership of the guard. The long-time commander-in-chief of the Hlinka Guard, Alexander Mach, accused the guard's commanders of their softness and looseness to blame for allowing the rebellion. Mach later, he admitted that he had really made a mistake in eliminating the preparations for the uprising because he knew about them but did not take action. German reports from that period also show that, especially among the Germans, a rumor has spread that if the guard were to have intervened earlier in the situation, the uprising would not have taken place.

It was clear that the Hlinka Guard had to be reorganized for deployment to defend the state. Jozef Tiso, after pressure from the Germans, allowed Otomar Kubala to be appointed chief of the Hlinka Guard. He was in good terms with the Germans in the past. In particular, he had very good relations with the German advisor for Hlinka Guard Viktor Nageler, with whom he organized the magazine *Our Fight*. It was necessary, however, that the former Chief Karol Danihel to resign. Officially, on September 6, the chief asked the president to release him, opening up the space to appoint Kubal.

It was clear to Kubal that, with the new demands placed on the guard, he had to fundamentally transform the organization. At 11 a.m. on September 8, 1944, he convened at the main Hlinka Guard headquarters a meeting of guardsmen commanders, where he issued guidelines for the upcoming work of the guard.

On the basis of the assessment of the situation was accepted the idea of creating so-called activated units, later called emergency units. For this reason, the activities of the Hlinka Guard and Hlinka Guard Emergency Divisions are often combined, which is, of course, justified, since the guard's commanders, especially at local level, often became commanders of the emergency services, which initially consisted mainly of members of the Hlinka Guard. On the other hand, the Hlinka Guard as an organization formally still functioned, but with few exceptions could not carry out their activities and gradually declined.

According to Otomar Kubala in a speech, the Hlinka Guard was to become the most decisive force whose response to the difficult moments of the nation was to be harsh and ruthless. The speech was also published in the first order of the chief of the Hlinka Guard of September 9, 1944, in which he tried to give guidelines for the forthcoming work of the guard.

In the first half of September, the guard had to change internally. For better information about specific units, Kubala ordered the establishment of a permanent telephone and radio service at each local and district headquarters. Each district commander was to send daily reports from the entire district, indicating the number of activated units and the status of the events that took place in his area. Reports were to be made by courier, to travel by train every day, and to headquarters at predetermined stops. The link was to always be, wherever possible, the same person dressed in a civilian suit, with the courier to legitimize each other and for maximum security. This would prevent the possibility of leakage of information to partisans, who could easily learn about the status or deployment of individual units. To prevent leakage of information to partisans, they were to introduce the use of passwords, which were to be changed every day for security.

Order Number 8 of September 18, 1944 established the use of the name emergency divisions of the Hlinka Guard or POHG (*Pohotovostné oddiely Hlinkovej gardy*). Another name used was the Flying Squads of the Hlinka Guard. Otomar Kubala commented on their tasks later: "Tasks of the Hlinka Guard Emergency Divisions is barracks guards, patrolling (at night), train control, occasional escorts and leisure training." Service in the Hlinka Guard Emergency Divisions also brought its members advantages.

Many of the members joined, not because of the guard's conviction, but to make themselves or families secure during wartime. In addition, a number of activated members of Hlinka Guard Emergency Divisions joined them for the reasons that they did not have to enlist in the renewing Slovak Army or dig the Germans trenches. To obtain as many members as possible, the commanders themselves promised potential candidates that if they joined the sections they would only serve in their place of residence and would not be engaged in combat. In a separate order, this practice was expressly prohibited by the chief of the Hlinka Guard, but apparently continued.

Complaints about the behavior of Hlinka Guard Emergency Division members gradually increased. It was not just about wearing uniforms, with which the guard had problems virtually from the beginning. For the Slovak citizen, the guardsman was supposed to be a model of discipline and bear certain values. In one of Kubal's orders, he writes:

> The member of the Emergency Divisions has to look pleasant from the outside neatly shaved and with a haircut. His gear must be clean, boots polished, uniforms fastened to the neck. His general behavior in the street, in public rooms and in society must be exemplary and proportionate to the military situation. The Hlinka Guard tape must be permanently sewn and can never be removed. The member of the Emergency Divisions without the tape will be disciplined.

Originally, guard members were paid 11.50 Slovak crowns per day, regardless of rank, paid out three times a month; later this became 1,500 crowns monthly for married men and 800 crowns for single men. Guardsmen often had to pay for food and uniforms out of their pocket, but their employers were required to continue to pay them their previous salary (they were later compensated by the government) and forbidden to fire them after returning from active service in the emergency divisions. Members were also entitled to additional food rations and cigarettes. Some members wore their old Hlinka Guard uniforms, others had Slovak Army or even *Wehrmacht* uniforms despite strict regulations requiring them to have appropriate uniforms. They were distinguished by a special ribbon on the left sleeve. Many emergency division members were frequently drunk, leading to quarrels with the regular army, German soldiers, and even the Slovak civilian authorities.

The initial actions of the Hlinka Guard Emergency Divisions against the partisans were hampered by difficulty of communication with headquarters. When communication with their superiors was not possible, local units collaborated closely with nearby German forces. Because the Germans did not trust them, the Hlinka Guard Emergency Divisions mostly performed auxiliary military tasks during the suppression of the uprising, rather than frontline combat. When Hlinka Guard Emergency Divisions units did confront the enemy directly, they often ran away; other Hlinka Guard Emergency Divisions dragged their feet when ordered into contested territory, foiling German offensives.

The first Hlinka Guard Emergency Division unit to join the fighting did not begin to engage in combat until the end of September, when the suppression of the rebellion was already well underway. It only suffered the loss of five killed and fifteen wounded, indicating that it was not involved in heavy fighting. This unit was also one of the most brutal in its treatment of captured Jews and partisans. The overall combat effectiveness of the Hlinka Guard Emergency Divisions was limited. Many of its personnel were middle-aged men with families, who took all opportunities to avoid danger. This tendency reduced morale among Hlinka Guard Emergency Division units and led to tensions with German forces, who had to take on dangerous engagements without help. One Hlinka Guard Emergency Division unit, training in the Bratislava area, rioted when it learned that it might be expected to fight against advancing Red Army forces. Many of its members deserted despite the death penalty. Partisan groups often set ambushes and lured Hlinka Guard Emergency Divisions units with anonymous tipoffs about Jews in hiding, a tactic that proved effective. German hopes of recruiting significant numbers of Hlinka Guard Emergency Division men into the *Waffen*-SS for deployment on the approaching Eastern Front never materialized.

The Hlinka Guard was sub-divided into various branches including Hlinka Guard 1st Class (men twenty to thirty-five years), Hlinka Guard 2nd Class (men thirty-six to sixty years), Hlinka Transport Guard, Hlinka University Guards, Hlinka Academic Guards, Hlinka Guard Abroad, Hlinka Guard Elite Storm Troopers-Emergency Divisions, Hlinka Mounted Guard, and Hlinka Flying Guard.

17

The Hlinka Guard and *Einsatzgruppen* H

Along with the German military forces, units of German security and *Einsatzgruppen* arrived in Slovakia. The *Einsatzgruppe* H of the Security Police and the Security Service were assigned to Western and Central Slovakia. The general staff resided in Bratislava and the commandos were deployed to the occupied territory.

Eastern Slovakia was occupied by members of Commando z.b.V. 27, controlled by the Commander of the German Security Police and the Security Service in Krakow. The priority of these units was to find and defeat everyone who supported the resistance as well as to deport or eliminate on the spot all Jews who survived in Slovakia. President Tiso and the Slovak government did not object in any way. On the contrary, they co-operated with the Nazi apparatus. The emergency divisions of the Hlinka Guard and field companies of the Hlinka Guard were made available to the commanders of the German forces. They also created rapid units of the Hlinka Youth. The Nazis and their Slovak collaborators arrested hundreds of citizens. They imprisoned them in various locations, where they were interrogated, tortured, and often executed.

Central Slovakia, where *Einsatzkommando* 14 was stationed with some Slovak units, saw some of the worst atrocities. Near Kremnička, the Nazis murdered 747 partisans, rebel soldiers, Jews, and Roma, including dozens of children, who were found in mass graves after the war. In Nemecká, the Nazis and their collaborators murdered 400–900 people. By the end of October 1944, the Nazis attacked Miezgovce and subjected dozens of local men to interrogation and torture. On December 27, 1944, the Nazis tortured and, before the eyes of the local people, executed three Slovak and one Soviet partisan in Medzibrod. In January 1945, the Nazis and their collaborators burned down Ostrý Grúň and Kľak, killing 148 civilians in addition to the few partisans they found. The residents of Skýcov were cast out of their homes while the village was looted and burnt in the middle of March, followed by the village of Kalište.

In early November 1944, Nazi *Einsatzkommando* 14 captured the rebel commanders Rudolf Viest, Ján Golian, and their entourage. After an interrogation by the *Gestapo*, Viest and Golian were brought before a special German court and sentenced to death. They were sent to the Flossenbürg concentration camp, where they were executed.

Einsatzgruppe H was one of the *Einsatzgruppen*, the paramilitary death squads of Nazi Germany. A special task force of more than 700 soldiers, it was created at the end of August 1944 to deport or murder the remaining Jews in Slovakia following the German suppression of the Slovak National Uprising. During its seven-month existence, *Einsatzgruppe* H collaborated closely with the Hlinka Guard Emergency Divisions and arrested 18,937 people, of whom at least 2,257 were murdered; thousands of others were deported to Nazi concentration camps—primarily Auschwitz. The victims included Jews, Romani people, actual or suspected Slovak partisans, and real or perceived political opponents.

Einsatzgruppe H and its two main component units, *Einsatzkommandos* 13 and 14, were formed in Brno, in the Protectorate of Bohemia and Moravia, upon the outbreak of the Slovak National Uprising, on August 28 or 29. Its commander was SS-*Obersturmbannführer* Joseph Witiska. Other German units were tasked with the military suppression of the uprising, *Einsatzgruppe* H's main focus was to implement the Final Solution in Slovakia. To this end, it intervened with the Slovak government and public life, carried out military actions against partisans, as well as committing massacres and roundups. The unit also submitted regular, detailed reports to Berlin concerning all aspects of life in Slovakia, including the military situation, Jews, public opinion, and culture.

Two days after the outbreak of the rebellion, Witiska met with Berger, the German ambassador to Slovakia, Hans Ludin, Erich Ehrlinger of the Reich Main Security Office, and Erwin Weinmann, the commander of the SS and SS intelligence service in the Protectorate. The object of this meeting was to discuss how to implement a radical solution to the Jewish question in Slovakia. Most Jews were captured during roundups. Either they were imprisoned at local prisons or else taken to the *Einsatzgruppe* H office in Bratislava, from which they were sent to Sereď concentration camp for deportation. In many cases, the local authorities provided lists of Jews. By this time, the Jews knew that deportation meant probable death, so many tried to flee, go into hiding, or otherwise avoiding arrest. The attitude of the local population was ambivalent. Some risked their lives to hide Jews, while others turned them in to the police.

Following the uprising, *Einsatzgruppe* H collaborated with the Hlinka Guard Emergency Divisions and a local German paramilitary organization, the *Heimatschutz*, to create an atmosphere of terror in rural Slovakia, perpetrating public executions and massacres of Jews, Romani people, and those suspected of supporting partisans. The success of *Einsatzgruppe* H was largely due to denunciations and the cooperation of the Hlinka Guard Emergency Divisions and the *Heimatschutz*, who were able to impersonate partisans due to their local knowledge and ability to speak Slovak. These collaborators participated in the massacres and aided with interrogations, as well as searching houses for Jews in hiding.

Einsatzgruppe H was organized hierarchically as were other *Einsatzgruppe* units. It was run from a central headquarters in Bratislava, where Witiska maintained an office at Palisády 42 with about 160 personnel. At its peak, the unit had six subunits with stationary headquarters: *Sonderkommando* 7a, *Einsatzkommandos* 13 and 14, and z.b.V. *Kommandos* 15, 27, and 29. Of these, *Einsatzkommandos* 13 and 14 and z.b.V. *Kommando* 27 were newly formed, while the other units had been transferred from other duties. Not all were subordinated to *Einsatzgruppe* H for the entirety of their activities in Slovakia; for instance, z.b.V. *Kommando* 27, which operated in eastern Slovakia from September 1944, was subordinated to the SD office in Kraków until January 1945. Except for z.b.V. *Kommando* 15, dissolved in February, the units continued to exist until the occupation of Slovakia by the Red Army, at which point most of the personnel fled into Moravia.

Einsatzkommando 13 was commanded by Otto Koslowski, Hans Jaskulsky, and then Karl Schmitz. A total 446 Jews were rounded up in western and central Slovakia by *Einsatzkommando* 13; they were held at Ilava prison before being deported from Žilina to concentration camps in Germany. On September 13 and 14, the unit did a roundup in Žilina, arresting hundreds of Jews who were held in Sereď and Ilava before their deportation to concentration camps, especially Auschwitz. Few survived the war.

Einsatzkommando 14, commanded by Georg Heuser, was the main unit of *Einsatzgruppe* H. Heuser had been the commander of the SS intelligence service in Minsk, where he had helped organize the mass shootings of Belarusian Jews. The unit was responsible for 2,876 murders, including the largest massacres on Slovak territory, the Kremnička massacre, with at least 747 victims, and Nemecká massacre, with some 900 victims. These massacres were committed in cooperation with the Hlinka Guard Emergency Divisions and the Hlinka Guard.

Einsatzkommando 29 and local collaborators committed the September 28 roundup in Bratislava, organized by Alois Brunner. On September 26, the Germans raided the Jewish Center, obtaining a list of Jews, with which they prepared the operation. On the night of September 28, 1,600 or 1,800 Jews in Bratislava were arrested and held in the Jewish Council's headquarters until 6 a.m., when they were loaded onto freight cars and transported to Sereď, arriving at 2 a.m. on September 30. They were deported to Auschwitz concentration camp later that month, where most were murdered.

According to *Einsatzgruppe* H's official records, the unit arrested 18,937 people: 9,653 Jews, 3,409 bandits (actual or suspected partisans), 2,186 defectors, 714 resistance members, 172 Romani people, and 546 others. Of these, 2,257 were subjected to *Sonderbehandlung* (summary execution). The unit captured the leaders of the uprising, Generals Jan Golian and Rudolf Viest, as well as a few American and British military personnel and German soldiers suspected of defeatism or homosexuality.

Until the outbreak of the uprising in late August 1944, the Hlinka Guard tried to limit the rights of the remaining Jews in various ways, despite the collapse of the restoration of deportations. The Hlinka Guards were ordered to follow the Jews in the districts and find out the names of those Jews or Czechs who were politically dangerous and who are not necessarily needed in the district either economically or otherwise. Prior to the outbreak of the uprising, the Hlinka Guard Highlands planned certain interventions in the area of the Jewish and Czech question. In addition to Jews and Czechs, they were also to observe suspicious individuals and, in particular, unknown persons to whom the security authorities were to draw attention.

As Hlinka Guard pointed out, an important part of their work was to monitor well-situated Czechs living in a luxurious life who, despite their status as a guard, behaved anti-state. In this period, various guardian schools remained places to exchange views and present radical ideas. The planned final solution thus came only with the German occupation, but it was no longer within the competence of the Slovak authorities to mitigate the Hlinka Guard's efforts to the extent that they had at least limited efforts until then. Control was already taken over by the Germans.

In September 1944, Sereď was transformed into a concentration camp with an SS guard under the command of Bratislava German Franz Knollmayer. The new contingent of SS soldiers proceeded to commit major atrocities against the prisoners, including torture, rape (though this was frowned on as a violation of racial hygiene laws), and murder. By the end of September, Knollmayer had been replaced by Alois Brunner, who had a mandate to finally resolve the Jewish question in Slovakia. Sereď became the main concentration camp for a second wave of deportations. In separate parts of the camp were imprisoned soldiers of the Slovak insurrectionist army, partisans, and people accused of supporting of uprising. Brunner organized eleven train transports, which deported prisoners to Auschwitz, Sachsenhausen, Ravensbrück, and Theresienstadt. The last transport left Sereď on March 31, 1945, shortly before its liberation by the Red Army.

About 13,500 Jews were deported in the second round including between 6,734 and 7,936 to Auschwitz and another 5,000 to Ravensbrück, Sachsenhausen, Bergen-Belsen, and Theresienstadt. From Slovakia, Ravensbrück received transports totaling 1,600 women and children, mostly Jews, and 478 male prisoners, including Jews, Romani people, and political opponents. About 1,550–1,750 men, mostly Jews, were deported to Sachsenhausen, while about 200–300 people were deported from Sereď to Bergen-Belsen, especially Jews in mixed marriages and some intact families of Jews. Between 1,454 and 1,467 Jews were deported to Theresienstadt, especially the elderly, orphans, and women with young children. About 200–300 Slovak political prisoners were deported to Mauthausen on January 19 and March 31, 1945. Many of those deported to the concentration camps in Germany were sent onwards to sub-camps of the main camps, where they worked mostly in war industries. On four transports from Sereď, selections were carried out at the camp with different cars being directed to Sachsenhausen, Bergen-Belsen, Ravensbrück, and/or Theresienstadt. Many details of the transports are unknown, because much of the documentation was destroyed by the perpetrators, requiring historians to rely on survivor testimonies. The influence of Catholic social teaching and National Socialism influenced interwar Slovakia and contributed to the eventual work of the Hlinka Guard and the Nazis.

A small group called *Náš Boj* (Our Struggle), which operated under SS auspices, was the most radical element in the Hlinka Guard. The case of the parish priests Karol Körper and Viliam Ries shows how the influential their work was. Körper's activities ranged from organizing the laity in the framework of the Catholic Action to the abstinence and hiking movements. He also engaged in politics. Already in the 1920s he not only joined Hlinka's Slovak People's Party but also the radical Rodobrana. When Alexander Mach founded the second daily paper of Hlinka's Slovak People's Party with the title *Slovenské Pravda* in 1936, Karol Körper became its chief commentator. By the end of 1939, he had written about 1,000 editorials with religious and national themes, criticizing the Prague government in the spirit of autonomism.

In foreign policy editorials, he concerned himself especially with the threat of Bolshevism, which he unmasked with regularity as the work of the Jews. At first, he criticized Nazism in the spirit of Papal encyclicals as a pagan cult of blood, but after the declaration of the Slovak state in March 1939, he began to openly praise Hitler and the *Wehrmacht* as guarantors of the national existence of the Slovaks. As a spiritual leader of the Hlinka Guard he appeared at public assemblies wearing its symbols and spoke on the radio in the spirit of its ideology. When the newspaper *Gardista* accused him of corruption, he gave up his position and switched to Tiso's moderate wing. However, he praised the German and Slovak leaders and the rule of one party, appealing to the Slovak people to bear sacrifices in the newspaper *Slovák*, at public assemblies and as a member of the Slovak parliament for the district of Ilava. Until 1943 he continued to praise the war as a form of spiritual purification.

While Karol Körper moderated after his initial radicalism, Viliam Ries openly progressed to a Nazi position and persisted with it until the end. Ries studied theology at Innsbruck and worked as a parish priest in the Banská Štiavnica area after his ordination. At first, he did not engage in the politics of the interwar period, but he wrote poems, which appeared under the pseudonym Ivan Javor in the publications of Hlinka's Slovak People's Party and Catholic cultural periodicals. This changed in the second half of the 1930s, when he became a member of Banská Štiavnica town council for Hlinka's Slovak People's Party and editor of its weekly paper *Štiavničan*. Ries's activity is an example of how the term National Socialism gained meaning in the Slovak context. Articles criticizing the social policies of the government or demanding social justice especially for local miners appeared ever more frequently in the *Štiavničan* during 1940. Ries, at this time both parish priest and commander of the Hlinka Guard at Svätý Anton, eventually provoked the authorities, and with the help of the Catholic Church hierarchy, he was transferred to the outlying parish of Sebechleby and was finally suspended at the beginning of 1942. He moved to Bratislava, where he became editor of the new magazine *Náš Boj* (Our Struggle) published by the Hlinka Guard radical Otomar Kubala in cooperation with German authorities. With Viliam Ries as its editor, *Náš Boj* developed into the most unambiguously radical pro-Nazi forum in the Slovak language. It spread racial anti-Semitism and celebrated Nazism attracting the extreme radicals in the Hlinka Guard.

Over the years, the Hlinka Guard was forced to compete with the Hlinka party for primacy in ruling the country. However, this was no longer an issue for the guard after the uprising, when the SS took over and shaped the Hlinka Guard to suit its own purposes. One Hlinka Guard unit operating in Lierny Balog rounded up sixty-five Roma men and forced them into a barn, then promptly set the barn on fire burning the entire structure and its inhabitants to the ground. Mass shootings of Gypsies families occurred in the valley of Vydrovo, and the Hlinka Guard massacred the entire Roma community of Ilija, Slatina, and Nresnice in November 1944.

Slovak Gypsies (Roma) were also persecuted by the Tiso regime as early as March 1939 but worsened greatly after the Slovak National Uprising. The German occupying authorities accused the Roma of complicity and insurrection, and then preceded with the wholesale roundups and mass killings of Gypsies throughout the region. The Hlinka Guard was used to do the dirty work, killing suspected Roma rebels in front of their wives and children, then murdering the entire family. An estimated 10,000 of the deportees died.

The death rate of those deported to concentration camps in Germany was around 25–50 percent. Of those deported to the Theresienstadt Ghetto, however, 98 percent survived. The high death rate at concentration camps such as Sachsenhausen, Bergen-Belsen, and Ravensbrück was due to the exploitation of forced labor for the war effort and inmates were murdered based on their inability to work, rather than their race or religion. Others died during death marches.

The exact number is unknown and impossible to determine due to discrepancies in the sources. For example, some Jews died or committed suicide before they were deported or during transport and were not counted consistently. The mortality rate was highest on the transports to Auschwitz in September and October, because there was a selection and most of the deportees were immediately murdered in the gas chambers.

18

The Auschwitz Concentration and Extermination Camp

The Auschwitz concentration camp was a complex of over forty concentration and extermination camps operated in occupied Poland. It consisted of Auschwitz I, the main camp in Oświęcim; Auschwitz II-Birkenau, a concentration and extermination camp built with several gas chambers; Auschwitz III-Monowitz, a labor camp created to staff a factory for the chemical conglomerate IG Farben; and dozens of sub-camps. The camps became the main destination for Slovak Jews.

After Germany invaded Poland in September 1939, the SS converted Auschwitz I, an army barracks, into a POW camp for Polish political prisoners. The first inmates, German criminals brought to the camp in May 1940 as functionaries, established the camp's reputation for sadism, beating, torturing, and executing prisoners for the most trivial reasons. The first gassings of Soviet and Polish prisoners took place in block 11 of Auschwitz I around August 1941. Construction of Auschwitz II began the following month, and from 1942 until late 1944, freight trains delivered Jews from all over German-occupied Europe to its gas chambers. Of the 1.3 million people sent to Auschwitz, 1.1 million died. Those not gassed died of starvation, exhaustion, disease, individual executions, or beatings. Others were killed during medical experiments.

As the Soviet Red Army approached Auschwitz in January 1945, toward the end of the war, the SS sent most of the camp's population west on a death march to camps inside Germany and Austria. In 1947 Poland founded the Auschwitz-Birkenau State Museum on the site of Auschwitz I and II, and in 1979, it was named a World Heritage Site by UNESCO.

Auschwitz I

A former World War I camp for transient workers, and later a Polish Army barracks, Auschwitz I was the main camp and administrative headquarters of the camp complex. Situated 50 km southwest of Kraków, the site was first suggested in

February 1940 as a quarantine camp for Polish prisoners by SS-*Oberführer* Arpad Wigand, the inspector of the *Sicherheitspolizei* (security police) and deputy of SS-*Obergruppenführer* Erich von dem Bach-Zelewski, the Higher SS and Police Leader for Silesia. Richard Glücks, head of the Concentration Camps Inspectorate, sent former Sachsenhausen concentration camp commandant Walter Eisfeld to inspect it. Around 1,000 meters long and 400 meters wide, Auschwitz consisted at the time of twenty-two brick buildings, eight of them two-story; a second story was added to the others in 1943 and eight new blocks were built.

Reichsführer-SS Heinrich Himmler, head of the *Schutzstaffel* (SS), approved the site in April 1940 on the recommendation of SS-*Obersturmbannführer* Rudolf Höss of the camps inspectorate. Höss oversaw the development of the camp and served as its first commandant. The first thirty prisoners arrived on May 20, 1940 from the Sachsenhausen camp in Oranienburg, Germany.

Crematorium I, First Gassings

Construction of crematorium I began at Auschwitz I at the end of June or beginning of July 1940. Initially intended not for mass murder but for prisoners who had been executed or had otherwise died in the camp, the crematorium was in operation from August 1940 until July 1943, by which time the crematoria at Auschwitz II had taken over. By May 1942, three ovens had been installed in crematorium I, which together could burn 340 bodies in twenty-four hours.

The first experimental gassing took place in or around August 1941, when Camp Leader Karl Fritzsch, at the instruction of Rudolf Höss, killed a group of Soviet POWs by throwing Zyklon B crystals into their basement cell in block 11 of Auschwitz I. A second group of 600 Soviet prisoners of war and around 250 sick Polish prisoners were gassed on September 3–5. The morgue was later converted to a gas chamber able to hold at least 700–800 people. Zyklon B was dropped into the room through slits in the ceiling.

Auschwitz II-Birkenau

After visiting Auschwitz I in March 1941, it appears that Himmler ordered that the camp be expanded. Construction of Auschwitz II-Birkenau, called a POW camp on blueprints, began in October 1941 in Brzezinka, about 3 km from Auschwitz I. The initial plan was that Auschwitz II would consist of four sectors, each consisting of six sub-camps with their own gates and fences. The first two sectors were completed, but the construction of B-III began in 1943 and stopped in April 1944, and the plan for B-IV was abandoned.

SS-*Sturmbannführer* Karl Bischoff, an architect, was the chief of construction. Based on an initial budget of 8.9 million Reichsmarks, his plans called for each barracks to hold 550 prisoners, but he later changed this to 744 per barracks, which meant the camp could hold 125,000, rather than 97,000. There were 174 barracks, each measuring 116 feet by 36 feet, divided into sixty-two bays of 43 square feet. The bays were divided into "roosts," initially for three inmates and later for four, with personal space of 11 square feet to sleep and place whatever belongings they had.

The prisoners were forced to live in the barracks as they were building them; in addition to working, they faced long roll calls at night. As a result, most prisoners in the men's camp in the early months died of hypothermia, starvation, or exhaustion within a few weeks. Some 10,000 Soviet POWs arrived at Auschwitz I between October 7 and 25, 1941, but by March 1, 1942 only 945 were still registered. They were transferred to Auschwitz II, where most of them had died by May.

Crematoria II-V

The first gas chamber at Auschwitz II was operational by March 1942. On or around March 20, a transport of Polish Jews sent by the *Gestapo* from Silesia and Zagłębie Dąbrowskie was taken straight from the Oświęcim freight station to the Auschwitz II gas chamber, then buried in a nearby meadow. The gas chamber was located in what prisoners called the little red house (known as bunker 1 by the SS), a brick cottage that had been turned into a gassing facility. The windows had been bricked up and its four rooms converted into two insulated rooms, the doors of which said *Zur Desinfektion* (to disinfect). A second brick cottage, the little white house or bunker 2, was converted and operational by June 1942. When Himmler visited the camp on July 17 and 18, 1942, he was given a demonstration of a selection of Dutch Jews, a mass killing in a gas chamber in bunker 2, and a tour of the building site of Auschwitz III, the new IG Farben plant being constructed at Monowitz. Use of bunkers I and 2 stopped in the spring of 1943 when the new crematoria were built, although bunker 2 became operational again in May 1944 for the murder of the Hungarian Jews. Bunker I was demolished in 1943 and bunker 2 in November 1944. Plans for crematoria II and III show that both had an oven room 98.4 feet by 36.9 feet on the ground floor, and an underground dressing room 162.2 feet by 26.0 feet and gas chamber 98 feet by 23 feet. The dressing rooms had wooden benches along the walls and numbered pegs for clothing. Victims would be led from these rooms to a 5-yard-long narrow corridor, which in turn led to a space from which the gas chamber door opened. The chambers were white inside, and nozzles were fixed to the ceiling to resemble showerheads. The daily capacity of the crematoria was 340 corpses in crematorium I; 1,440 each in crematoria II and III; and 768 each in IV and V. By June 1943, all four crematoria were operational, but crematorium I was not used after July 1943. This made the total daily capacity 4,416, although by loading three to five corpses at a time, the special workers were able to burn some 8,000 bodies a day. This maximum capacity was rarely needed; the average between 1942 and 1944 was 1,000 bodies burned every day.

Auschwitz III-Monowitz

After examining several sites for a new plant to manufacture Buna-N, a type of synthetic rubber essential to the war effort, the German chemical cartel IG Farben chose a site near the towns of Dwory and Monowice, about 4.3 miles east of Auschwitz I. Tax exemptions were available to corporations prepared to develop industries in the frontier regions under the Eastern Fiscal Assistance Law, passed in December 1940. In addition to its proximity to the concentration camp, a source of cheap labor, the site had good railway connections and access to raw materials. In February 1941, Himmler ordered that the Jewish population of Oświęcim be expelled to make way for skilled laborers; that all Poles able to work remain in the town and work on building the factory; and that Auschwitz prisoners be used in the construction work.

Auschwitz inmates began working at the plant, known as Buna Werke and IG-Auschwitz, in April 1941, and demolishing houses in Monowitz to make way for it. By May, because of a shortage of trucks, several hundred inmates were rising at 3 a.m. to walk there twice a day from Auschwitz I. Because a long line of exhausted inmates walking through the town of Oświęcim might harm German–Polish relations, the inmates were told to shave daily, make sure they were clean, and sing as they walked. From late July, they were taken to the factory by train on freight wagons. Given the difficulty of moving them, including during the winter, IG Farben decided to build a camp at the plant. The first inmates moved there on October 30, 1942. Known as KL Auschwitz III-Aussenlager (Auschwitz III sub-camp), and later as the Monowitz concentration camp, it was the first concentration camp to be financed and built by private industry.

Measuring 890 feet by 1,610 feet, the camp was larger than Auschwitz I. By the end of 1944, it housed sixty barracks, each with a day room and a sleeping room containing fifty-six three-tiered wooden bunks. IG Farben paid the SS 3–4 Reichsmark for nine- to eleven-hour shifts from each worker. In 1943–1944, about 35,000 inmates worked at the plant; 23,000. Thirty-two a day, on average, died as a result of malnutrition, disease, and the workload. Within three to four months at the camp, the inmates were reduced to walking skeletons. Deaths and transfers to the gas chambers at Auschwitz II reduced the population by nearly a fifth each month. Site managers constantly threatened inmates with the gas chambers, and the smell from the crematoria at Auschwitz I and II hung heavy over the camp.

Life in the Camps

Born in Baden-Baden in 1900, Rudolf Höss was named the first commandant of Auschwitz when Heinrich Himmler ordered on April 27, 1940 that the camp be established. Living with his wife and children in a two-story stucco house near the commandant's and administration building, he served as commandant until November 11, 1943, with Josef Kramer as his deputy. Succeeded as commandant by Arthur Liebehenschel, Höss joined the SS Business and Administration Head Office in Oranienburg as director of *Amt* DI, a post that made him deputy of the camps inspectorate.

Richard Baer became commandant of Auschwitz I on May 11, 1944 and Fritz Hartjenstein of Auschwitz II from November 22, 1943, followed by Josef Kramer from May 15, 1944 until the camp's liquidation in January 1945. Heinrich Schwarz was commandant of Auschwitz III from the point at which it became an autonomous camp in November 1943 until its liquidation. Höss returned to Auschwitz between May 8 and 29 July 29, 1944 as the local SS garrison commander to oversee the arrival of Hungary's Jews, which made him the superior officer of all the commandants of the Auschwitz camps.

About 6,335 people, 6,161 of them men, worked for the SS at Auschwitz over the course of the camp's existence; 4.2 percent were officers, 26.1 percent non-commissioned officers, and 69.7 percent rank and file. In March 1941, there were 700 SS guards; in June 1942, 2,000; and in August 1944, 3,342. At its peak in January 1945, 4,480 SS men and 71 SS women worked in Auschwitz.

Most of the staff were from Germany or Austria, but as the war progressed, increasing numbers of German language speakers from other countries, including Czechoslovakia, Poland, Yugoslavia, and the Baltic states, joined the SS at Auschwitz. Not all were ethnically German. Guards were also recruited from Hungary, Romania, and Hlinka Guard in Slovakia. Camp guards, around three-quarters of the SS personnel, were members of the SS-*Totenkopfverbände* (death's head units). Other SS staff worked in the medical or political departments, or in the economic administration, which was responsible for clothing and other supplies, including the property of dead prisoners. The SS viewed Auschwitz as a comfortable posting; being there meant they had avoided the front and had access to the victims' property.

Life for the Inmates

The day began at 4:30 a.m. for the men, and earlier for the women, when the block supervisor sounded a gong and started beating inmates with sticks to make them wash and use the latrines quickly. Sanitary arrangements were atrocious, with few latrines and a lack of clean water. Each washhouse had to service thousands of prisoners. In sectors B-Ia and B-Ib in Auschwitz II, two buildings containing latrines and washrooms were installed in 1943. These contained troughs for washing and ninety faucets; the toilet facilities were sewage channels covered by concrete with fifty-eight holes for seating. There were three barracks with washing facilities or toilets to serve sixteen residential barracks in B-IIa, and six washrooms/latrines for thirty-two barracks in B-IIb, B-IIc, B-IId, and B-IIe. The washroom was badly lit, full of draughts, with the brick floor covered by a layer of mud. The water was not drinkable and had a revolting smell.

Prisoners received half a liter of coffee substitute or herbal tea in the morning, but no food. A second gong heralded roll call, when inmates lined up outside in rows of ten to be counted. No matter the weather, they had to wait for the SS to arrive for the count; how long they stood there depended on the officers' moods, and whether there had been escapes or other events attracting punishment. Guards might force the prisoners to squat for an hour with their hands above their heads or hand out beatings or detention for infractions such as having a missing button or an improperly cleaned food bowl. The inmates were counted and recounted.

After rollcall, to the sound of "form work details," prisoners walked to their place of work, five abreast, to begin a working day that was normally eleven hours long and longer in summer. A prison orchestra, such as the Women's Orchestra of Auschwitz, was forced to play cheerful music as the workers left the camp. Kapos (prisoners who collaborated with the Nazis to serve in leadership or administrative roles) were responsible for the prisoners' behavior while they worked, as was an SS escort. Much of the work took place outdoors at construction sites, gravel pits, and lumber yards. No rest periods were allowed. One prisoner was assigned to the latrines to measure the time the workers took to empty their bladders and bowels.

Lunch was three-quarters of a liter of watery soup at midday, reportedly foul tasting, with meat in the soup four times a week and vegetables (mostly potatoes and rutabaga) three times. The evening meal was 300 grams of bread, often moldy, part of which the inmates were expected to keep for breakfast the next day, with a tablespoon of cheese or marmalade, or 25 grams of margarine or sausage. Prisoners engaged in hard labor were given extra rations.

A second rollcall took place at 7 p.m., in the course of which prisoners might be hanged or flogged. If a prisoner was missing, the others had to remain standing until the absentee was found or the reason for the absence discovered, even if it took hours. On July 6, 1940, rollcall lasted nineteen hours because a Polish prisoner, Tadeusz Wiejowski, had escaped. Following an escape in 1941, a group of prisoners was picked out from the escapee's workmates or barracks and sent to block 11 to be starved to death. After rollcall, prisoners retired to their blocks for the night and received their bread rations. Then they had some free time to use the washrooms and receive their mail, unless they were Jews. Jews were not allowed to receive mail. Curfew was marked by a gong at 9 p.m. Inmates slept in long rows of brick or wooden bunks, or on the floor, lying in and on their clothes and shoes to prevent them from being stolen. The wooden bunks had blankets and paper mattresses filled with wood shavings. In the brick barracks, inmates lay on straw.

Approximately 800–1,000 people were crammed into the superimposed compartments of each barracks. Unable to stretch out completely, they slept there both lengthwise and crosswise, with one man's feet on another's head, neck, or chest.

Sunday was not a workday, but prisoners had to clean the barracks and take their weekly shower and were allowed to write (in German) to their families, although the SS censored the mail. Inmates who did not speak German would trade bread for help. Observant Jews tried to keep track of the Hebrew calendar and Jewish holidays, including Shabbat, and the weekly Torah portion. No watches, calendars, or clocks were permitted in the camp.

Women's Camp

About 30 percent of the registered inmates were female. The first mass transport of women, 999 non-Jewish German women from the Ravensbrück concentration camp, arrived on March 26, 1942. Classified as criminal, asocial, and political, they were brought to Auschwitz as founder functionaries of the women's camp. Rudolf Höss wrote of them: "It was easy to predict that these beasts would mistreat the women over whom they exercised power.... Spiritual suffering was completely alien to them." They were given serial numbers 1–999. The women's guard from Ravensbrück, Johanna Langefeld, became the first Auschwitz women's camp Lagerführerin. A second mass transport of women, the 997 Jews from Poprad, Slovakia, arrived on the same day. According to Danuta Czech, this was the first registered transport sent to Auschwitz by the *Reichssicherheitshauptamt* (RSHA) office IV B4, known as the Jewish Office, led by SS-*Obersturmbannführer* Adolf Eichmann (Office IV was the *Gestapo*.) A third transport of 798 Jewish women from Bratislava, Slovakia, followed on March 28, 28.

Women were at first held in blocks 1–10 of Auschwitz I, but from August 6, 1942, 13,000 inmates were transferred to a new women's camp in Auschwitz II. This consisted at first of fifteen brick and fifteen wooden barracks in sector B-Ia; it was later extended into B-Ib, and by October 1943, it held 32,066 women. In 1943–1944, about 11,000 women were also housed in the Gypsy family camp, as were several thousand in the Theresienstadt family camp.

Conditions in the women's camp were so poor that when a group of male prisoners arrived to set up an infirmary in October 1942, their first task, according to researchers from the Auschwitz museum, was to distinguish the corpses from the women who were still alive. Gisella Perl, a Romanian–Jewish gynecologist and inmate of the women's camp, wrote in 1948:

> There was one latrine for thirty to thirty-two thousand women, and we were permitted to use it only at certain hours of the day. We stood in line to get into this tiny building, knee-deep in human excrement. As we all suffered from dysentery, we could barely wait until our turn came, and soiled our ragged clothes, which never came off our bodies, thus adding to the horror of our existence by the terrible smell that surrounded us like a cloud. The latrine consisted of a deep ditch with planks thrown across it at certain intervals. We squatted on those planks like birds perched on a telegraph wire, so close together that we could not help soiling one another.

Langefeld was succeeded as Lagerführerin in October 1942 by SS-*Oberaufseherin* Maria Mandl, who developed a reputation for cruelty. Höss hired men to oversee the female supervisors, first SS-*Obersturmführer* Paul Müller, then SS-*Hauptsturmführer* Franz Hössler. Sterilization experiments were carried out in barrack 30 by a German gynecologist, Carl Clauberg, and another German doctor, Horst Schumann.

Medical Experiments in Block 10

Block 10, Auschwitz I, is where medical experiments were performed on women. German doctors performed a variety of experiments on prisoners. SS doctors tested the effectiveness of X-rays as a sterilization device by administering large doses to female prisoners. Carl Clauberg injected chemicals into women's uteruses in an effort to glue them shut. Prisoners were infected with spotted fever for vaccination research and exposed to toxic substances to study the effects. In one experiment Bayer, then part of IG Farben, paid 150 Reichsmarks each for 150 female inmates from Auschwitz, who were transferred to a Bayer facility to test an anesthetic. A Bayer employee wrote to Rudolf Höss: "The transport of 150 women arrived in good condition. However, we were unable to obtain conclusive results because they died during the experiments. We would kindly request that you send us another group of women to the same number and at the same price."

The most infamous doctor at Auschwitz was Josef Mengele, the "Angel of Death," who worked in Auschwitz II from May 30, 1943, at first in the Gypsy family camp. Interested in performing research on identical twins, dwarfs, and those with hereditary disease, Mengele set up a kindergarten in barracks 29 and 31 for children he was experimenting on, and for all Romani children under six, where they were given better food rations. From May 1944, he would select twins and dwarfs from among the new arrivals during selection. He and other doctors would measure the twins' body parts, photograph them, and subject them to dental, sight and hearing tests, X-rays, blood tests, surgery, and blood transfusions between them. Then he would have them killed and dissected. Kurt Heissmeyer, another German doctor and SS officer, took twenty Polish Jewish children from Auschwitz to use in pseudoscientific experiments at the Neuengamme concentration camp near Hamburg, where he injected them with the tuberculosis bacilli to test a cure for tuberculosis. In April 1945, the children were killed by hanging to conceal the project.

A Jewish skeleton collection was obtained from among a pool of 115 Jewish inmates, chosen for their perceived stereotypical racial characteristics. Rudolf Brandt and Wolfram Sievers, general manager of the Ahnenerbe, a Nazi research institute, delivered the skeletons to the collection of the Anatomy Institute at the *Reichsuniversität* Straßburg in Alsace-Lorraine. The collection was sanctioned by Heinrich Himmler and under the direction of August Hirt. Ultimately, eighty-seven of the inmates were shipped to Natzweiler-Struthof and killed in August 1943.

Punishment Block 11

Prisoners could be beaten and killed by guards and Kapos for the slightest infraction of the rules. Common infractions included returning a second time for food at mealtimes, removing your own gold teeth to buy bread, breaking into the pigsty to steal the pigs' food, putting your hands in your pockets.

Flogging during rollcall was common. A flogging table called "the goat" immobilized prisoners' feet in a box, while they stretched themselves across the table. Prisoners had to count out the lashes and if they got the figure wrong, the flogging resumed from the beginning. Punishment by "the post" involved tying prisoners' hands behind their backs with chains attached to hooks, then raising the chains so the prisoners were left dangling by the wrists. If their shoulders were too damaged afterwards to work, they might be sent to the gas chamber. Prisoners were subjected to the post for helping a prisoner who had been beaten, and for picking up a cigarette butt. To extract information from inmates, guards would force their heads onto the stove, and hold them there, burning their faces and eyes.

Known as block 13 until 1941, block 11 of Auschwitz I was the prison within the prison, reserved for inmates suspected of resistance activities. Cell 22 in block 11 was a windowless standing cell. Split into four sections, each section measured less than 11 square feet and held four prisoners, who entered it through a hatch near the floor. There was a small vent for air, covered by a perforated sheet.

Selection and Extermination Process

From 1942, Jews were being transported to Auschwitz from all over German-occupied Europe by rail, arriving in daily convoys. The gas chambers worked to their fullest capacity from May to July 1944, during the Holocaust in Hungary. A rail spur leading to crematoria II and III in Auschwitz II was completed that May, and a new ramp was built between sectors B-I and B-II to deliver the victims closer to the gas chambers. On April 29, the first 1,800 Jews from Hungary arrived at the camp. From May 14 until early July 1944, 437,000 Hungarian Jews, half the pre-war population, were deported to Auschwitz, at a rate of 12,000 a day for a considerable part of that period. The crematoria had to be overhauled. Crematoria II and III were given new elevators leading from the stoves to the gas chambers, new grates were fitted, and several of the dressing rooms and gas chambers were painted. Cremation pits were dug behind crematorium V. The incoming volume was so great that the *Sonderkommando* resorted to burning corpses in open-air pits as well as in the crematoria.

Selection

Of the 1,095,000 Jews deported to Auschwitz, around 205,000 were registered in the camp and given serial numbers; 25,000 were sent to other camps; and 865,000 were killed soon after arrival. Adding non-Jewish victims gives a figure of 900,000 who were killed without being registered.

During selection on arrival, those deemed able to work were sent to the right and admitted into the camp to be registered, and the rest were sent to the left to be gassed. The group selected to die included almost all children, women with small children, the elderly, and others who appeared on brief and superficial inspection by an SS doctor not to be fit for work. Practically any fault, scars, bandages, boils, and emaciation, might provide reason enough to be deemed unfit. Children might be made to walk toward a stick held at a certain height; those who could walk under it were selected for the gas. Inmates unable to walk or who arrived at night were taken to the crematoria on trucks; otherwise the new arrivals were marched there. Their belongings were seized and sorted by inmates in an area of the camp in sector B-IIg that housed thirty barracks used as warehouses.

Inside the Crematoria

The crematoria consisted of a dressing room, gas chamber, and furnace room. In crematoria II and III, the dressing room and gas chamber were underground; in IV and V, they were on the ground floor. The dressing room had numbered hooks on the wall to hang clothes. In crematorium II, there was also a disinfection room. SS officers told the victims they had to take a shower and undergo delousing. The victims undressed in the dressing room and walked into the gas chamber; signs said bath or disinfection room. A former prisoner testified that the language of the signs changed depending on who was being killed. Some inmates were given soap and a towel. A gas chamber could hold up to 2,000; one former prisoner said it was around 3,000.

The Zyklon B was delivered to the crematoria by a special SS bureau known as the Hygiene Institute. After the doors were shut, SS men dumped in the Zyklon B pellets through vents in the roof or holes in the side of the chamber. The victims were usually dead within ten minutes; Rudolf Höss testified that it took up to twenty minutes. Leib Langfus, a member of the special work unit, buried his diary (written in Yiddish) near crematorium III in Auschwitz II. It was found in 1952, signed A.Y.R.A:

> It would be difficult to even imagine that so many people would fit in such a small room. Anyone who did not want to go inside was shot or torn apart by the dogs. They would have suffocated from the lack of air within several hours. Then all the doors

> were sealed tight and the gas thrown in by way of a small hole in the ceiling. There was nothing more that the people inside could do. And so they only screamed in bitter, lamentable voices. Others complained in voices full of despair, and others still sobbed spasmodically and sent up a dire, heart-rending weeping.... And in the meantime, their voices grew weaker and weaker.... Because of the great crowding, people fell one atop another as they died, until a heap arose consisting of five or six layers atop the other, reaching a height of one meter. Mothers froze in a seated position on the ground embracing their children in their arms, and husbands and wives died hugging each other. Some of the people made up a formless mass. Others stood in a leaning position, while the upper parts, from the stomach up, were in a lying position. Some of the people had turned completely blue under the influence of the gas, while others looked entirely fresh, as if they were asleep.

Use of Corpses

Special work unit members wearing gas masks dragged the bodies from the chamber. They removed glasses and artificial limbs and shaved off the women's hair; women's hair was removed before they entered the gas chamber at Bełżec, Sobibór, and Treblinka, but at Auschwitz it was done after death. By February 6, 1943, the Reich Economic Ministry had received 3,000 kilograms of women's hair from Auschwitz and Majdanek. The hair was first cleaned in a solution of Sal Ammoniac, dried on the brick floor of the crematoria, combed, and placed in paper bags. The hair was shipped to various companies, including one manufacturing plant in Bremen-Blumenthal, where workers found tiny coins with Greek letters on some of the braids, possibly from some of the 50,000 Greek Jews deported to Auschwitz in 1943. When they liberated the camp in January 1945, the Red Army found 7,000 kilograms of human hair in bags ready to ship.

Just before cremation, jewelry was removed, along with dental work and teeth containing precious metals. Gold was removed from the teeth of dead prisoners from September 23, 1940 onwards by order of Heinrich Himmler. The work was carried out by members of the special work unit, who were dentists. Anyone overlooking dental work might themselves be cremated alive. The gold was sent to the SS Health Service and used by dentists to treat the SS and their families; 50 kilograms had been collected by October 8, 1942. By early 1944, 10–12 kilograms of gold were being extracted monthly from victims' teeth.

The corpses were burned in the nearby incinerators, and the ashes were buried, thrown in the Vistula river, or used as fertilizer. Any bits of bone that had not burned properly were ground down in wooden mortars.

Death Toll

At least 1.3 million people were sent to Auschwitz between 1940 and 1945, and at least 1.1 million died. Overall, 400,207 prisoners were registered in the camp: 268,657 male and 131,560 females. A study in the late 1980s by Polish historian Franciszek Piper, published by Yad Vashem in 1991, used timetables of train arrivals combined with deportation records to calculate that, of the 1.3 million sent to the camp, 1,082,000 had died there, a figure (rounded up to 1.1 million) that Piper regarded as a minimum. That figure came to be widely accepted.

The Germans tried to conceal how many they had killed. In July 1942, according to Rudolf Höss's post-war memoir, Höss received an order from Heinrich Himmler, via Adolf Eichmann's office and SS commander Paul Blobel, that "All mass graves were to be opened and the corpses burned. In addition the ashes were to be disposed of in such a way that it would be impossible at some future time to calculate the number of corpses burned."

Earlier estimates of the death toll were higher than Piper's. Following the camp's liberation, the Soviet government issued a statement, on May 8, 1945, that 4 million people had been killed on the site, a figure based on the capacity of the crematoria. Höss told prosecutors at Nuremberg that at least 2.5 million people had been gassed there, and that another 500,000 had died of starvation and disease. He testified that the figure of over 2 million had come from Eichmann. In his memoirs, written in custody, Höss wrote that Eichmann had given the figure of 2.5 million to Höss's superior officer Richard Glücks, based on records that had been destroyed. Around one in six Jews killed in the Holocaust died in Auschwitz.

Conclusion

National Socialist policies of racial superiority brought into the Slovak society a new dimension of anti-Semitism, which was evident in Slovakia since the nineteenth century, but only gained monstrous proportions during the period of 1939 to 1945. The dramatic fate of approximately 89,000 men, women and children of Jewish nationality is a rebuke of the Slovak nationalism, which resulted during World War II in a form of an unspeakable brutality and still manifests itself in thought and action of a certain group of the Slovak population.

An anti-Jewish campaign was launched after the declaration of the Slovak autonomy in 1938 and the presentation of a solution to the Jewish question became one of the main attributes of the governmental policy of the emerging authoritarian and totalitarian regime. On the night of November 4–5, 1938, the autonomous government with the help of the Hlinka's Guards prepared the forced deportation of Jews to the south of Slovakia which was given to Hungary after the Vienna Award. The Slovak State, established on March 14, 1939 under the Constitution of July 1939, was called the Slovak Republic and opened the road for the implementation of Slovak nationalism. The authoritarian regime in the so-called solution of the Jewish question showed its anti-democratic, anti-human and ultimately anti-Christian side.

Official propaganda together with the government's anti-Semitic policy provoked hatred against Jewish citizens. After the Slovak–German negotiations in Salzburg during the summer of 1940, the fate of thousands of Jews began to be addressed according to the German model and racial principle. After those negotiations, a special German adviser for the solution of the Jewish question, Dieter Wisliceny, arrived in Slovakia. In September 1940, the Slovak parliament conferred full powers to the government to solve the Jewish question within one year. The German adviser suggested a simple plan of seizure the income and assets of Jewish co-citizens, which should lead to solving the question of the removal of Jews from Slovakia. The act of conferring full powers for one year to the new government brought literally hundreds of anti-Jewish decrees and regulations of national or regional scope. The government policy systematically excluded

Jewish population from the economic and public life and premeditatedly deprived them of social, civil, and finally human rights. Up to September 1941, the Jewish community was intentionally impoverished and this mass of people deprived of their rights. They became an uncomfortable social burden for the state.

The most critical moment was the publication of 198/1941 Sl.z. Regulation of September 9, 1941 on the Legal Status of the Jews. The government regulation contained up to 270 paragraphs and was the most comprehensive regulation issued during the existence of the first Slovak Republic. This regulation was an almost exact or true copy of the German laws against the Jews and defined a solution of the Jewish question in Slovakia on strictly racial basis. Compared with other countries as Italy, France, Hungary, Romania, the Netherlands, Austria and others. The consequences of the treatments directed against Jewish citizens had tragic consequences in early 1942, when the eviction of Jews from Slovakia started being prepared.

On March 25, the first transport of 1,000 young people left for Auschwitz, situated in occupied Poland. The act of eviction of the Jewish people began with these words: "Jews can be deported from the territory of the Slovak Republic." The deportees lost all movable property and citizenship. The cost of eviction was 500 Reichsmarks per person and was to be funded from confiscated Jewish property. The parliament of the Slovak Republic which approved the emigration law on May 15, 1942, managed to insert exceptions meant to save thousands of Jewish citizens. However, until transports were stopped in October 1942, around 58,000 people were transported from Slovakia.

Deportation was accompanied by various acts of violence by the security forces. Inhuman treatment of the Jewish population provoked outrage among the public and church leaders. A large number of Jews were saved from deportation because of the dedication of the Slovak population, church and government officials who disagreed with the procedure of other government officials and pressed for a stop of the transports, which they achieved in October 1942. After that, despite the German pressure, no Jews were deported from Slovakia until 1944. After the arrival of the German Army in August 1944, deportation restarted. Nazis together with the Hlinka's Guards deported from Slovakia about 13,500 Jews. Almost all of the deported perished in Nazi camps under appalling conditions.

The Hlinka Guard is still perceived in society very contradictory. Already at the time of its existence, the Slovak society was divided in its view of the guard. On the one hand, there were sympathizers who associated it with the "golden times" of Autonomous Slovakia and the First Slovak Republic, willing to overlook its excesses. Some believed the group was influenced by ideology, but in the opposite direction, while others believe the guard acted to enrich themselves while acting on the anti-Semitic prejudice of society. Yet some perceive the guard as an instrument of the Nazis that was unavoidable. Whatever the motive and purpose, the results speak for themselves.

Altogether over 70,000 Jewish citizens of Slovakia died in concentration camps, the largest percentage in Auschwitz-Birkenau. Approximately 80 percent of the Jewish population of Slovakia perished during the Holocaust. The Hlinka Guard played an important role in the deportations of the Slovak Jews to Auschwitz and other labor and death camps.

Bibliography

"Auschwitz Birkenau: German Nazi Concentration and Extermination Camp (1940–1945)," *World Heritage List, UNESCO*

Bauer, Y., *Jews for Sale: Nazi-Jewish Negotiations, 1933–1945*, (New Haven: Yale University Press, 1994

Büchler, Y., "First in the Vale of Affliction: Slovakian Jewish Women in Auschwitz, 1942," Holocaust and Genocide Studies Volume 10, Issue 3, Winter 1996; "The deportation of Slovakian Jews to the Lublin District of Poland in 1942," *Holocaust and Genocide Studies, Volume 6, Issue 2, 1991*

Cichopek, A., *Beyond Violence: Jewish Survivors in Poland and Slovakia, 1944–48*, (Cambridge: Cambridge University Press, 2014)

"EuroDocs," *European Studies*, (Provo: Harold B. Lee Library, Brigham Young University)

Fatran, G., *Die Deportation der Juden aus der Slowakei 1944–1945* [The deportation of the Jews from Slovakia 1944–45]. (Bohemia: Zeitschrift für Geschichte und Kultur der Böhmischen Länder, 1996)

"Governmental regulation of legal status of Jewish people," EuroDocs, European Studies, (Provo: Harold B. Lee Library, Brigham Young University, 1941)

Hilberg, R., *The Destruction of the European Jews*, (New Haven: Yale University Press 2003)

Holocaust Education & Archive Research Team, www.HolocaustResearchProject.org

Jelinek, Y. "Storm-troopers in Slovakia: the Rodobrana and the Hlinka Guard." *Journal of Contemporary History*, 6(3), 1971

Kamenec, I., *On the Trail of Tragedy: The Holocaust in Slovakia*. Translated by Styan, Martin, (Bratislava: Hajko & Hajková, 1991)

Kubátová, H., and Láníček, J., *The Jew in Czech and Slovak Imagination, 1938–89: Antisemitism, the Holocaust, and Zionism*, (Leiden: Brill Publishing, 2018)

Mandel, L., *The Tragedy of Slovak Jewry in Slovakia*, (New York, 1950)

Niewyk, D. L., *The Columbia Guide to the Holocaust*, (United States: Columbia University Press)

Rotkirchen, L., *The Destruction of Slovak Jewry*, (Jerusalem: Yad Vashem, 1961)

Sniegon, T., *Vanished History: The Holocaust in Czech and Slovak Historical Culture*, (New York: Berghahn Books, 2014)

Slovak National Archives, Bratislava, Slovakia

Sokolovič, P., *The Flying Squads of Hlinka Guard: Coming to Terms with the Slovak Wartime Past*, (Trnava University of Ss. Cyril, 2015); *Hlinkova garda 1938–1945*, (Bratislava: National Memory Institute, 2009)

Špiesz, A., Bolchazy, L. J., and Caplovic, D., *Illustrated Slovak History: A Struggle for Sovereignty in Central Europe*, (Mundelein: Bolchazy-Carducci Publishers, 2006)

Vlcko, P., *In the Shadow of Tyranny: A History in Novel Form*, (Vantage Press 1973)